Here's the thing. I really can't remember how all this started. One minute I was making my way through arrivals at Auckland International Airport to the sound of recorded chirruping native birds, the next I was out there experiencing it for real, tramping in the bush, asking locals ridiculous questions, and driving through places I never knew existed let alone how to pronounce. In fact I've been politely murdering place names up and down the country for the past two years now, and sometimes I'm still unsure why.

I suppose initially this little odyssey of mine sprang from a desire to become better acquainted with the country I now call my adopted home. In 2003, still reeling from the culture shock of moving from London to the Kapiti Coast, I realised I wanted to get to know more about its history, its landscapes, its foibles, its 'can do' attitude, its wine, possibly its cheese too, but most of all its people. Living in Paraparaumu I also realised that it wasn't just going to land in my lap. No, if I wanted to uncover more of the real New Zealand I would have to prise myself out of my comfy armchair and into my comfy driving seat. Fortunately the road in question was State Highway 1 and it went practically past my front door.

State Highway 1, SH1, is New Zealand's mother road, a Kiwi Route 66. Interrupted only by that choppy stretch of water known as Cook Strait, it runs the entire length of the country, 2026 kilometres in all, from Cape Reinga in the north to Bluff in the south. It spans plains, rivers, deserts and mountain ranges; it skirts oceans, lakes and hills, and at times bores through solid rock on its unerring path southwards (or northwards if you're a South Islander). It also touches the lives of roughly 80 per cent of all New Zealanders on a daily basis, passing through more than 300 towns including the nation's five biggest cities, namely Auckland, Wellington, Christchurch, Hamilton and Dunedin.

Armed with such overwhelming statistics, I knew I had to do something. The trouble was what, exactly. The plan in the end was simple. I would travel the length of State Highway 1, stop in every town on the way and do, see or experience one thing in each. Wherever possible I would stick close to the main drag unless I felt the need to cheat and take a slight detour, but even then I'd never stray more than a few kilometres off the highway. I would travel in manageable stages from north to south, stopping in B&Bs or at friends' houses where I could to save money. And I would undertake this trip in short bursts – periods not much longer than a week – so as not to use up my entire holiday allowance in one go without my wife and family, and thus hopefully avoid a messy divorce.

Now I can't claim to be totally original in my quest. I'm sure many people down the years have done the whole *Goodbye Pork Pie* thing, either by car or on foot. In 1960, for example, A.H. Reed of publishing fame decided to walk from North Cape to Bluff at the ripe old age of 85. He travelled the whole way by road too, so whenever relevant I shall be consulting old Reedy to find out what he got up to, or to seek his advice.

A few other things while I'm at it. First, when I began writing this book it became evident there was no way I could include absolutely everything I wanted to about the towns I visited. 'What you have in mind would end up longer than the Bible' were the nervous words of my publishers, so in the name of brevity I have kept things, well, brief. This was also aided in some towns by my distinct inability to find anything to do.

Second, the activities I have chosen in each place by no means comprise a definitive list, merely the '1 Thing' I plumped for while I was there. Indeed, since I completed my quest a number of possibly better options have been brought to my attention. My advice then, should you ever find yourself in a similar position, is to do whatever floats your personal boat.

Third, I am well aware that there are no set rules to translating Maori place names. 'Transliterating' can get you into all sorts of trouble, and probably has, but as a rule if the translations are good enough for *The Reed Dictionary of New Zealand Place Names* then they've been good enough for me.

Fourth, I would also like to say right now that it is not my intent to upset anyone, and I apologise humbly in advance should this be the case. Likewise if you think I haven't done your town justice. And if my observations seem flippant at times, it is probably due to English ignorance rather than any desire to offend or take the mickey.

Last, and by no means least, thanks for reading this book. I hope you get as much enjoyment from reading it as I did writing it. And so now, never mind the kicks on Route 66, let's have some fun on State Highway 1 ...

Cape Reinga See Columbia Bank, where oceans meet. *Te Paki* Surf the dunes. *Waitaki Landing* Visit the holiday complex (and don't confound the locals). *Karatia* Find Karatia. *Tangaoke* Spot a fernbird (or any old bird). *Te Kao* Buy a kumara. *Ngataki* See the cemetery. *Waihopo* Picture Waihopo's prolific past. *Te Raupo* Sample some Raupo bread (you may have to make it first). *Houhora* Visit New Zealand's northernmost tavern. *Pukenui* Take in the spectacular views of Mount Camel. *Raio* Visit the Wagener Museum. *Waiharara* Visit Gumdiggers Park. *Waipapakauri* Have a drink at the Waipap Hotel. *Waimanoni* See the Marae. *Awanui* Climb the staircase at the Ancient Kauri Kingdom. *Kaitaia* See de Surville's anchor in the Far North Regional Museum. *Rangitihi* Find Rangitihi. *Pamapuria* Stay out of trouble. *Victoria Valley* Check out Queen Victoria's breasts. *Mangataiore* Spot Tracey's Bridges. *Mangamuka Gorge* Stop at the lookout. *Mangamuka* Find out about the taniwha. *Mangamuka Bridge* Take a walk around the Omahuta Kauri Sanctuary. *Umawera* Visit the Umawera Tea Rooms. *Rangiahua* Find the ancient mooring post (difficult). See the 'Historic Place' (easy). *Waihou Valley* Visit the Northland Firehouse Museum. *Okaihau* See the old train tunnel (right next to SH1). *Lake Omapere / Puketutu* Find the battle site (with the landowner's permission, the aid of a decent map and someone to read it correctly). *Teahuahu* Climb the hill. *Ohaeawai* Visit St Michael's Church on the old battle site. *Pakaraka* Visit the Holy Trinity Church. *Moerewa & Kawakawa* Check out the two toilets. *Waiomio* Visit the glowworm caves. *Ruapekapeka* Visit the pa. *Towai* Have a drink in the Towai Tavern and take the hole-in-one challenge. *Akerama* Discover more about the origin of the name Akerama. *Hukerenui* Visit the Happy Huka pub. *Waiotu* Go fishing in the Waiotu River. *Whakapara* Go fishing again, or post a letter to Panguru. *Otonga* Discover the racehorse link. *Waro* See/visit Waro Limestone Reserve. *Hikurangi* Visit the Hikurangi Museum. *Kauri* Find a kauri. *Kamo* Visit Whangarei Falls (yes, yes, I know...). *Whangarei* Find the clock that tells the correct time at Clapham's Clocks. *Otaika* Visit The Paper Mill. *Puwera* Experience heat, or the landfill site, but not simultaneously. *Oakleigh* Call in at the service station. *Mata* See the big apple. *Ruakaka* Take in the beautiful views of Bream Bay. *Uretiti Beach* Go to the beach. *Waipu* Visit the Heritage Centre, or drink a whisky. *Brynderwyn* Visit the Skyliner Café. *Pukekaroro* See the remains of the kauri tramline, or the memorial. *Kaiwaka* See the lights at night, and visit Eutopia. *Topuni* Stand by the river and consider that you're only 15km from the east coast. *Te Hana* See the bronze sculptures, or spot the pig sign. *Wellsford* Buy something from Trish & Kev's 2nd hand shop. *Wayby* Visit the Wayby Art Gallery. *Waiwhiu* Walk to Waiwhiu Kauri Grove (weather and physical fitness permitting). *Dome Valley* Sheepworld! *Warkworth* Sit by the river and take in the beautiful view. *Pohuehue* Take the Moir Hill Walkway to the waterfall. *Puhoi* Visit the pub (or The Art of Cheese if the pub's too full). *Waiwera* Watch a movie in the hot pools (and pray it's not Top Gun). *Hatfields Beach* Wander on the beach. *Orewa* Walk on the beach again. Play Mini Golf. Or for a saltier experience, sample some liquorice. *Silverdale* Visit Wainui Historical Village. *Auckland* Take the Sail NZ America's Cup challenge. *Bombay* Spot the cairn. *Pokeno* Find some evidence of JenniferAnn.com or see the Queen's Redoubt. *Mercer* Buy some cheese from Albert. *Meremere* Spot someone with a mullet. *Rangiriri* Visit the pa site and Heritage Centre. *Lake Ohinewai* See the lake. *Huntly* Visit/see the power station (as if you could miss it). *Taupiri* See the royal graveyard. *Hopuhopu* Find a gumboot. *Ngaruawahia* See the Turangawaewae House. *Horotiu* Paint a plate at Splashy™. *Te Rapa* Visit NZ's second-largest branch of The Warehouse. *Hamilton* Gamble $100 at the Sky City Casino. *Tamahere* Don't scare anyone. *Pukeroro* PYO strawberries. *Cambridge* Take the Equine Stars Walk of Fame. *Karapiro* Visit Gavin and Judy en route to the dam. *Tirau* See the Info Site corrugated iron dog. *Putaruru* Take the Te Waihou walkway to the blue spring and have a drink. *Lichfield* Spot the cheese plant. *Tokoroa* Walk around the Talking Poles. *Kinleith* See the mill. *Atiamuri* Check out the Hatupatu rock. *Wairakei* Visit the Wairakei Terraces. *Taupo* Go trout fishing on the lake. *Wharewaka/Waitahanui/Hatepe/Hallett's Bay/Motutere/Mission Bay/Waitetoko/Te Rangiita/Tauranga-Taupo* Take in the beautiful lake views. *Motuoapa* Visit the Echo Cliffs. *Turangi* Visit the Tongariro National Trout Centre. *Rangipo/Desert Road* Admire the scenery. *Waiouru* Visit the Army Museum. *Hihitahi* Visit the Forest Sanctuary. *Turangerere* Enjoy the new road. *Ngawaka* Play New Zealand's finest 12th hole. *Bennetts Siding* See the timber mill. *Taihape* Chuck a gumboot. *Winiata* Enjoy the beautiful countryside. *Ohutu* Spot the disused building. *Utiku* Gravity Canyon/Wool Shop. Your choice … *Manui* Spot the sandstone gorges. *Mangaweka* Go kayaking on the river. *Ohingaiti* Visit Porky's Bits and Pieces. *Mangaonoho* Spot the Makohine viaduct. *Vinegar Hill* Go camp(ing). *Hunterville* Experience the shemozzle. *Silverhope* Try the wine. *Rata* See the old butter factory. *Poreua* Visit the Amazing Maze. *Greatford* See St Martin's Church. *Bulls* Discover as many 'bull' puns as you can in half an hour. *Ohakea* Visit the Air Force Museum. *Sanson* Sit in the rugby stand. *Carnarvon* Try an ice cream at the Waireka Honey Shop. *Oroua Downs* Visit the Sheepskin Factory Shop. *Himatangi* See the buoy. *Foxton* Climb the de Molens windmill. *Poroutawhao* Locate Te Rangihaeata's pa. *Levin* Go walking in the Papaitonga Scenic Reserve. *Ohau* Find somewhere open. *Kuku* Spot a wood pigeon. *Manakau* Take a break at the Kirk Wood Café. *Otaki* Visit Te Rauparaha's grave at the Rangitea Church. *Te Horo* Stay the night at Jenkins Cottage. *Waikanae* See a kiwi at the Nga Manu Nature Reserve. *Paraparaumu* Take a trip to Kapiti Island. *Paekakariki* See the amazing view. *Pukerua Bay* Buy a book at Archway Books. *Plimmerton* Visit the Te Rauparaha monument. *Paremata* Jump off the bridge. *Porirua* Watch kickboxing (or go shopping). *Tawa* Have a drink. *Johnsonville* Climb Mount Kaukau. *Wellington* Get a tattoo at Roger's.

Cape Reinga to Kaitaia.

The first time I sit down in the car, I lie.

'Where you off to, sir? Just travelling around?'

'Up north. Stopping in Kaitaia.'

'You're not going all the way up, are you?'

The car rental man talks as if I were attempting to scale Mount Doom, not simply driving the five hours or so north of Auckland. I decide appeasement is the better part of truth.

'Nah. Not me.'

It has come to my attention that if you rent a car in New Zealand the insurance doesn't cover you on what are politely referred to as 'unsealed roads' or what I call gravel. New Zealand boasts a great many of these roads, 34,000 kilometres of them from a total of 92,000 kilometres, in fact. In some places they trickle into the main asphalt highway like nervous tributaries, in others they are the only link to the outside world. One thing's for sure, they can all be treacherous. Thus the car rental companies are very specific about the rules, and my guy is no exception.

'You can go pretty much anywhere you like, it's unlimited mileage, only be sure to avoid the roads which aren't tarmacked. There's usually a notice up to say "NO RENTAL CARS BEYOND THIS POINT",' he says, posting up the words emphatically on an imaginary signpost. 'Or something like that,' he adds, a touch embarrassed at his zeal.

'Right you are,' I say.

One day later I hit gravel. To be fair, I have given the matter plenty of thought before breaking the rules. Officially, the last 20 kilometres or so of the route north from Waitiki Landing

A small epic journey down New Zealand's mother road.

The 1 Thing.

Bob Moore.

First published in 2006 by New Holland Publishers (NZ) Ltd
Auckland • Sydney • London • Cape Town

www.newhollandpublishers.co.nz

218 Lake Road, Northcote, Auckland, New Zealand
14 Aquatic Drive, Frenchs Forest, NSW 2086, Australia
86–88 Edgware Road, London W2 2EA, United Kingdom
80 McKenzie Street, Cape Town 8001, South Africa

The excerpt from *The Story of a New Zealand River* is reproduced
by permission of the Richards Literary Agency, Rangi Cross and the
estate of the late Jane Mander.

ISBN-13: 978 1 86966 136 6
ISBN-10: 1 86966 136 2

Managing editor: Matt Turner
Editor: Leigh Bramwell
Design: Dee Murch
Cover design: Seven Ltd, Bevan Tonks

A catalogue record for this book is available from the National
Library of New Zealand

10 9 8 7 6 5 4 3 2 1

Colour reproduction by Image Centre Limited, Auckland
Printed in China at Everbest Printing Co

Contents

For Claire, George & Arthur

The 1 Thing.

Acknowledgements

I would like to thank the following:
Claire my wife, for her patience and support throughout. Travelling companions *Nick Ward*, *Stephen Dalley*, *Barbara Moore*, *George Moore*, *Paul Wilkinson*, *Arthur Moore*, *Val Harris* and *Steve Harris*.
Bob Bamber & family for their kindness. *Matt Turner* for taking a chance on a first timer. *Jamie Bichan* for the tattoo template.
Leeann Morgan and *Anthony Dreaver* for their research help. And lastly *Stewart Baxter* for finding and returning my camera. Thank you.

up to Cape Reinga are not classed as State Highway 1 yet, but as Bret de Thier states in *Highway One*, his photographic homage to New Zealand's main road, they are bound to be in the near future. Besides, it doesn't feel right to start my journey inland, and more to the point I'm buggered if I'm going to drive all the way up here only to be denied the chance of spectacular coastal scenery by insurance small print. Anyway, when I reach Waitiki there is no prohibitive sign as predicted by the rental man.

'Sod it,' I say, out loud, to no-one in particular, and drive on.

Now I don't know how many of you have driven on an unsealed road in a Toyota Starlet but as a near-death experience I can thoroughly recommend it. Even a moderate volume of traffic on these roads can produce compacted ridges on the surface like indelible tank tracks. To the naked eye they don't appear anything much to be wary of. To the Starlet, however, they may as well be oil-coated marbles. Though exhilarating in a masochistic kind of way, it is also embarrassing. Of the few other cars I have met this morning, all have roared past me as if on rails, and all have been 4x4s. I swear I could hear their drivers sniggering.

Here I am, half an hour into the last 20 kilometres and still there's no hint that the road, or the land, is coming to an end. All I get is a yellow sign which advises me, without a hint of irony, not to exceed 35 kilometres per hour at a certain corner. Who are they kidding? I haven't hit 35 since Waitiki.

I'm just on the verge (sometimes literally) of wondering how I can have taken the best part of an hour to travel such a short distance on a deserted road when I see it: my first glimpse of open ocean and a tantalising flash of white water, the very first item on my checklist. Sure enough, a bone-jangling two minutes later the dunes unfold on to a tarmac car park (oh now you use bloody tarmac), and all my concerns are instantly forgotten as I survey the magnificent scene in front of me.

Cape Reinga, as every respectable Kiwi knows, is the most northern tip of New Zealand accessible by car. Much more than this it is also a wahi tapu, a deeply spiritual place for Maori. For here is Te Rerenga Wairua, 'the place of leaping', where the spirits of the dead travel to the underworld (reinga) by climbing down the roots of an 800-year-old pohutukawa and into the ocean on the final journey back to their ancestral home of Hawaiki. To preserve and respect Maori cultural heritage there is no public access to the beach itself. A sign even prohibits eating or drinking in the vicinity. A good thing too. Who wants Coke bottles and crisp packets polluting your pohutukawa?

Half-falling out of the car, I stagger straight up the headland that overlooks the entire scene. I'm not disappointed. It is a gorgeous morning with excellent visibility, a perfect start to my odyssey. Over to the left is the stunning Te Werahi Beach, a picture-perfect bite-mark of yellow sand and deep blue sea arcing away towards Cape Maria van Diemen and Motuopoa. To my right is the sacred cliff and beach itself, much smaller than I had envisaged somehow, but beautiful nonetheless. And there, down in front of me, is what I have come to see.

Not just a place of departure, Cape Reinga is also a meeting place. Here the Pacific Ocean and the Tasman Sea come together in a clash of white waves, creating a maelstrom of conflicting currents which fizz and swipe at each other on the surface of the water. It's called Columbia Bank and the ocean is relentless around here. Since 1808 more than 140 vessels have sunk in these coastal waters.

I click off a few shots from the top, sweeping around to create the kind of hit-or-miss David Hockney-esque panorama so detested by my wife. A waste of film, apparently. Determined to waste some more, I head down to the lighthouse, an elegant white-painted wooden structure set on a narrow promontory 165 metres above Columbia Bank. Early morning clear blue sky, crashing white waves, unpredictable gusts of wind – the whole experience is so breathtaking that even were I in company I would feel compelled to remain silent. Unfortunately this sentiment is not shared by two German tourists who march up, tearing at the peace with harsh syllables and bushy moustaches. The moment has gone.

There are plans to build a visitor centre here at the Cape. I can only hope they make a better job of it than at Land's End in the UK where a similarly dramatic stretch of coastline has been transformed into a cheap tea-tray theme park. It couldn't happen here though, could it? These and other questions rattle around my head as I drive my personal judder-box on the road south. The journey has begun.

Apparently there are wild horses roaming the **Te Paki** region. I can't say I have seen any, but they would have to be pretty damn wild to keep me away from the famous Te Paki sand dunes. Trouble is, the dunes are a little way from the road, and you have to cross Te Paki Stream to get there, quicksand and all. If you don't know what you're doing, and I'm pretty sure I don't, the results can be disastrous. Stopping at Te Paki Station I ponder my options. Should I wait for a coach and hitch a ride? No. Should I hitch a ride with another car? Good idea, but I am the only car in sight.

Or am I? What is this vision of spray-painted metal rolling towards me, coming to rest by the station? It looks like a heavily decorated VW combi van, with a heavily decorated driver to boot. He has a variety of tattoos and facial piercings, some of which look like they must really hurt.

'Hey man, you OK?'

I explain my dilemma. I want to go to the dunes, but my car isn't up to it.

'No problem,' says the driver and introduces himself as Jim. 'Jump in. I'll take you. Got a board in the back, too.'

According to *The Reed Dictionary of New Zealand Place Names*, my Bible for approximate Maori translation, Te Paki means 'the fine weather', and they're not joking. Man, it is hot, and I'm not even carrying the board. The warm wind and loose sand are sucking the very energy out of me. Even my sweat droplets are sweating – which, I am soon to discover, is not good when you're about to be immersed in sand.

While I rest, Jim clambers up to the top to take the first run. This is good. Not only does it give me time to get my lungs working normally again, but never having surfed or snow-boarded in my life I can also study and copy his technique. Jim carves his way elegantly down the slope and then comes jogging towards me, eyes ablaze.

'That is awesome, dude,' he says. 'You gotta have a go.'

'That's what I'm here for,' I say, bluffing desperately. I don't think Jim buys it for a second, especially not when I start questioning him about technique.

'How do I slow down?'

'Why would you want to do that?' he smiles, a crazy glint in his eye.

I start climbing. The fine, hot sand engulfs my feet as I grunt and sweat slowly upwards. With my turned-up shorts, white legs and T-shirted paunch, the only way I could look more English would be to wear a knotted hanky on my head. I reach the top slick with sweat.

I drop the board, look out to sea and take deep breaths, trying to calm myself. At base camp Jim is wondering what the hold-up is. He repeatedly gives me the thumbs up, recognised international sign language for 'Let's go', soon followed by a beckoning hand gesture, recognised international sign language for 'Hurry the fuck up, English dude.'

There is nothing else for it. I clamber gracelessly onto the board, lie down and push off. Bump, bump, bump, whoosh, JesuuuuuuUUUUUSSS! Clinging on for dear life, I hurtle down the hill at a speed faster than anything I have achieved in the Toyota Starlet. Luckily I remember Jim's advice to keep my mouth shut. For a good proportion of the ride I extend that advice to include my eyes as well. Eyelashes, ears, hair, arm-pits, pants ... I never knew I had so many nooks and crannies. I should have worn a nose clip, too. I'll be picking sand out of inconvenient areas for the rest of the day. It is over almost as soon as it begins, a sentiment I'm sure practically any male in the world can relate to. But what a rush.

Jim is still giggling foolishly when I return with the board.

'Man, you should have seen your face. Choice! You going again?'

In the spirit of true cowardice I politely decline. Back at my car we say our farewells and wonder aloud if our paths will cross again, though I suspect we both secretly know they won't. Not on this journey at least. Bless you, Jim, wherever you are.

By **Waitiki Landing**, the start proper of SH1, I'm mildly euphoric at the feel of wheel on tarmac again. I pull into the northernmost store and camping ground in New Zealand to buy some film.

'Do you have any APS film?'

'What's it for?'

'A camera.'

'Oh. I don't think so.'

I buy two disposable cameras. Pulling off the forecourt I notice for the first time that my baking hot car is making a strange electrical noise, like a metallic cow lowing. It doesn't seem to affect the performance of the engine, however – that is still as sluggish as ever. Without actually knowing it I pass through **Karatia**, looking over to the left at the beautiful, pure white silica sands of Parengarenga, and on to **Tangaoke** which, I am informed, is not an Argentinian dance-cum-sing-along, but a town with good fernbird habitat due to the nearby swamp. All I see are some particularly suicidal pukeko.

Te Kao has a gastronomically auspicious past. The name translates as 'the dried kumara' because the village used to produce such a hefty crop that much of it had to be dried and stored for later use. The resulting powder was then either rehydrated when needed, or carried as a snack on journeys. A packed lunch, if you will.

I am here simply to buy a kumara in its natural form, so it's handy that there's a dairy. The affable owner doesn't question my odd solitary purchase, although he does notice that the early morning sun has burnt my arm and seizes the opportunity to flog me some sun lotion.

'You wanna be careful, my friend.'

Before long I am through **Ngataki**, too, which as far as I can tell consists purely of a small cemetery on a hill, and on to **Waihopo**.

'If ever a place had characters and stories, Waihopo did. If ever a place was different, Waihopo was.' So says Alice Evans, a member of the famous Subritzky family of this region, in her fascinating memoirs *Mount Camel Calling.*

Gumdigging was Waihopo's claim to fame. Kauri gum was originally used by Maori for lighting fires, chewing and in some cases for moko (tattooing). However, from the late nineteenth to early twentieth centuries, the great clumps of fossilised kauri tree resin prevalent in this swampy area were dug up mainly by Pakeha settlers and shipped off to Europe and the USA where they were melted down for use in lacquers, high quality varnishes and for lining fruit and jam tins. The Subritzky family, renowned among other things for having kept a pet monkey, thrived upon this export, their ships trading the New Zealand coast, Pacific Islands and Australia. And in turn Waihopo thrived upon the community which built up around the gumdiggers.

Not so these days. I drive past a garden littered with clapped-out cars, see the remains of something which may have been the old school shed, and that is about it. There isn't even a road sign to mark the place, let alone a plaque to commemorate the hive of industry which enlivened this once bustling little town. Such a shame.

Moving swiftly on I soon find myself at **Te Raupo**, the name a reference to the native reed which grows here and whose pollen was once greatly prized by Maori for breadmaking. The ingredients for a loaf were simple: pollen and water, which was mixed into a glue, put into baskets and then steamed in a hangi. However easy the cooking method, everything else connected with making raupo bread seems a right old palaver, as the Reverend Richard Taylor tells us in *Te Ika-a a Maui: New Zealand and its inhabitants 1840s*:

> The process of making bread from the *oua*, or pollen of the *raupo*, is curious, both on account of the patience required to collect sufficient for the purpose, and for religious rites connected with it and the great stress they laid upon religion in aiding their efforts to procure it. It is also remarkable for the number of words belonging to the process, which is proof of the value put upon this article of food.

So it seems unlikely then that I will actually find anyone here who still makes raupo bread, but I might just find someone who remembers eating it, like a member of the Subritzky family perhaps, if any remain in this area. Certainly there's a Subritzky Road just over there, and hang on, there's a mailbox with the name 'Subritzky' painted on in what looks like paper correction fluid. In for a penny. I park up and knock on the door. No answer. Either no-one is home or they are all too busy out the back scoffing pollen bread from a flax basket and watching their pet monkey dance.

FIGHTING EARNS A 3-MONTH BAN
FROM THE PUB FOR BOTH PARTIES

You could never call the **Houhora** Tavern a classy joint. But to anyone who subscribes to the philosophy that pubs are for drinking in, it's ideal. It's homely in a rough sort of a way and there are fish and boar heads mounted here and there, a couple of pool tables, and a noticeboard crammed with photos, postcards and a scattering of posters including the one mentioned above, possibly a remnant of former landlord William Henry Evans (King Bill), who helped to put this place on the map.

From 1907 when he took over until his death in 1950, the colourful King Bill stamped his own particular brand of raw authority over this tavern and the surrounding area. Previously a rather rough pub, Houhora was subjected to a zero tolerance-style clean-up by the man who was rarely seen without a shabby old overcoat. (When his housekeeper decided to bury one particularly soiled example of his favourite attire, afraid he might try to wear it around the pub, he dug it up again.) And woe betide the punter who pointed out the error of his ways, or pushed him into opening up until he was good and ready. King Bill was master of the bar and anyone not playing by his rules also risked legal action, as he served as the local Justice of the Peace. That and local postmaster, storekeeper, gum tycoon, farmer, racehorse breeder and taxi driver.

In those times, gumdigging times, Houhora was the place to be seen on the Aupouri Pensinsula, boasting stables, kennels, a race track, a dance hall (the biggest in the Far North), a store, a post office and even a billiards room which must have seemed the height of opulence. The post office and shop buildings remain to this day in the pub car park, but alas they are only empty shells, and the original hotel is now a private bar. Playing safe, I head for the public bar with its eccentric collection of memorabilia.

Very much part of the fixtures and fittings are three locals who at 12.15 pm are chatting and laughing in a manner which suggests they are about to settle in for the afternoon. The most vocal of the three reminds me of Harry Dean Stanton in the opening scenes of *Paris, Texas*, only with a slightly bigger beard. Sorry, strike the word 'slightly' there. It is huge. You could stuff a cushion with it, if you were so inclined. Not wishing to upset the hirsute status quo, I nod a greeting, order a handle of beer, and settle down at an adjacent table.

The three are obviously good mates, although an unlikely trio. With the Harry Dean Stanton look-alike sits another bearded Pakeha guy, a kind of Kenny Rogers gone wrong, and a younger Maori woman. All three are drinking jugs of beer at a steady but respectable rate, and all three are clearly practitioners of the art of taihoa.

The parasitic plant known as taihoa has lent its name to a state of mind up here in the Far North. A tough vine which mats together to impede horses, carts and even heavy machinery when in abundance, taihoa was a great hindrance to early settlers, clogging roads and entangling many a beast of burden. Like a rat caught in a snake's mouth, the more the horse struggled the more it became ensnared. Thus victims of the vine's wiry grip were forced to endure taihoa, literally 'wait a while'. This came to represent either a negative image of procrastination as found in many a hot country (the Spanish *mañana*, for example) or a positive one of taking time to reflect, recharge one's batteries and untangle life's woes in a considered and mature manner. I think I know which applies to these three: it seems they plan to get well and truly taihoa-ed today.

It looks like it's going to be fun. Even the current landlord has a tinge of green to his eye as he wheels the lawnmower out back in preparation for some strenuous activity in the baking midday heat.

'Are you going to be a noisy bugger all day, then?' asks Harry Dean Stanton.

'Nah, ten minutes should do it,' the landlord replies.

'Only ten minutes? You can go and do mine after if you like,' pipes the woman. It's all good stuff. I'm in New Zealand's northernmost pub, the banter is class, the beer is chilled and it's a glorious day, as testified by the landlord on his return ten minutes later.

'Bloody hard work,' he says, wiping sweat from his brow.

'Do you good,' says Harry, raising his glass. The gesture he receives from the landlord in return is far less amicable.

Distinctly hostile too, I discover, are the origins of the name Houhora, literally 'the drying of the feathers'. Supposedly, a young Maori chieftain on a raid was chased up Ninety Mile Beach by the people from the southern end. In desperation he ran across the peninsula to where the hotel now stands and swam for it towards the settlements on what is now called Mount Camel. However, he was caught and slain, and his feather headdress laid out to dry on a rock. Nice.

Pukenui is positively thriving by comparison with everywhere else I have been so far. Opposite the wharf road stands what in Far Northern terms must count as a shopping mall;

dairy, post office, café, bar and even a takeaway outlet. As well as a fairly steady stream of custom, a large group of teenagers is hanging out on the wooden benches outside, eating fish and chips, talking loudly and showing off in that way only teenagers seem to find appealing. A car pulls up towing a trailer of brightly coloured canoes – a giant pencil-case of Day-Glo yellow, blue and orange. In the harbour modern yachts are bobbing gently on their moorings, and there is my '1 Thing', Mount Camel, lying supreme and supine (or whatever the camel equivalent is) in the distance.

Mount Camel was named by Captain Cook in 1769 because he said it lay on 'a desart [sic] shore', and for its similarity in shape to a camel kneeling. Thus far none of the pictures I have seen of Mount Camel have looked remotely like this image, and I did wonder whether maybe the scurvy or the sea air had gotten to old Cooky at this stage of his voyage. But now I'm beginning to see just what he meant. It does indeed look like a camel readying itself to take on a passenger. I take it all back. Before Cook arrived, the local Maori, never having seen a camel in their lives, had quite rationally referred to Mount Camel as Mount Whale. I suppose I can kind of see this too, although the camel definitely does it for me. And that's not a phrase I thought I'd ever utter.

For a close-up view I travel to **Raio**, pausing in the little café and picnic area at the back of the Wagener Museum. Here, Mount Camel is so near you can almost stroke it; indeed at low tide it is possible to walk across to the headland. Not today: the tide is in. I'm also disappointed that the museum, once unrivalled for its displays of Maori artefacts and gumdigging memorabilia, is now more of a holiday park, with only a small selection of Wilfred Wagener's collection remaining. At the counter I am told that due to lack of profit most of it has recently been auctioned off in Auckland. The final straw came when the tourist buses from Paihia decided to miss it out as an attraction on their route. And that, as they say, was that.

Gumdiggers Park at **Waiharara** is a short grunt through

manuka and kanuka, which are to the Far North as cypress trees are to Tuscany, marching across the skyline. Here in the eerie silence you'll find a re-creation of a gumdigger's camp. A motley collection of canvas shacks marks where only a century or so ago men, women and children ground out their trade from sun-up till sundown, six days a week. Not far from camp I come across a small, unfinished hole which still contains a kauri stump. No, my mistake. The nearby placard points out that this is not one kauri stump but two. Something has struck the two giant trees with such force that one has impaled the other, and let's not forget, these are big trees. There is a theory that the huge kauri forests which yielded all the gum here were decimated millions of years ago by a meteor-powered tsunami from somewhere out in the Tasman Sea. The waves are said to have been over two kilometres high. From what I can see, the evidence seems fairly compelling.

Before I even arrived here I liked Waiharara for its name. Waiha, in Maori, is a specific type of kumara. Rara means 'there'. Put them together and roughly translated you get 'There's kumara there'. Personally, I love this particular brand of place naming. I would be delighted if they were to rename London 'Therestoomanypeoplethere', or dub Llandrindod Wells 'Theresbuggerallthere'. Perhaps Dylan Thomas would approve of the latter, too.

Even I could have a stab at translating **Waipapakauri** by now as 'swampy ground where the kauri grows'. But to me it also means another pub. Built in 1904, the Waipapakauri Hotel is the last remaining building of a complex set up to serve the gumdiggers. Our friend A.H. Reed stopped here in 1960 and inadvertently met an amateur critic in the public bar who told him in no uncertain terms that one of his books sucked big time. Maybe I had better watch out.

It being a Sunday, the pub is humming. Every table is packed with good keen men chatting, drinking and watching the Black Caps versus Pakistan on the screens. It's rowdy, smoky, friendly. I order a Macs Gold and stand at the bar.

Before you can say 'There's kumara there', a man walks in wearing a checked shirt, shorts and gumboots, his hair sticking straight up, giving the effect that somehow even his rubber footwear has not prevented him from being successfully electrocuted.

'G'day, Alf,' says the barmaid. 'Who's your hairdresser?'

'Same as yours by the look of it,' Alf replies, quick as a flash, deadpan. Brilliant. I don't want to leave, but my quest calls me on.

A standard wooden building from the outside at least, the marae in **Waimanoni** recently staged a meeting on the settlement of the Treaty of Waitangi. I find it difficult to imagine anywhere in this sun-baked and peaceful landscape hosting anything so politically charged. More in keeping with the area seems the Ancient Kauri Kingdom at **Awanui**, with its shop delighting in all things carved and kauri. I'm not here to buy though, not really. Centre stage for me is the Giant Staircase, just part of a huge kauri log extracted from a nearby swamp in 1994, the largest of its kind ever. Now it stands as the superb centrepiece of the Kingdom, and an irresistible way of enticing people upstairs to the coffee shop.

I really should take a photo, so I ask a pleasant South African couple if they wouldn't mind doing the honours, yours truly standing portly beside it.

'Oh, that's a good idea, John,' says Mrs S.A. 'We should do that, too.' But John obviously struggles with my camera, something I don't discover until the film is developed. Not since my own father attempted to take a picture of Reims Cathedral, the second largest in France, and missed, has a photographic subject so successfully evaded capture. John forgets the staircase and zooms in on me, with a vaguely woody background.

And so it's on to **Kaitaia** on a balmy Sunday afternoon, where the smell comes close to that of Bali, or Kuta at least, a pungent, slightly abrasive odour stabbing at my nostrils, dry heat mixed with curry. But there the comparison must end. Unlike Jalan Legian, main street Kaitaia is as dead as the proverbial moa apart from a church congregation belting out hymns on one side of the street, and a karaoke bar belting out something quite different on the other. 'The Lord's My Shepherd' *vs* 'Suspicious Minds'. Heaven *vs* Hell, or vice versa depending on your standpoint.

I'm on my way to the Far North Regional Museum, a little deflated at having just been called 'Saggy Arse' by some teenager outside the bottle shop. The curator is much more polite, and gives me a guided tour of the glass cabinets containing kauri gum and a copy of the famous Kaitaia Carving uncovered from deep in a swamp here in 1921, depicting a main central figure with, unusually for traditional Maori carvings, chevron markings outside it.

'Where's the original?' I ask.

'In Auckland,' she replies, begrudgingly. Of course. Gone the same way as the Wagener no doubt.

Fish hooks carved from whale bone, a fine example of a Maori ceremonial cloak, my first complete moa skeleton (just a baby), there's plenty here including some of the remains of the *Rainbow Warrior*, the Greenpeace ship so outrageously scuppered in Auckland harbour by the French secret service in 1985, resulting in the death of a photographer. And talking of strained Franco-Kiwi relations, here is the main attraction. No, not the ball from the 1999 Rugby World Cup semi-final, but the huge iron bulk of de Surville's anchor.

Jean-François-Marie de Surville was a French explorer who flirted with the coast of New Zealand at the same time as Cook. Indeed, both captains were caught in the same storm on 28 December 1769 around the area of the North Cape. It was de Surville who fared the worse. He nearly lost his ship the *St-Jean Baptiste* in Doubtless Bay, and was forced to cast off two of his three anchors, almost certainly a factor in his decision not to stay and explore New Zealand, along with the fact he had also recently had an argument with local Maori over a dinghy. So he sailed off to different shores, sadly having his ship and crew seized in Peru, and dying in the surf there while trying to secure aid and refreshment for his scurvied men. His anchors, though, were found over 200 years later, and housed in New Zealand museums; one originally in Whangarei but now at Te Papa, and one right here in front of me, the earliest official souvenir of European involvement in New Zealand. Wow. It might not float everyone's boat (if that's a decent metaphor to use about an anchor), but I can't help feeling impressed that this hunk of black metal symbolises a meeting of two hitherto alien cultures. My reaction surprises me, and pleases my guide no end.

'In Wellington they hang their anchor from the ceiling,' she says. 'You just don't get the scale of it there. But here ...'

She certainly has a point. Laid out across the floor it is an impressive sight, maybe six metres long. My guide enthuses on, but once the initial hit has faded, my attention wanders. Well, you can only get so excited about an anchor, can't you?

Kaitaia to Kawakawa.

On the way out of Kaitaia a road sign warns of 'AGED PERSONS'. Aged Persons? Whatever happened to Elderly or Old People? The last time I heard terminology like that was in a Dickens novel. I'm still chuckling inwardly when at approximately 10.30 am I cruise into **Rangitihi**. At approximately 10.31 am I cruise straight out the other side. It is almost as if someone, possibly an aged person, has forgotten to put the Rangitihi sign out. 'Aw, Jeez, Wendy. It was your turn today.'

Never mind. It's on to **Pamapuria**, the Maori interpretation/mispronunciation of Pamphylia, which is what the Reverend Joseph Matthews christened this settlement way back in the 1830s. Nice of him, I think, although why he named a remote part of Northland after a coastal plain in southern Turkey where St Paul first entered Asia Minor to preach the gospel is beyond my powers of investigation.

My research on Pamapuria informs me that nearby Takahue kids now come to Pamapuria school because theirs was burnt down by land protestors in 1973; and that as recently as 2003, disputes here, again over land, resulted in State Highway 1 being blocked and a man arrested for, among other things, threatening to kidnap a policeman.

Fortunately for me, today all seems quiet, the worst criminal act on view being a couple of old people, sorry, aged persons, out mowing their lawns and wearing particularly malicious-looking sunhats.

I am soon approaching the town of **Victoria Valley**, named of course in honour of Queen Victoria, or Kuini Wikitoria as Maori called her. I'm not so sure she would have been amused had she known why the valley was dedicated to her though, albeit with the best intentions. The two rounded hills here are supposed to symbolise her breasts, homage enough to make any queen colour a little, I imagine, with the possible exception of Latifah.

A short drive through regal cleavage later brings me to **Mangiataiore**. There's not much to report here, either. So I kick on to the lower slopes of **Mangamuka Gorge**. The gorge itself is a vast tableau of green, a jungle of trees and ferns clinging to the slopes and plateaux of this spectacular natural feature. Like so much of New Zealand's bush landscape, it is the kind of vegetation you can imagine an explorer in an unrealistic pith helmet hacking their way through on a grainy 1950s film set. And no doubt in the past some poor sods must have done exactly that, not least the people who blazed this trail in the first place.

The road twists and turns constantly, climbing up and up to its full height of 346 metres above sea level with banked cambers and rock walls that eclipse the sun and threaten to lure you over the edge. In fact I am surprised to encounter only one white cross on the entire way up. Not that it seems to put off the locals at all. Climbing sedately in the Electric Cow, I manage to collect a string of cars behind me. Presumably they are ignoring the signs that warn of falling rocks for the next 13 kilometres, so I pull over to allow those with a death wish to scoot past.

Conveniently, my stopping place turns out to be a viewing point with a panorama looking all the way back to Kaitaia. It is incredible just how much the scenery has changed in that short distance. From gentle, sun-scorched undulations to vivid green hills and bush in no more than 20 minutes. Like a new country.

Manga means 'stream', and muka refers to the nikau palm which thrives in these parts. Beyond this however, **Mangamuka** is also the name of one of the legendary taniwha or water spirits which allegedly roam the length and breadth of the country and are especially prevalent in the Hokianga. It is said that two taniwha, Arai-te-uru and Niwa, guard the north and south heads of the entrance to the harbour. These latter-day Scylla and Charybdis are reputed to lash out with their tails to stir up the waters and bring misfortune to any waka (canoe) that dares to enter. Arai-te-uru has a family, a brood of younger taniwha who are responsible for many of the geographical features of the area, such as the Waihou Valley and Lake Omapere. Mangamuka was one of these offspring who, after carving a channel with his nose through solid rock (Mangamuka Gorge), was blinded by a tupua (shape-shifting spirit) and retreated eventually to die in the bay not far from Kohukohu, Motitui Island, where he is said to lie today.

At the garage by **Mangamuka Bridge** the attendant gives me perfect directions to the Omahuta Kauri Sanctuary. He also sports a dazzling outfit. No bland corporate uniform for this chap. Resplendent in a string vest, bright red tartan shorts and knee-length white socks accompanied by, yes, you guessed it, a pair of brown leather sandals.

'You have a good day,' he shouts. He's already made certain of that.

So far I have seen plenty of dead kauri: stumps, logs, offcuts shaped into both attractive and unattractive objects. But I am yet to see a full-grown specimen alive in its natural habitat. The Omahuta Tree Sanctuary promises to change all that. Now, as anybody who has watched *Logan's Run* will testify, a sanctuary is not always the easiest place to reach. I can vouch for this as 20 minutes later, red-cheeked and wheezing heavily, I am struggling up a hill cursing my lack of fitness.

I've seen pictures of mature kauri in books and on the Internet, but nothing can really prepare you for your first glimpse of one of these giants. Even from a distance I can tell it is a monster. And as I near my goal, tramping through the lush undergrowth, the sight only becomes more impressive.

The kauri truly is a tree-hugger's dream, especially if you enjoy working in teams. From a shoot, it grows at a steady 30 centimetres a year to start with, rising straight up to stick its neck higher than any surrounding trees. In middle age it then spreads its canopy and, much like a human, adds to its girth. And then adds, and adds some more, except a kauri manages somehow to keep a pretty much uniform girth from ground to branch level. Oh, and then it lives for a thousand years or so.

The biggest living kauri in New Zealand today, Tane Mahuta or 'Lord of the Forest', is to be found in the Waipoua Forest, unfortunately too far south of my current route. It is estimated to be over 1200 years old, and about 67 metres high, with a girth of around 13 metres from its base up to branch level. But even this is slim stuff compared with some kauri on record. One felled at Mercury Bay on the Coromandel Peninsula had a ground to branch level distance of 23 metres, a girth of 22 metres and a diameter of 7 metres. That's one hell of a potential staircase.

The rest of the walk through Omahuta Kauri Sanctuary is a treat. The pathway snakes through marshy swamp and thick vegetation alike, right up beside these massive trunks. It is like walking through a green New York, carefully watching the ground yet always with one eye on the towering skyscrapers above you. At times I feel dwarfed, insignificant; at others I'm reminded of just how fragile these giants can be, a fallen kauri spanning the trail at one point forcing me to duck underneath, its hollow cadaver big enough to accommodate several Electric Cows, or so it seems on reflection when I get back to the car, panting and desperately in need of a decent cup of tea.

'What can I get ya?' asks the woman at the **Umawera** Tea Rooms.

I'm assuming she's the new owner, since it was auctioned off about a year ago. Her husband sits at one of the other picnic-style tables, reading a paper.

'Just a pot of tea, please,' I answer, sounding painfully English. 'How long have you been here?'

'About a year,' she says. Spooky.

'So are you a local, or did you move here? If you don't mind me asking,' I add, not wishing to come over too pushy.

'Woodlands,' she replies, a place down the bottom of the South Island, just north of Invercargill. It seems like quite a drastic move, from the south of the South to the north of the North, and I tell her so.

'Seems quite a drastic move,' I say. 'From the south of the South to the north of the North.'

'Yeah. Well, we fancied a change. Things were a bit too quiet down there.'

I look around. Apart from the Tea Rooms there is very little else man-made to be seen in any direction. Rolling countryside with birds singing, insects chirruping. No car noise. Nothing. I don't know whether she is serious or just having a laugh at my expense. Her expression never betrays the slightest hint of irony. If she is joking it is genius. If not, the last leg of my trip in the South Island promises to be a right bag of laughs.

Before leaving I feel a minor urge to visit the toilet. I refrain, however, and get back out on the highway: I'm saving it up for a much more auspicious location just a few stops along.

According to most translations, **Rangiahua** means either 'Great' or 'To approach the sky'. We assume this has something to do with the relatively tall hill ahead. I say 'we' because on this, my second visit to this particular town, I'm now accompanied by a friend of mine, Nick Ward, writer of the movie *Stickmen*, who's here to help me find an ancient puriri tree originally used by Maori as a mooring post. Reed mentions it in his book. He also talks of a hotel and store up on the hill, run by a certain Mr Harry Cheeseman, all of which I spectacularly failed to uncover on my first trip here.

We park up beside the river and start searching. My map shows houses up on the hill which simply aren't there. No shop, no hotel, nothing. In fact, apart from a shell of a place we have passed on the road here, the only man-made object on view approximating a home is the ramshackle barn across by the bridge which Nick points out.

'Where?' I ask.

'Over there,' Nick replies. 'The one with the two dogs outside the front and the man unloading something from the boot of his car ...'

The man is named Dave and proves very affable, much more so than I think I may ever be towards two portly, unshaven men who turn up at my gate.

'G'day,' bellows Nick, brimming with confidence. I am just relieved the dogs are tied up. 'I wonder if you can help us...'

We introduce ourselves and Dave shakes both our hands in turn with his own oil-stained paws. He then proceeds to shed absolutely no light whatever on the history of his home or its surroundings.

'I'm only renting,' he explains apologetically. 'Been here for about a year.'

Of course. This is becoming a worrying trend in Northland. I ask about the hotel and shop, to be greeted by a blank expression.

'Nah,' says Dave, a man economical with his words. 'Not any more. Used to be a sandworks here.' He motions towards the corrugated iron shed behind him. 'Boats up from the coast.'

I want to ask him about the puriri tree, but I think all three of us realise we are onto a loser.

Never mind. Further up the road is a New Zealand Historic Places Trust sign which reads 'HISTORIC PLACE'. Intrigued, we take a look at the small plinth in the lay-by.

THE BARON CHARLES DE THIERRY
ESTABLISHED HIS HOME IN 1837 ON
THE TERRACE 250 METRES SOUTH
OF THIS PLAQUE ON LAND GIVEN
BY THE CHIEFS PATUONE AND NENE.

In 1820, after fleeing the French Revolution, Baron Charles-Phillippe-Hippolyte de Thierry arranged from the UK for land to be bought for him in the 'New World', presumably not for the purpose of building a supermarket. He supposedly paid the bargain price of 36 axes for just over 40,000 acres, or so he thought. Unfortunately it took him a further 15 years to make it down here, by which time the Maori chiefs, understandably presuming no-one was coming to claim it, had re-sold the land to other Europeans, and rightfully for a much higher price. However, in an act of extreme generosity the chiefs Patuone and Nene offered the errant Gaul a smaller slice of land, as long as he renounced his previous claim. With little choice in the face of such kindness, de Thierry accepted. And then modestly declared himself not only the principal pioneer colonist, but 'King and Sovereign Chief of New Zealand'. Those Frenchies, huh?

Eccentric he may have been, but de Thierry's nationalistic bluster was also a contributing factor in Britain's desire to annex New Zealand for itself, in turn giving rise to the Treaty of Waitangi. And now here we are, standing right beside this land, just 250 metres from the first Kiwi 'Chez Thierry'. You can't help but feel a little humbled. Unfortunately, it is obviously not a feeling shared by everyone who stops in this lay-by. So whoever you are, 'Nero', or possibly 'Nerd' – the person who sprayed the monument with bright blue graffiti, anyway – you could do a lot worse than follow the advice of Mr Garrett, a former deputy headmaster at my old school: 'There are a lot better ways to make your mark on the world.' Although possibly not as luminous.

Waihou Valley owes its name to the same legend as Mangamuka. Indeed, Waihou is said to be the taniwha who carved both the valley which bears his name and Lake Omapere, where he quite literally curled up and died.

Not marked on my map, however, the Northland Firehouse Museum, which I'm now approaching, is a shock of vivid red surrounded by a scattering of ex-service fire engines. A grey-haired man is merrily knocking the crap out of some paving slabs as I pull up the drive.

'My little boy would love this,' I venture as a starter, referring to the fire engines rather than the general whacking of paving slabs. Mind you, either would be true.

'Yeah. Mine used to. That's how all this started.'

My new friend, now close to retiring, was originally in the fire service. No surprise there, then. One day he proudly brought home a model of a fire truck for his son, like the one he used at work. And then another. And it went from there.

'I just kept collecting. My son did, too. He was a fireman for a while, but then he started a family and moved away, so now it's up to me. Kids, eh? Let me turn the lights on for you.'

We walk through into the garage. The fluorescent tubes flicker on to reveal an obsession: glass cabinets crammed with neatly displayed models of fire trucks, fire helicopters, flashing lights, extinguishers, hoses and helmets adorning every inch of the walls from ceiling to floor.

'Don't forget the upstairs, too,' he says, before sauntering off to punish some more slabs.

Upstairs holds all the uniforms, dozens of them on racks, from fire services across the globe, and more helmets including a shiny golden one from the 1880s NZ Fire Service, and a particularly alarming example sprayed liberally with bitumen from a tanker blaze. Thankfully, the wearer only suffered minor shoulder burns, according to my host. He is noticeably less forthcoming about the 9/11 FDNY uniform, however, perhaps as a mark of respect.

'What a lot of stuff,' I say, eruditely.

'Yes. I need to sort it out better but it's just me these days,' he sighs, wistfully rubbing the back of his neck. 'I'm retiring in two years, so I'll try and do it then, build a new structure and get these trucks inside so they don't rust away.' It seems a massive undertaking for one man. 'If I didn't keep hold of this stuff it would just get thrown away or auctioned off to some bugger in Auckland,' he adds. Now where have I heard that before?

'Don't forget to sign the book, will you?' he says. 'It helps me get Lotto funding.'

Before long I am on my way to catch a train in **Okaihau**. Unfortunately, and in a role reversal of my 34 years experience as a rail passenger, I am late for that train. About 17 years too late, in fact.

There's puppies in an apple box and pipis in a sack,
Ridin' the Okaihau Express,
But no-one knows the difference
        when they're drippin' from the rack,
Ridin' the Okaihau Express.

So goes one verse from the traditional New Zealand song by Peter Cape entitled, of course, 'The Okaihau Express'. Ah, they don't write 'em like that any more, which some might suggest is a good thing. The song pays tribute to the railway that used to link Okaihau with Otiria and the Auckland line just 20 kilometres to the east. Like so many of New Zealand's railways since the war, this stretch of line closed down, unable to compete with the relative cheapness and efficiency of road transport. In 1950 New Zealand had a railway network of about 5700 kilometres. By 1990 that figure had been reduced to just 3500 kilometres. The Okaihau line did well to survive until 1987.

Today, though, you'd never know the railway existed here, were it not for the 1926 rail tunnel which you pass on the right as you come in, running as it does through a grassy bank to the main street. Of course these days it connects nowhere to nothing, its dank innards merely a magnet for the usual litter you'd expect (empty beer cans, condom wrappers) and some you wouldn't, such as a bottle of Kiwi shoe polish and a whiteboard marker. How do these things get here? 'Ah, Trace, the bloody whiteboard marker's stuffed.' 'No worries, Col. Just chuck it in the tunnel and get another one of out the box.'

The name Okaihau, I find out from the local dairy, can be pronounced both 'Okay-how' and 'Okay-who'. As in 'Okay, how did that dog get in here?' or 'Okay, who is going to clean that up?' Literally translated as 'the wind eater' or 'one who eats wind' (as opposed to talking it or passing it, presumably), Okaihau was first established as a European-style township in 1862 by a bunch of Canadian settlers who set up home and began clearing the land for farming. The railway followed soon after. But before both the Canadians and the trains, it was the British Army that steamed into this part of the world.

As you head east along this stretch of State Highway 1 you pretty much follow in chronological order of battle the First New Zealand War, the initial period of unrest caused by Maori dissatisfaction with the overbearing British interpretation of the Treaty of Waitangi. So as I trundle towards what used to be Te Mawe pa at Puketutu on the shores of Lake Omapere, my first encounter is happily to be with the opening site.

I have with me copies of the sketches of the battle of Puketutu pa, drawings and watercolours by Major Cyprian Bridge and Lance-Sergeant John Williams, both members of the British 58th Regiment present on the day of 8 May 1845. The fading scenes show an innocuous-looking wooden fort by the shores of Lake Omapere surrounded by scores of well-drilled, smart British troops armed with everything from musket to long-range cannon. But the paintings tell only part of the story.

I also have a fellow navigator again in Nick – someone with whom to discuss options and help find the pa, someone to turn off electric fences and offer a helping hand out of boggy marshes, and someone to give me at least a 50/50 chance of survival should an irate farmer take umbrage at us crossing his land and take a potshot. To avoid the last of these fates, we think it best to ask at the nearest farm before trying to locate the exact site from the map. We are soon in earnest conversation with a mother and daughter. I show them the paintings.

'Oh, yes! There's the lake! Crikey, I had no idea!' exclaims the mother. 'We've only been here a year,' she adds, almost apologetically. I've heard that line somewhere before. She is very amenable though, inviting us to follow the cattle runs as long as we shut gates.

'We're not going to get shot at, then?'

'No,' she says. 'Not on a Monday.' I'm pretty sure she is joking, but you never really know, do you?

We park the car further up SH1 beside a gate, and strike off southwards on foot. Our target is the larger of two small promontories jutting into Lake Omapere. 'Easy,' we think, a spring in our step. 'That must be it there.' And indeed we are right. Unfortunately, in the next couple of minutes we manage to persuade ourselves otherwise and cut further across country, much to our regret. The electric fences become more prevalent, as do the marshes. Still, historically, we are in good company.

In 1845, led by Lieutenant Colonel Hulme, the British Army trudged this very same route, hampered by lashing rain and boggy conditions. 'Never passed so miserable a night,' wrote the soldier artist Bridge. Things didn't improve for them during the battle, either. After ineffectual rocket bombing, Hulme sent 216 men on a suicide mission to take the pa. They were caught in a pincer attack between Hone Heke's men inside the pa and Kawiti's men hiding in the bush, and were forced to retreat, exhausted.

It's a feeling we can relate to. Nick has just clipped his testes on an electric fence, and five minutes ago in the woods I had a fish dropped on my head by an irate nesting bird. To add insult to injury, we have also just walked five kilometres out of our way to find the pa site when all it should really have taken was a short, effortless stroll across two fields.

Still, we're here now and the scene is beautiful, the sun glistening on the lake. In fact, it is difficult to imagine a battle ever unfolding in such idyllic surroundings, but then I guess that's the same with many old battle sites. Sadly, there is nothing here to mark the historic event, and I can't help thinking that this should be addressed somehow. Just a signpost, or a plinth maybe, anything to commemorate those who gave their lives unnecessarily by the shores of Lake Omapere.

Our goal achieved, Nick and I trudge back to the car, older if not wiser men.

Teahuahu is not far away, which in some ways is a god-send, in others not so great. Sure, it means only a brief jaunt down the highway, but considering we have just put ourselves through an unnecessarily arduous flog across marshland, cows and electric fences, the prospect of then climbing a 373-metre volcanic cone is not one we attack with relish. 'The view, Moore,' I tell myself, 'think of the view, the satisfaction. Not the aching calf muscles.'

It's not going to work, though, especially when Nick points out we're losing light fast, and we still have to 'do' Ohaeawai, our next stop on SH1, today. Whatever my legs think, and I'm guessing they approve, logic necessitates that instead of traipsing up its flanks we stop and admire Teahuahu, home of Kuratopepa pa, from below. I feel a little let down.

Ah well, I console myself that the site itself may even be tapu, or if it isn't then it probably should be, especially considering the events that unfolded here shortly after those on the shores of Lake Omapere.

The Battle of Teahuahu was an all-Maori affair. Matters came to a head when Te Taonui and Waka Nene, Nga Puhi loyal to the Crown, stormed in to take Heke's pa here during his absence. This displeased the chief greatly, and along with his ally Te Kahakaha he resolved to recapture it. They ought to have, too. The odds were with them, outnumbering the men within the newly occupied pa almost three to one. But somehow it just never happened. The plan was good – a two-pronged attack with Heke taking on Nene on one side, and Taonui and Te Kahakaha battling it out on the other. Only this time no-one was trapped in the middle. After much vicious armed combat and many musket volleys, Waka Nene held his ground against Heke, while around the other side during one particularly reckless advance, Te Kahakaha was gunned down and mortally wounded. On hearing this, Heke lost it. He stripped off his clothes and weapons and ran screaming across the battlefield to where his friend lay dying, at which point his men thought discretion the better part of valour and retreated at the double. At some point in the process, too, Heke was shot in the thigh, though fortunately for him it was just a flesh wound. And so, his forces having fled, his friend dead and he himself wounded, Heke slunk off under cover of darkness back to Ohaeawai. All in all, 12 June 1845 was not a good day at the office. Still, it could have been worse. At least Heke survived to fight on another day, and his experiences at Teahuahu may have served to steel his resolve. He never lost another battle.

The only battle Nick and I are beginning to lose is against the light. And so, like Heke, we, too, slink off in the encroaching darkness towards **Ohaeawai**.

Turn left at the T-junction by the Ohaeawai Hotel and you stay on State Highway 1. Take a short detour right on State Highway 12 and you'll soon see a 'MONUMENT' signposted off to the right through a gateway. This leads you to St Michael's Church, a small and unremarkable wooden building, nothing much to look at in itself, but we're here for the site more than what now sits upon it.

The hills either side loom darkly over Nick and me as the sun begins to set. Almost subconsciously we assume a respectful, subdued air as we wander around the headstones. It's a gloomy place, even for a cemetery. There are two memorial stones of the battle here, the famous cross on the south-east side of the church and a more recent plinth by the entrance gate. I remember from James Belich's historical documentary that at least one of the stone walls of the graveyard is positioned directly over the outer wooden wall of the old pa, a faint echo of history in what is, after all, a truly important site in modern military history. For it was here at Ohaeawai, during the third battle of the First New Zealand War, that the Maori 'invented' trench warfare, in a plan masterminded by that wily old warlord Kawiti, also of Nga Puhi.

In addition to building a triple palisade, Kawiti ordered the construction of an underground network of communication tunnels and bomb shelters within the pa, to keep his men safe from the inevitable British bombardment which started on 24 June 1845. The plan worked. By the time the British, led by the arrogant Colonel Henry Despard, believed they had pounded Kawiti's army out of existence, they were in fact still relatively unscathed. Another disastrous British charge saw 33 men dead within seven minutes, and Despard's name destined for military infamy. In fact the Duke of Wellington was heard to remark that only distance saved him from a court martial.

In the present day, Nick and I take a last look around the gravestones before heading back to the car. As we exit the graveyard Nick explains that the bottles of water sitting on a rock by the gate are a Maori custom.

'You use them to wash the dead spirits from you,' he says.

I sprinkle my hands liberally, glad to be leaving here and heading back to the pub, where these days Happy Hour is Tuesdays 6–7 pm, Saturday is Karaoke with Kara, and the locals are nothing but friendly.

There's not a lot to **Pakaraka**, or 'pa of the karaka' (a berry-bearing tree), but what fruits it bears, both physical and historical, are certainly worthy of note. Hone Heke was born here, and buried here, too, in a cave known as Umakitera. These days the town lives in the charming shadow of possibly the cutest little church I've ever seen. In fact, Holy Trinity Church is so cute it makes me want to wear a flat cap, socks and sandals, tow a caravan and set up a picnic on a trestle table in the lay-by, just so I can sit and eat egg-and-cress sandwiches, drink tepid tea and marvel at it. It is fantastic. A harmonious combination of white-painted timber and grey slate roof in the Gothic Revival style, surrounded by a white picket fence.

Pakaraka's church is a memorial to Henry Williams, leading figure of the Church Missionary Society in New Zealand during the mid-1800s and original translator of the Treaty of

Waitangi, although I don't think we should hold that against him. It was built by his wife, Marianne, and family after his death in 1867, and the two lie here side by side in the cemetery. As a monument to the life of a loved one, they don't come much better.

The road curves south-east out of Pakaraka to, let's see, **Moerewa**. Oh. A quick wrinkle of the nose. Then **Kawakawa**. Ah, well, maybe not so bad then. Now, I am sure anyone who has ever been this far north will not be surprised at this reaction. Hell, even people in Moerewa will be expecting me to put the boot in. It would be easy, and I imagine they'd be used to it by now. Well, time out there, Dr Marten.

Only a couple of kilometres yet worlds apart, separated by a trio of humpback bridges to quicken the pulse of any respectable Scalextric fan, Moerewa is the ugly duckling to Kawakawa's beautiful swan, on the surface at least. Whereas Moerewa has a grubby, industrial railway siding, Kawakawa has a romantic train track running up the middle of the high street, with daily steam trains to Opua in the Bay of Islands. Similarly Kawakawa's shop frontages and houses are bright as the proverbial buttons while many of Moerewa's houses are in disrepair or in dire need of a lick of paint. I'm sure you're beginning to get the picture. And the cause of such a marked difference in fortunes for these two towns? Well, you could say it's a tale of two toilets, and I plan to visit both while I'm here. In fact they are the reason I have been crossing my legs since the Umawera Tearooms. We'll start with Kawakawa.

Kawakawa's public toilet was designed by renowned Viennese artist and architect Friedrich Hundertwasser, a resident here in his later years, and it is superb, possibly creating a new psychiatric condition which will henceforth be known as 'toilet envy'. Finished in 1999, it could be described as a kind of psychedelic Persian palace, with colourful ceramic mosaics and bottle glass windows offset by a grass roof and a living tree integrated into the design structure. In other words a masterpiece, and as a result the town has flourished.

Moerewa, too, has a new public toilet, finished around the same time, only they had to fight tooth and nail to get it. Without the considerable kudos of a world-famous artist backing the project, it took a community festival and local initiative called Te Puna i Keteriki to bring about their functional stone building, now brightly decorated with murals of native flora and fauna. Incidentally, the name Te Puna i Keteriki comes from a Maori whakatauki or saying which talks of 'the knitting of people when peace is made'.

So you see, although to most eyes there is no comparison, both toilets here have a history worthy of note, which is why I choose to 'spread the love' by making free use of both today. And if you're ever on holiday heading up towards the Bay of Islands via State Highway 1 and you see the smart, new wooden sign for Kawakawa, do drop in and take a look around this revitalised town, including its top-notch toilet. But don't stop there. Carry on to Moerewa to check out their toilet, too, and help the town that translates as 'to float on high like a bird' live up to its name. They've earned it just as much.

Kawakawa to Whangarei.

'Let's see if we can find Elvis,' says Ariana, our guide, as we enter the caves at **Waiomio**.

Blimey, don't say this is where he's been hiding all along. She is in fact referring to a large eel which scavenges in the rock pools at the cave mouth. A few steps in and sure enough, there's the King himself, lying black and immobile, peering up at another herd of strange creatures in the daily procession past his home. I'm on the tour with a young family, and one of the kids attempts to stir him with a tiny pebble, much to the consternation of her mother, but Elvis is having none of it.

'He must be grumpy today,' Ariana says. 'Can you see Priscilla anywhere?'

A quick hunt reveals no sign of Elvis' companion eel.

'Ah, no wonder he's grumpy, then,' she concludes, and leads us on into the cave proper.

As we climb the wooden stairs to the upper tier I discover that these caves are home not just to an abundance of glow-worms (yet to be seen) but also to a fascinating tale of Maori heritage and, if my hearing is up to scratch, that Ariana herself is a direct sixteenth-generation descendant of the protagonist. The story goes that over three centuries years ago Hineamaru, a famous ancestress of the Ngatihine tribe, came to Waiomio from the Hokianga with her father Torongaere and her brothers. On exploring the valley of her new home she was intrigued to find tawa berries which had been trodden on although none of her party had ever travelled that way. Later, she also smelt smoke which seemed to be coming from a nearby hill. On further investigation Hineamaru discovered this cave, and 150 metres or so within she came across a woman named Roku sitting by a fire. Roku explained she was hiding from her husband, Haumoearangi of the tribe Ngatitu, as he had beaten her severely. Legend has it that she hid here for more than a year before being discovered. Standing here in Roku's Kitchen as it is now called, I can only marvel at her resourcefulness and be chilled by the desperation that forced her to live in these dank, dark surroundings for such a long time.

I'm lagging behind, however, as the kids are much more interested in what's happening further down the 200-metre trail. Even with Ariana's lamp beaming out in front, we begin to see the first few specks of neon blue dotting the ceiling of the cave. First, though, comes an impressive collection of stalagmites and stalactites.

'This is what we call the Tom Toms,' says Ariana, shining her light on two musical ridges in the side wall of the cave. 'Hard and hollow. Have a go. Play us a tune.'

Some of us duly oblige, and we walk on past more pools containing another resident eel, this time named Michael Jackson. Careful, Ariana; this is supposed to be a kids' tour. And as if on cue, we soon arrive at two huge, phallic stalactites. 'Fingers', she calls them, but I have a lower opinion.

Then it's on to the highlight of our tour, the glowworms themselves, and the part of the cave known as the Milky Way. It is stunning, and when the lamp is turned off and we are left in the pitch black to gaze at the celestial beauty above us the effect is breathtaking – myriad dots on the ceiling, as if the stars have come down to create a heaven on earth. No wonder Ariana has developed a neck problem from all the looking up she has done during her tours. You can't blame her. The cave is mesmeric. And all from something as simple as gnat larvae.

On the road again, signposts are back in fashion. I turn left on to gravel once more and commence the winding climb to **Ruapekapeka**, 'the bat's nest', scene of the final showdown in the First New Zealand War and now rightfully a historic reserve. In 1845 it took the British Army with all its equipment just over three weeks to travel this short distance through the bush, whereas today I make the same journey in roughly 20 minutes. Mind you, presumably the soldiers had to build this road, and what they found at the end of it would put even their experiences of Ohaeawai in the shade.

At the car park I leave the Electric Cow in the late afternoon sun and enter the pa through the ornately carved wooden gate. My climb up the final section of the hill takes me to the inner compound, a markedly different scene these days although some of the old trench outlines remain. The Maori cannon still sits at the centre of this lush plateau, pointing forlornly west-wards in a final gesture of defiance.

Its defences masterminded again by Kawiti, the pa at Ruapekapeka was a trap waiting to be sprung. Safe within its palisades and complex network of hollows and tunnels, local Maori withstood more than two weeks of constant bombard-ment before retreating into the woods in an attempt to ambush the chasing British soldiers. Their dastardly plan didn't work, but Ruapekapeka served once again to show the British what they were up against and forced Governor Grey to pursue peace, in the north at least, in more diplomatic ways.

When in places like this I'm never sure whether it's the knowledge that life-changing events occurred here that lends them such a definite presence, or whether they are imbued with something else, something deeper. I suspect the former, but sometimes it's almost comforting to believe the latter. Either way, Ruapekapeka must have been an amazing fortress for those short three or four months of activity.

The **Towai** Tavern has quite a history. Established in 1872, it has also been known as 'the grasshopper house' after moving location twice in its lifetime. It started out about a kilometre away from its current site, down the hill near the stream, but in

1933 was moved up the hill on rollers by a tractor. Apparently it took three days to shift, and the bar never closed during that time. I presume crampons were provided for patrons.

It's still a beautiful old building today, although you don't really get to appreciate fully its original colonial-style balcony unless you cross the busy SH1.

'Hot enough for ya?' asks the beaming landlord. 'That'll see you right,' he says, pushing a lager my way. I grab it as gratefully as my armful of research notes will allow and walk on through to the only empty table in the beer garden, receiving a few strange looks from a group of bikers in the process. It's the 'He's in a pub and he's got books and stuff' variety of stare.

The tavern has a 'Hole in One Challenge' on the green situated down the hill. The reward for achieving the nigh impossible is $1000, but there are a couple of other minor prizes involved, too. Getting on the green earns you an extra ball, while scudding your way through a conspicuous truck door window somewhat closer to the tee gets you a free beer. The odds are against me, but it's too good an opportunity to miss so I pay my money and line myself up with three balls.

To hoots of derision from the bikers, my first shot scoots harmlessly down the hill to the left, coming to rest in long grass. My second ball is even worse; after a poor contact it ends up no more than three metres away. I'm beginning to wonder whether this was such a good idea after all. But my final attempt has the crowd gasping. It soars gracefully through the air, looping down right at the flag, bounces a metre in front of the hole and skips on past and off the back of the green. Damn my lack of backspin.

'Not having another go?' asks the landlord when I take my empty glass back to the bar. I decline politely, explaining that I think I have outdone myself already. Besides, I still have a distance to go this evening so it's back into the Electric Cow and off down the road, passing a sign for Dawson's Bridge and wondering idly whether there's a Dawson's Creek underneath.

Akerama is said to be the Maori form of Aceldama, the

Field of Blood, first referred to in the Old Testament as the place where Cain killed his brother Abel. According to the Acts of the Apostles in the New Testament, it was also the land Judas bought with his blood money. What this has to do with a sleepy backwater in New Zealand I am unsure. But then there's St Matthew, whose gospel takes the slightly different view that Judas didn't buy the land at all; the chief priests did so after his suicide, using his blood money for the specific purpose of having somewhere to bury strangers or foreigners. It all clicks into place. Perhaps Akerama is so called because it was originally a graveyard, presumably for the new settlers who were arriving more and more frequently by the mid-nineteenth century. Today it is as quiet as a graveyard too, so I move on.

The land on which **Hukerenui** now sits was originally bought from local Maori by the Crown in 1875. At the time it was thought of as little more than swamp but in 1887, after a deal of to-ing and fro-ing with the Land Office over its suitability for settlers, Hukerenui South as it was then called (Towai was Hukerenui North) it came into being as a community. The first years were tough going. The Waipuakakahau Stream to the north was prone to flooding, from whence presumably came the name Hukerenui, or 'large cascade'. And if persistent rain didn't foil crops in winter and spring, then scorching hot sun parched the earth in the summer. Add to the mix a plethora of natural plagues such as locusts and crickets, and the outlook was by no means rosy for this young town. Matters were not improved in 1888 when a fire devastated over a third of the nearby Puhipuhi forest, a lifeline for those settlers whose livelihood relied on kauri logging or gumdigging.

Still, despite losing over half of its original number through illness or plain disillusionment, the community pulled together in true Kiwi fashion to stick it out. The discovery of silver in Puhipuhi was just the morale boost they needed, and although the finds were shortlived, it proved a launching pad for local commerce. By 1904 the railway had brought even greater prosperity. As the terminus on the line north from Whangarei,

Hukerenui boasted a railway station and a goods and engine shed. The town also benefited from a temperance boarding house, a post and telegraph station, a public hall, a local store, a blacksmith shop, a bootmaker and a butcher, as well as a school and a hotel.

With the exception of the last two, they're gone now – even the store and the post office. The school is still a fair size by all accounts, catering for five- to 13-year-olds from towns all around the area, and other little communities which have seen their own amenities disappear with the march of time.

But there remains the Hukerenui Hotel – or the Huka, which has recently evolved into the Happy Huka. The sole slice of original history in the town, the Huka was opened around 1890 by one Carl Rasmussen, who also owned one of the two local stores. It is of a very similar style to the Towai Tavern up the road, and like its pub twin it, too, has been moved from its original location. In the Huka's case, though, it was a downhill slide, not an uphill one. The trip was short but tricky, taking several weeks using bullock teams and timber jacks to slide the pub down the slope. Happily, as in Towai, the landlord managed to keep the bar open during the move.

Today the Happy Huka sits proudly beside SH1 (on the left as you travel south), a beacon for passing trade like me with my orange juice, and local farm and forestry workers of the area who have arrived to watch the rugby.

I'm reaching wetter, swampier country, although I doubt the ancestors of Hukerenui would agree with me. **Waiotu** turns out to be a tiny place, in fact without the map I'd be struggling to find it at all. The name Waiotu literally means 'pool or stream of Tu', or Tumatauenga, Maori god of war. It is said that ceremonies were carried out here in his honour, in the Waiotu River which runs close by. These days the only rituals performed near the waters are those of anglers waiting patiently for their next bite. According to Fish and Game New

Zealand, just by the road and railway bridge is a promising spot for trout fishing, both up and downstream. Today, however, no-one is rising to the challenge, not even at dusk when the fish are said to be gagging for it. I sit ruefully in the car at the side of the road and wish I had brought a rod. Then again, my angling skills leave a lot to be desired. So for this evening at least, the trout of Waiotu can sleep soundly in their river beds.

Whakapara is another tiddly place, most of it huddling around the swampier area by the old road north. Indeed, the main street is still called Old North Road, its more recent cousin SH1 taking the higher ground to the east, presumably to avoid flooding from the river.

The name Whakapara means 'to make a clearing in a bush', which I presume is exactly how the old Maori town originated – someone asked where they should live, and the chief said 'let's make a clearing in that bush.' Simple. With the advent of Europeans the clearing and the population grew considerably and by the end of the 19th century Whakapara was a thriving timber town with two mills nearby. Nowadays it doesn't even have a Post Shop. Still, at least it got to keep its original name, a fact I discovered purely by accident on Google. The search engine returned no results for Whakapara, but asked me whether I meant 'Whakarapa'. Not noticing the subtle change, I clicked on the link and was bombarded with information on Dame Whina Cooper of hikoi fame. It turns out she was instrumental in renaming her home town of Whakarapa, 100 kilometres away in the Hokianga, as Panguru, because the post office sorters in Whangarei and Auckland always confused the mail.

There is one twist in the tale. As far as I can make out, Dame Whina Cooper's hikoi started from Te Hapua in the Far North and pretty much followed State Highway 1 all the way down through Northland, which means the route must have missed out Panguru but ironically gone straight through Whakapara here.

I'm still pondering this as I enter **Otonga**, 'the place of the south wind' although an ill wind for me. Wanting inspiration for my '1 Thing', I am desperate for information here. My research tells me only that SH1 has been upgraded here recently and there was a problem with sediment control. Oh, and that there is a racehorse called Otonga Ripper. Fascinating stuff.

Next stop is **Waro**, literally a 'deep pit or chasm'. I am wondering if the naming of the place was a prophetic intuition on the state of the road surface around here when, quite startlingly, the tops of the limestone rocks for which I have been searching loom out of the bush.

You can take a wander through the Waro Limestone Reserve, an ancient geological outcrop which according to www.whangareinz.com 'looks like a giant has tossed the toys out of the playpen'. If you're a keen amateur rock climber you can scale them, too, with cliff heights from 9 to 18 metres. Or if, like me, you're not keen on either of these options, you can avoid the treacherous sink holes, caves and getting your thumb caught on a crampon, and simply admire the view.

It is 10 am. I'm with my friend Nick again, and we're cruising into **Hikurangi**, home of the famous Salty Dog bait ('That's the bugger you need' as the radio ad goes) and the Hikurangi Historical Museum. Sitting on the kerb outside are two 'aged persons', a man and a woman, drinking tea.

'You're lucky you caught us,' says Yvonne, obviously the mouthpiece of the duo.

'Not really,' I say. (I'm not being a smartarse – the Internet told me the Hikurangi Museum is open 9.30 – 11 am Tuesdays, Thursdays and the first Saturday of every month.)

'We've done our research, see,' adds Nick.

Yvonne's eyebrows rise as she looks at her husband as if to say 'We've got a couple of live ones here, Arthur,' and beckons us into the main building.

Hikurangi is an old coal mining town, and it used to be a

thriving one at that, with its very own dairy (the cow variety), courthouse and a railway station to deal with the coal and the stone quarried in these parts. Inside the museum buildings (which include the old courthouse) you'll find all kinds of paraphernalia from the last century, especially if, like us, you get the gold star treatment from Yvonne.

'What's that?' asks Nick, pointing at an unusual plastic object in a glass cabinet.

'An artificial kneecap,' says Yvonne. 'One careful owner.'

Like any mining town Hikurangi has seen its fair share of disaster, but probably no blacker day than when tragedy struck the Ackers family in February 1933. One by one, brothers James (24), Jack (20) and Albert (18) were overcome by poisonous 'black damp' fumes while checking out an air shaft for their father. Jack died trying to rescue his brothers. A fourth son wanted to attempt a rescue as well, but the gathering crowd of local men wouldn't let him. A triple funeral was held, and the whole community mourned. The last mine closed here in 1948.

'Is that Piano Hill?' I ask, pointing out of the window.

'No!' says Yvonne, affronted. 'That's our Hikurangi mountain! Piano Hill's that way. Got its name from the bridge which spanned the river there, made from slats of wood, and every time a cart or vehicle went over it played a plinky plonky tune.'

We walk from room to room, Arthur turning off the lights behind us, and around the back to see the old jailhouse. Two cells, no rock. One cell has been set up as a police office, the door of the other asks: 'Have you seen the prisoner?' I lift up the flap to reveal … a mirror.

'That's very profound, Yvonne,' I say. 'Very existential.'

Nick looks in, too.

'He's a handsome bugger, mind,' he says, to Yvonne's amusement.

Back outside (don't forget those lights, Arthur) we are joined by another likely old lad, Ted. I ask him about our next stop,

Kauri, and whether there are any kauri trees left there.

'There was a real beauty there about fifteen years ago, but they cut it down. You might find some little ones, maybe, on private land.' He strokes his chin pensively. 'There used to be much bigger ones around, you know, some forty-five-foot round. You want to go over to the forest really, or up north.'

I explain I've just come from up north.

'Ah,' he says, 'I heard they had one up there it took a day to walk round. Mind you,' he adds, a twinkle in his eye, 'it was on the edge of a cliff.'

It's stock sale day in **Kauri** and the market entrance is crowded (by country standards) with trucks, jeeps and cars. However, a few of the farmers are walking away as Nick and I park up.

'Is it over, then?' I ask one farmer in a long waterproof.

'Nah,' he replies, 'the sheep are over. The sheep are always first, then cows, then pigs. Go on in and have a look.'

We stumble clumsily across the crumbling wooden walkways which span the crumbling wooden pens, witnessing various cows and pigs being booted to stand up for the crowd as the auctioneer rants like a racing car continually changing gear.

Frankly, there's not much to see, so we soon leave to start our quest proper. Taking Ted's advice, we turn up the driveway of a home surrounded by a generous plot of land. The lady of the house seems taken aback by my question.

'Are there any kauri trees in Kauri?'

'Crikey,' she says, literally scratching her head. 'Do you know I've never really thought about it.'

She assures us there are none on her land as her husband would have mentioned it. She suggests maybe we'll have more luck up the hill on the other side of SH1, but we don't. At our second, third, fourth and fifth stops, husbands and wives all give us a similar reaction of utter bemusement. I can't quite believe no-one has ever considered this before. I mean, it's the name of the town. Then again, maybe you'd just take it for granted.

'There might be a little one up there in the bush,' one lady ventures hopefully, waving in a general westerly direction.

'But not in the town?' I ask.

'No. Sorry.'

Nick and I decide to call it quits, and swear that if we ever come back here we will plant a kauri just for the sake of local identity.

'The Falls. That's about it.'

'You're sure?'

'Yep.'

The woman at the Shell Station is quite adamant that this is the only worthwhile attraction in **Kamo**, even though strictly speaking the falls are in Tikipunga, roughly two kilometres away. 'Second after that, it's this place,' she says, sweeping her arm in reference to the mini mart in which we're standing. Whangarei Falls it is, then.

I'm not disappointed. After an intuitive (read sparsely sign-posted) drive it's a short walk from the car park to surely one of the most picturesque waterfalls in the north. There's no doubt about it, Whangarei Falls are magnificent. The water at the top is little more than a trickle, and yet the majestic way it cascades down the 25 or so metres to the deep green, rock-lined pool at the bottom causes everyone present to stand and stare in awe. Even Germans.

Of course there are always those people who, in their eagerness to get back to nature, will take this kind of thing too far, and today is no exception. One guy sits on the basalt rocks mid-stream at the top, meditating like a hippy in a 1970s psychedelia movie and forcing himself into everyone's photos. I'd like to see him do that at Niagara.

Perhaps the most surprising fact about Whangarei Falls is that they are so close to the city centre. So once I've had my fill of tranquillity, it is only a 10-minute journey into **Whangarei**. Our destination is Clapham's Clocks, and finding it is no problem, thanks to a tall clock/sculpture thing piercing the sky nearby, and then directly outside, a rather large sundial possessing a 22.6-metre gnomon. Forgive me, it's not every day I get to use that word.

The interior of the museum is not quite what I am expecting, though, with one exception: there are a hell of a lot of clocks here, over 1600 in fact. Once the collection of the eponymous Archibald Clapham, they are now housed in what the brochure describes as a 'futuristic building' but what I would refer to as a prefabricated metal shack. Don't let me put you off, though. We're here for the clocks, and with this many on offer you can't go wrong. Alarm clocks, cuckoo clocks, ornate clocks, French bird clocks, grandfather clocks, Disney clocks, moving eye clocks, German clocks, Swiss clocks, Dutch clocks, clocks in the shape of fish, clocks with flashing lights, matchstick clocks, Big Ben clocks, musical clocks, digital clocks, Meccano clocks, football clocks, mice running up clocks, hourglasses and a whole display case of watches. To avoid the deafening chorus of hundreds of timepieces all marking the hour at the same time, they've been set at different times. But surely at least one must be telling the correct time, I ask the lady at the front desk. She laughs and simply points to her own watch, giving me her tourist comedy routine. 'Actually,' she confesses, 'it's the big grandfather clock there.' An English Black Oak Cased Clock, apparently, with a Westminster chime. So now you know.

After the subdued clicks, whirs, ticks, tocks and chimes of the museum, back outside the baking heat and gleaming brightness of a Northland summer come as quite a shock. I wander around the waterfront, drinking in the mellow atmosphere. Whangarei may be more of a large town than a city, but from what I can see you can't really argue with their refreshingly honest advertising slogan: 'Whangarei – It's a great place.'

Whangarei to Auckland.

Whether by design or oversight, they seem to have made getting out of Whangarei much more difficult than getting in. After a huge roundabout with no signposts, I guess right and put myself back on SH1, where I pass the Kauri Clock Factory. Not today, thank you. The nature of my quest also precludes me from picking up a solitary hitchhiker this morning. Sorry, mate, but you really wouldn't want to stop as often as I intend to, and firstly today at **Otaika**.

Proving that you can't always 'transliterate' Maori words and expect to come up with a true translation, Otaika means either 'to eat raw fish' or 'the place to lie in a heap'. If the two are even remotely connected I certainly won't be sampling the local sushi. Instead I'll park up and have a nose around The Paper Mill, a real-life paper-making facility set up in 1989 'to lift the self-esteem of intellectually disabled people'. I go on a small tour of the works and watch as several students mash up strips of waste paper to filter through their frames. It truly is a great little set-up; the paper-makers are having a real laugh and their enthusiasm is infectious. I pay $30 for a home paper-making kit and get called a 'big spender'.

Puwera means 'heat' and they're not joking either. It's boiling here today and my notes tell me that the only thing of note is a landfill site, producing the sort of unsavoury combination that persuades me easily to move on to **Oakleigh**, with its train station, wharf and service station. I call in at the latter where one of the attendants kindly wipes down the windscreen of the Electric Cow. A good job, too, or just down the road I wouldn't be able fully to appreciate the majesty of the first true passing lane I can remember encountering on the road so far. There is no-one to overtake here but that's not the point. I sate myself with the knowledge that I could if there were, and arrive at my next stop the fresher for it.

Mata, here at least, is said to mean 'flint' or 'quartz', and today it still possesses a quarry. However, I'm here to see the Big Apple – the shopping centre that is, with its huge plastic sign proudly trumpeting its existence to the world and looking rather more like a tomato than an apple. We're about as far away as possible from anything resembling a 'city that never sleeps'. This is more like a 'town that permanently dozes' but hey, you can't argue with a loaf of bread for just $1.20. Bet you couldn't find that in Manhattan.

I'm looking forward to **Ruakaka**, 'the parakeet's nest', as I've heard the views of Bream Bay are spectacular here. I'm not disappointed. This stunning eastern coastline is skirted by a generous stretch of sand, and on a clear day like today Bream Head is dominating. My only regret, and that of the locals I imagine, is that the vista is partially spoiled by the oil refinery at Marsden Point up the coast. Further exploration around Ruakaka itself reveals the Bream Bay Hotel and some really rather posh houses, presumably because the town is on the outer limits of the Auckland weekend retreat zone and as such is in the process of being massively redeveloped. Whatever the reason, Ruakaka seems a perfect place to take a break, let the kids paddle safely and, if parents are feeling particularly adventurous, check out the local patchwork club. No, honestly. I hear it's dog eat dog in the embroidery world. And as for macramé, well …

It would be fair to say that **Uretiti Beach**, just a couple of kilometres down the road, delivers more of the same beautiful scenery only without any of the amenities. A road sign encourages inactivity: 'Relax – you're still over 2 hours from Auckland' it says, tongue firmly in cheek, all adding up to the archetypal New Zealand day out, and I for one won't spoil things by butting my Pommie nose in where it's not wanted. Instead, I resolve to tootle on down to **Waipu** and kick a few Scots out from under their cairns.

'I'm on a B-road heading for the sea,' croons the singer of Scottish band Trashcan Sinatras on my car stereo, very pertinently as it happens, as I turn off SH1 and down Nova Scotia Drive, the northern entrance to the town.

They're proud of their Scottish heritage in Waipu, and rightfully so. The short history of the town carries an amazing story of surely one of the longest ever migrations, from the Highlands of Scotland to New Zealand via Nova Scotia. This community was carried by seven ships halfway around the world and led by one Norman McLeod, a controversial hardcore Calvinist minister who had already effectively been ejected from the Presbyterian Church in Scotland. Nevertheless, under his guidance the new settlers managed to transform a damp and often cold outpost of the new world into a thriving, self reliant town. A small slice of Scotland in Northland, if you like. Some attribute McLeod's success to the fact that he lost none of his austerity, reflected in, it is said, his taking issue with the Lion Rampant statue in the main street. Allegedly, Big Norm deemed the Lion's penis offensive and had it removed. He also banned dancing and even Christmas in the town.

You can still see the lion statue, no longer rampant of course, in the main street outside the Waipu Heritage Centre where you can immerse yourself in total Jockdom. First settled in 1854, Waipu still holds a Highland Games event on 1 January every year, and to celebrate the 150th anniversary of the town recently they even invented their very own tartan.

It's only a short hop from Scotland to Wales, then, through Waipu to the Brynderwyn Hills, a curiously Cambrian moniker for an area otherwise dominated by Maori names. It's 2.30 pm on a summer afternoon, yet the sky is so dark that some cars have their headlights on. 'STOP AT THE TOP' yells a painted sign on a corrugated iron roof, and do you know, I just might. The actual town of **Brynderwyn** sits on the far side of what is more accurately called Pilbrow Hill, but I could do with a video-less rest and a nice cup of tea right now, so the Skyliner Café it is. The view from the top is worth a few dollars in itself, a fabulous land and seascape stretching from Waipu Cove to Bream Head. It seems odd that someone has seen fit to recreate the exact same scene in a mural right underneath the actual view. Maybe they use it on cloudy days.

I get back in the Electric Cow and out on to SH1 for the short journey down the hill into Brynderwyn that a passenger bus failed to make on 7 February 1963. After a short rest at the crest of the hill, the bus driver found his brakes had failed. Though he valiantly used gears, handbrake and body strength to wrestle the vehicle down the twists and turns of this steep incline, his increasing momentum into the final corner saw the bus crash through a wire fence and roll down a 30-metre slope to the Piroa Stream. Fifteen people died that day in one of New Zealand's worst-ever bus accidents.

Later on my left comes the well-known landmark of Baldrock or Pukepohutu (Hill of Stone), so called for its large rocky knoll which juts out distinctly from the surrounding lower slopes of greenery. But Baldrock wasn't always so bald. Until recently its pate poked out from a huge kauri forest, as described in *The Story of a New Zealand River*, Jane Mander's pioneering Kiwi novel from the early twentieth century:

> Towering arrogantly above all else, on the crests and down the spurs, stood groups of the kauri, the giant timber tree of New Zealand, whose great grey trunks, like the pillars in the ancient halls of Karnak, shot up seventy and eighty feet without a knot or branch, and whose colossal heads, swelling up into the sky, made a cipher of every tree near.

Both fire and over-enthusiastic logging have long since put paid to such dominant woodland around here, and although a new generation of kauri is growing, the bluestone crest points skywards, lonely, or at least most of it does. After the fire killed off the last of the previous forest, the landowner became inter-ested in the stone itself and some of it was cut out in the early 1900s and sent to various sites around the country. Apparently a few blocks of Baldrock stone can be seen to this day in a bus shelter outside St Paul's Church, Symonds Street, Auckland.

To my satisfaction it turns out that Jane Mander spent part of her childhood living in **Pukekaroro**, my next stop. It was here, among other towns in the region where her father sought kauri to mill, that she found the inspiration for her novel. In turn she has also unwittingly provided me with a further head-ache in trying to trace the origin of the name Pukekaroro.

It translates literally as 'hill of black-backed gulls': straight-forward enough you might think, a nesting place perhaps, but so far I have discovered two different sources. The less grue-some version revolves around the story of how a landing party of Nga Puhi warriors were trying to locate the pa here in order to attack it. They saw the gulls fly over this hill and knew the river and the pa must be close, hence the name. The second and infinitely more interesting version has it that the fortified pa in question frequently changed hands, and after each battle the gulls gathered in their thousands to feast on the flesh of the resulting corpses. And now there is the Jane Mander version, which suggests that the name stems from the great flocks of gulls which would circle the hill for days before the advent of a storm. All in all, a fine quandary for the amateur researcher.

I'm not here to see gulls, but to see if I can make out the remains of the old tramline which used to transport timber down to the river, and which also makes an appearance in Jane Mander's novel, as her protagonist's husband struggles to establish his business in this rough terrain.

I turn down Mountain Road because rumour has it that the old piles of the tramline bridge can still be seen at low tide by Point Ernie. Unfortunately it's now high tide, so I console myself by reading the tramline memorial plaque by the side of the road here, around which someone has kindly placed empty beer cans.

The name **Kaiwaka** is not, as I immediately presumed, the literal 'food canoe', but a reference to the fast-flowing Kaiwaka river destroying or 'making a meal' of said canoes. The term can also be applied to the art of hollowing out a canoe, which makes sense, much more sense in fact than Kaiwaka's recent penchant for illuminations, an activity which has earned it the title 'Little Town of Lights'. It all started in 1997 when the church was adorned with angel lights. Since then many other local businesses have followed suit, and now the town boasts lighting sculptures that include a motorbike, scissors, saw, postbox, sailing ship, fireman's ladder and more. I'm very much looking forward to seeing the spectacle in this settlement of just 450 people or so, but while I wait for it to get dark, I have a contrast of cafés to visit.

The first, on the northern outskirts of Kaiwaka, is the German Café. As I pull into the car park I ponder the intriguing name. What is so German about it? The building is wooden and unsurprising. Two llama (llamas? llamae?) are grazing on the grassy patch out front. I don't recall the llama being native to Bavaria, but I could be mistaken. Maybe I'll find out more inside. Nope. No real clues here either. Granted, my cup of tea and meat pie seemingly have no sense of humour, but I don't find them particularly Germanic so I resolve to ask the girl behind the gift counter.

'Excuse me', I say, interrupting an elderly lady with a tiki spoon mid-sale. 'Why is this called the German Café?'

The girl offers a withering look. I get the feeling I am not the first to utter these lines. 'Because the owners are German,' she says, flatly, and wraps the lady's souvenir in a paper bag.

What a difference, then, to the warm welcome at Eutopia, a beautiful if bizarre sculpted structure at the southern end of town. Think mini Elven Taj Mahal or Brighton Pavilion, and you may be close. Add a bridge, fountain, pedestals, gardens and even a pizza oven, and you'll be even closer. Talk authoritatively about the *ferrocement* construction style, plaster on a wire framework which eventually sets as hard as concrete, and you can go to the head of the class.

Eutopia is the vision of Peter and Raewyn Harris, a couple truly living the dream, although the dream to me looks like a hell of a lot of hard work. They have built this place from scratch themselves, room by room, feature by feature, and when fully finished it promises to be quite a spectacular sight. That's not to say that parts of it aren't beautiful right now, but even a layman like me can see that the complex is far from completion. To help fund their compulsion, and presumably to help keep themselves in necessities, they have turned part of the complex into an organic café. It's nothing too flash as yet but the coffee is good, the toasties hit the spot and, believe me, it sure beats being surrounded by old ladies slurping their tea and marvelling at stuffed toy souvenir sheep wearing woolly jumpers with a New Zealand logo on the front.

I note also that despite luring me into a false sense of security by looking not unlike the father from The Modern Parents in *Viz* comic, Peter is also quite a canny businessman. As I leave to catch the lights of Kaiwaka he manages to soft-sell me a copy of his self-published book, *Fantastic Ferrocement*, at $35 a pop. I don't mind, though. I think he's probably earned every cent.

Topuni is situated on the western edge of one of the narrowest parts of the North Island. Not that you'd think it from a casual glance of the map, but the distance from the Topuni River (which joins up with the Kaipara Harbour) to Mangawhai Heads on the east coast is a mere 15 kilometres. The only other facts I know about Topuni are that 1) it used to have a sawmill, 2) it now has a scenic reserve, and 3) it gets its name from a Maori cloak made from dogskin and woven flax which was ceremonially draped over places or people to signify power and authority over them.

Flax also plays a part in the history of **Te Hana**, literally 'the glow', the name given to a Maori flax garment coloured with red ochre. One of my friends addicted to television's 'Shortland Street' informs me that Te Hana is also a nurse in New Zealand's favourite soap. Personally, I'll always be more entertained by signs like the one off to the right, which shows a cartoon pig with a speech bubble advertising pork for just $4.99 a kilo. The pig looks unnervingly happy about this state of affairs, almost as if he just hasn't made the connection. 'Pork? What, me? Ah, get away with you.'

I'm now into the district of Rodney, a fact of which I am reminded not a few metres later by a sign that reads 'AUCKLAND WELCOMES YOU'. Blimey. I knew it was a big city, but not this big. And well before the outskirts of the great metropolis, there's **Wellsford**, whose main thoroughfare on SH1 reminds me for the first time since Kawakawa of what I would call a typical New Zealand street: awning-covered rows of shops, cafés, bars and dairies, people milling around chatting, looking in windows, waving at passing cars … you get the general idea. The whole scene would be near idyllic were it not for the driving rain which is hitting the Electric Cow almost horizontally out there. Maybe this is why I now find the Albertland & District Museum shut when it professes to be open seven days a week until 6 pm.

I take this point up with Trish in Wellsford's fantastic second-hand shop.

'It's shut? Really?' she says, and then shrugs her shoulders in resignation. 'Yeah, we're a bit slack with stuff like that here. I expect where you're from it's all twenty-four seven, eh?' she adds, presumably in reference to my Pom accent.

'Yeah,' I reply, 'Paraparaumu's just crazy.'

She smiles. 'They've got a big second-hand shop in Paraparaumu too, eh?'

'Statue Bargain Barn,' I affirm.

We chat about the general high standard of New Zealand's second-hand shops, and then Trish asks me what I'm doing in this neck of the woods. I explain my quest.

'So I guess I was asking myself what one thing I could do in

Wellsford. Any suggestions?'

Trish wrinkles up her nose. 'Nah. You got me there.'

Then I have an idea. 'Tell you what,' I say, 'if there's anything in this store that is typical of Wellsford, I'll buy it. How's that? What would you say represents Wellsford here?'

'Well, I represent Wellsford, but I don't think Kev would like it if you bought me.'

She rightly suggests I should quit bugging her and look around for the answer myself, so I unleash myself on as comprehensive a collection of used items as you could ever wish to see in one place. I pore over vases, obscure novels, ancient typewriters with missing keys, crumbling blocks of old kauri gum, but nothing really takes my fancy, or gives me a solution as to what I could possibly do in Wellsford on a wet Monday at 3.45 pm. And then, just as I am losing hope, one item practically sings out from the shelves. On a shelf of cups, mugs and various other drinking vessels sits a glass with a handle, the immortal words 'BOOZE IS THE ANSWER' written on the side. Here it is, my moment of clarity. I grab my prize and take it up to Trish.

'Yeah,' she laughs, 'that'll be about right.'

I pay my two dollars and leave, a very happy man. If I could only put the glass to some use right now I would be even happier, but there's no rest for the writer, as they say, and before long I'm back on the main drag and approaching town number 61 on the journey south, the tiny settlement of **Wayby**. And tiny is the word. In fact, were one to replace the 'W' with an 'L' I don't think many outsiders would quibble over the accuracy of the name, which was actually decided upon at a public meeting way back when. Apparently, as the Great North Road ran through the district, Wayby was chosen because the road was, quite literally, 'the way by'. There's no arguing with that kind of logic, and no bloody sign of life here until I brake sharply at the sight of a sign for the Wayby Art Gallery. Fantastic.

An electric sensor guard frog croaks as I walk up the path in search of life. For quite a while there doesn't appear to be any, but a cheery voice shouts 'Hello there!' and scares the life out of me. It belongs to Noelene. The Art Gallery is in fact her home, and she has converted the back room into a place to show off her own exploits with the brush. Thirty or so works of various size adorn the walls, each one showing a typical New Zealand landscape or country scene. 'I paint for pleasure, really,' she says, 'but it's nice to make a sale now and then. Makes it all worthwhile somehow.'

It is then I realise I am being gently held to ransom by an amiable old lady and I get the feeling there is no way I'm getting out of here easily without buying one of her paintings. I resign myself to my fate and choose a picture. If anyone out there has tips on how to refuse a hard sell from someone who reminds you of your own granny, I'd love to hear from them.

Right, then. Caution. Geographical anomaly approaching. My next two stops will be visited in reverse order. I think. The reasoning for this is simple: to reach **Waiwhiu** Kauri Grove it's easiest to start your walk at **Dome Valley**. Thus it is with fresh drizzle in the air that I pull up in the car park at the Dome Valley Tearooms to start a fairly gentle climb through forest to the Dome Lookout, about a kilometre away. Thankfully I've remembered to bring my water bottle this time, as well as something equating to waterproofs, so the 20 minutes or so to the platform leaves me rosy cheeked and in good shape to appreciate the views across the Mahurangi Peninsula and Hauraki Gulf beyond. Or at least it would were they not completely obscured by low cloud. I decide to knock the rest of the walk on the head and retire for the day, back to Whangarei to put my Wellsford tankard to good use.

'Disneyland? Universal Studios? Busch Gardens? You can keep 'em, mate. I've been to Sheepworld and it's shear heaven.' That's how to write a cheesy ad for Dome Valley's major tourist attraction, and there's even an element of truth to my verbal frolicking.

Sheepworld is all things sheep for every sheep enthusiast, and particularly for children. Every day at 11 am and 2 pm, kids can marvel as the dogs bring the sheep down the hillside to the pen and then watch them being sorted and shorn. Heck, you can even have a go at shearing one yourself if you feel so inclined. I don't. No, I'm just hanging around here waiting for the famous duck assault course to start. When it does, it is all I dreamt it would be and more. With the latent threat of a stick up their tail feathers, the ducks quack and waddle their way around ramps and through hoops to the general hilarity and applause of all spectators. The only obstacle missing is the flaming hoop, but I guess this would be tempting fate.

Down the road a bit I find the most tranquil and charming place I have visited so far. **Warkworth** was founded in 1853 by an Englishman called John Anderson Brown who thankfully resisted the urge to call it Brownville and instead named it after his hometown in Northumberland. Boat-building, orcharding, lime mining and cement manufacture all played a part in the initial industry for the town; indeed you can still visit the old Portland Cement works should the mood take you. But then why on earth would you want to when Warkworth has so much else to offer. It's a supreme example of what New Zealand river towns used to be like and exactly what I imagine Whangarei to have been before commercialisation.

I was going to make the Warkworth District Museum in Parry Kauri Park, with its two towering kauri trees, my '1 Thing' for the town, but now that I'm settled on a bench by the river in the Lucy Moore Memorial Park I've changed my mind. I expect you would, too. The sun is glinting off the water, the native greenery on the far bank stretches as far as I can see without the hint of a manmade structure, and there's that perfect sense of peace, coupled with the sweet smell of freshly cut grass in the air. After the hectic schedule of the past few days, it's marvellous to sit here and do nothing for a change. I mention this a little later to the woman at the Info Centre.

'Ah,' she says. 'Maybe it's a good job you didn't go to the

museum, then. You might have started hugging those kauris.'

After a short, relaxed wander through Warkworth's alley-ways, it's time for another date with my walking shoes on the Moir Hill Walkway at **Pohuehue**. This walk should be extremely manageable, even for me. It's just a short tramp to the waterfall down in the valley. I'm greeted in the gravel car park by several chickens who are very pleased to see me, obviously expecting food. It's funny but I can't see any houses nearby. Do people drop their poultry off in lay-bys and then pick them up at the end of the day? Also present are two elderly persons in a combi van who look on appalled as I wrestle to attach my camera to my belt, partially dropping my trousers in the process. I smile but they don't smile back.

The track to the stream is quite a sharp decline and leads to a neat little wooden bridge. Now this *is* picture-postcard New Zealand: vivid green foliage, clean, earthy scents, the faint chatter of bird noise and the gurgle of water flowing softly over cool rock. Even most of the traffic noise from SH1 is drowned out by the dense bush and the slope.

I turn left on the far side of the bridge and follow the teeter-ing path to where it splits off for serious trampers tackling the ascent to Moir Hill. I can't locate the waterfall – perhaps it's near this muddy grass to my right – but the whole experience has been so refreshing that I'm really not bothered missing it. After struggling back up the bank to the car, I emerge from the bush panting, sweating and smiling all at once, much to the consternation of the elderly couple in the combi van who don't appear to have moved in the last half hour. There is now a faint look of disgust on the woman's face. God only knows what she thinks I've been doing in there but it appears to have put her off her flask of tea.

Over the impressive Pohuehue viaduct and past the fantas-tically named Hungry Creek Road, I'm drawing ever closer to **Puhoi**, famous for its well-documented origins and not purely because of the cheese made here nowadays.

Imagine this if you will. It's the mid-19th century. You're

married, a mother of five young children, living in a small town not far from Prague. Times are hard. Those three vicious bedfellows of poverty, hunger and disease are stalking the land like Jerry Collins on the fringe of an opposing maul. Then one day your husband returns home with the promise of free land, work and a pastoral existence in a far-off country. Before you know it your scant belongings are packed, and along with 76 other adventurers you and your family are off to a new life. You take a 106-day voyage by boat to New Zealand, crammed in with a load of English, Scots and Irish people whose language you don't speak. Parts of the crossing are pretty damn rough, and during one particularly powerful storm a load of loose timber kills your husband. Freshly widowed, now a single mother of five, you finally arrive in Auckland to find it an unimpressive collection of ramshackle buildings. From here you and your fellow immigrants are paddled up the coast and then up a river by a group of dark-skinned people you have heard are cannibals. The further upstream you go, the denser the forest, until you are finally dumped on the bank in a small bush clearing. Two nikau whare, just 10 metres long, await your entire party, and nothing else. Welcome to the Promised Land.

This is the concise version of Mrs Lawrence Turnwald's introduction to Puhoi, and believe me the unabridged account makes for even grimmer reading. What would you have done? Wondered what on earth you'd been thinking when you agreed to come here? Resolved to get the hell out as quickly as possible? Dropped to your knees and wept? You won't be surprised to hear that Mrs Turnwald and her fellow founders of Puhoi did all three. Unfortunately once the tears were over they realised that with no money and nowhere else to go there was little choice but to eke out an existence with what they had. The community survived through grim determination. The Puhoi Bohemians worked hard – many of them for 16 hours a day – to forge something from nothing.

Today the setting is idyllic in the extreme. I pass a Catholic shrine, a museum, a beautiful white wooden church, the local dairy and the much-favoured Puhoi pub with its beer garden full of Aucklanders and bikers. I buy a pint and like A.H. Reed before me settle down to eat my lunch near the river – what else but a cheese baguette, the contents of which come from just down the road at a cheese factory called The Art of Cheese. Children laugh, men with beards discuss the price of petrol and a young mother explains her preference for Chardonnay over Cabernet Sauvignon. It's such a far cry from tales of Puhoi past and the unfortunate demise of Mrs Lawrence Turnwald.

Having proved herself worthy of any task thrown at her in the establishment of the new settlement, and having survived adversity that would turn a lesser person's heart to putty, Mrs Turnwald came to a most untimely end at the hands of one of those closest to her. Her son was cleaning his rifle one day when it accidentally discharged straight at her. She died a few days later of her wounds.

As I drive out of Puhoi I thank my lucky stars that my introduction to New Zealand consisted of a bar, dinner with friends and a warm hotel room.

Back on SH1, I stop the car at the crest of the hill to appreciate the view. Stretching out to the east are the estuaries of the Puhoi and Waiwera rivers, meandering lazily towards the ocean through plains of lush green. I wish I could take the river route to **Waiwera** myself, instead of the short journey down the hill to where the mobile oyster van sits in the car park. I pull up outside the first hotel I see and check in. A brief kip and then it's time to hit the town. I fancy a movie, followed by some light supper. Which is lucky.

The curative hot springs at Waiwera, literally 'hot water', were known to Maori for generations before Europeans came to these shores. They would dig holes in the sandy beach here and lie down in the mineral waters that collected. In 1845 Robert Graham, Superintendent of the Auckland Province, recognised Waiwera's tourist potential, bought 20 acres of foreshore land here and immediately built a hotel. The source of the water supply was traced back up into the hills and then piped to 20 baths in the new resort. It was probably the first such enterprise in New Zealand.

Today the Waiwera Thermal Spa Resort is as popular as ever, something I soon find out as I pay my entry fee and slip into the changing rooms at 7.30 pm. If I wanted I could indulge my corpulent frame in any of the Fountain, Seal, Selby, Sapphire and Opal Pools, or career gracelessly down the Short and Sharp, Gut Buster, Squeeze, Bob's Mistake (far too prophetic), the Twister, the SPEEEED Slide or the Black Hole. Or I could lounge around in the water and watch a movie in the Movie Pool. No choice really, then. I wonder what's playing.

Unfortunately, not long after I willingly embrace the welcoming 38°C waters, the new movie starts. *Top Gun*. Just brilliant. I'm guessing Tom Cruise is a local favourite after part of *The Last Samurai* was filmed in this region. I hope so. There really is no other excuse.

Still, I think, supping my first beer of the evening, it could have been worse. *Far and Away* worse. Several beers and a fine plate of nachos later and I'm laughing about it. And is it my imagination or am I really beginning to feel the benefits of my little dip? I feel very fluid. Marvellous.

Stumbling back to the hotel room at closing time, I notice for the first time that my room backs directly onto SH1 just at the point where vehicles accelerate to make it up the hill. I spend a restless night punctuated by bizarre dreams about toppling kauri trees. Puhoi, Tom Cruise and nachos. Maybe I should have taken it easier on the cheese today.

There's work going on to prevent the dunes eroding at **Hatfield's Beach,** a glorious little cove just a kilometre on down the road, named after Alec Hadfield (what's a consonant between friends?), one of the first Europeans to realise the curative powers of the waters at Waiwera. I can't help thinking that SH1 is partly responsible for the erosion here, and that somehow a constant stream of daytrippers from Auckland has compounded the problem.

Up another hill and winding down the other side I'm knocked bandy again by the breathtaking view of **Orewa** beach, a golden stretch of sand tapering off into the distance. The local council has had the foresight to build a viewing platform here, and I just can't believe there is such an open expanse of beautiful sand so close to a major city with absolutely no-one on it. Well, nearly no-one. I feel it my duty to kick off my shoes and socks and wander up to the gentle ocean waves. You could play a mean game of beach cricket here, when the tide's out.

After drying my feet on yesterday's damp towel, I drive up to the centre of town in search of coffee, and possibly lunch. To my delight I instead find a shop called Windmill which specialises in all things Dutch, from clogs to cheese to cookies. My eye, however, is particularly taken by the liquorice counter. I'm a sucker for liquorice, and soon I'm piling a load of assorted black tubes of pleasure into a paper bag, including salty versions. I've never tasted salty liquorice before, and to be honest I don't think I ever will again, unless held at clog-point.

Back on SH1, I catch my first glimpse of the Skytower rearing its pointy mast in the distance, and then I'm heading back in time again as I sail into **Silverdale**.

Silverdale was originally known by Maori as Te Weiti after a headland at the mouth of the river. Once settlers arrived this name was soon bastardised by Europeans into The Wade, a reference to the boggy conditions of the road in these parts, or possibly the river, although at times it was difficult to tell the difference. It remained The Wade through the initial timber and gumdigging eras until it was decided the name didn't really promise a warm welcome to visitors, especially with nearby Waiwera outdoing it in the tourist stakes. So in 1911 a town meeting was called to select a new name. New Jerusalem, a hot contender, was ultimately rejected, as was Muddale, a curious suggestion. Neither Swamptown nor Bogville was on the list but Silverdale was, and Silverdale was chosen. Whether it was a reference to the proliferation of poplar trees in the area, or an enticing lure for silver prospectors, or simply because it sounded good, the truth is unclear. Certainly there were no significant reports of silver being found here.

The riches Silverdale has to offer today come in the form of the Wainui Pioneer Village, a nugget's throw from the modern shops. Established in 1969 by the Wainui Historical Society which uses the Parsonage here as its headquarters, the collection of buildings is a noble effort to preserve some of the rich history of the area, from Maori times right through to the mid 1950s and beyond. I walk the Time Trail, basically a tour from building to building, none of which appears to have started its life here. For example, the Chapel is thought originally to have lived in Auckland High Street before being shipped here in 1860, and the Post Office, although built in 1929, was only recently donated. Musical buildings.

The schoolhouse especially carries reminders of how much life has altered in a century. Rules of good manners are posted on boards for children: 'Be Respectful to your teachers and help them as much as you can; their work is difficult and trying.' True enough in any age, yet hardly helped either by some of the *Rules for Teachers 1915*: 'You MAY NOT dress in bright colours'; 'You may UNDER NO CIRCUMSTANCES dye your hair'; 'You MAY NOT ride in a carriage or automobile with any man unless he is your father or brother'; and my personal favourite: 'You MAY NOT loiter downtown in icecream stores'.

It takes me an age to turn right out of Silverdale across a particularly busy stretch of road. **Auckland** is near, very near now. It's 4 pm and I'm looking forward to a beer and a friendly face. I'm up and over the Auckland Harbour Bridge clip-ons before I know it. Now all I have to do is navigate the motorway junctions correctly. Last time I was here I crossed the bridge three times trying to reach the city centre. On this occasion, however, I sail through to Dominion Road like a seasoned Jafa and as a result feel very proud of myself. I only hope pride will not, as the saying goes, come before a fall.

Auckland to Hamilton.

It is a truth universally acknowledged that wherever you travel in the world, you cannot escape Phil Collins. And believe me, I have tried. It all started in childhood, Worcestershire, England. *In the Air Tonight. I Missed Again.* All through high school Phil haunted me like a stalker, not hurrying love, that was all-ing and then unforgiveably turning up at both original Live Aid concerts. I remember his grinning face at the piano in Philadelphia as I cursed the day Concorde had ever been conceived. 'This afternoon I was in London. Funny old world, innit.' No, Phil, it wasn't.

As I grew older and travelled, geography provided little respite. I was *Sussudio*-ed in Swansea, *Easy Lover*-ed on Exmoor (which sounds interesting but, let me assure you, is quite the reverse), and what should have been *Another Day in Paradise* in Paris was ruined for at least five minutes, although it seemed longer. It always does with Phil. Since then I've been *I Can't Dance*-d in Florida, Budapest, right across Germany, Spain, Hong Kong, Slovenia, New York, Seattle, and even the Cook Islands. Probably the cruellest blows of all have come recently thanks to my son, by whom I am regularly *Tarzan*-ed and *Brother Bear*-ed in my very own living room. And now, here I am in Auckland, 'Last, loneliest, loveliest of all' according to Kipling. He, however, revelled in a lifetime where the word Genesis referred only to the Bible.

I have no idea which song is playing as Nick and I walk through an otherwise welcoming open bar door, but it hits us like a wall of Puhoi cheese. That's Phil. It's not going to get to me today, though. Oh no. Because today is rather special.

I've already booked us in for the main event, but first we're sampling the delights of 5° Below, the vodka bar with a difference. The name refers not to the temperature at which the vodka is served so much as to the room temperature at which it is served. Much like Iceland's famous Ice Hotel, 5° Below is Auckland's Ice Bar where all the furniture, decorations, hell, even the bar counter and glasses are made of ice. Of course such frosty décor necessitates warm clothing and thankfully all the gear is provided. Unfortunately they only give out the Russian hats to staff, but coats, mittens and boots are all donned, and no sooner are we kitted up than it's time to get Absolut-ed up.

I don't quite know what to expect as we step through to the inner sanctum. A blast of Arctic air perhaps, or a stray penguin from Kelly Tarlton's Underwater World. In the event, it's neither. The drop in temperature is quite pleasant, nowhere near as cold as I imagined, and a real tonic for a blocked nose. Nick and I shuffle up to the bar, gazing around in wonder at the ice sculptures and ice seats covered with animal skins. In our state of chilly excitement we ask the barmaid all the questions she's no doubt heard before, such as does she catch more colds working here, can you hold parties here, and how long are staff allowed to stay inside (no, no and an hour and a half). Then we both order something with vodka and cranberry.

'You have to drink it quick,' says the barmaid, 'or the fruit juice starts to freeze.'

Two drinks later and before we know it it's time to leave. I don't think I'll ever have a better stiffener in my life, although I'm not sure the yachties would necessarily recommend it until afterwards. Big clue. Later today we are going to take part in the Sail NZ America's Cup Experience, and not merely the two-hour freesailing version but the three-hour match race between *NZL40* and *NZL41*, two custom-built yachts that played some kind of role in the America's Cup. If you're assuming that I know very little about sailing, you're right. But what I do know, and can see in front of me, is the very tangible effect that New Zealand's America's Cup win and subsequent defence had on what was previously a rundown part of the waterfront. Today the redeveloped Viaduct Harbour is buzzing with bars, swanky restaurants and tourists. I overheard one Aucklander at the Empire Tavern last night mention that it is definitely passé for locals these days, but that's fine by me. I'm here to race.

We check in at the kiosk and after a short wait are ushered down to the yachts where the captains go through the obligatory safety check and dish out the rules: 1) Always wear your lifejacket, like Colin Meads told you; 2) Don't fall in, it's cold; and; 3) Keep your hands away from the ropes or you're liable to lose a finger or two. Seemingly sound advice. We're divided into teams and welcomed aboard *NZL41* along with five crew and 10 other punters. This is it. My first yachting experience.

Motoring sedately out of the harbour under engine power we are told our duties as guests will involve mainly grinding, leaving the tacking and gybing to the professionals. I have no idea what the man is talking about but dutifully stand next to the winch thing for the sails as instructed. Ah, so this is what grinding means.

'Hello. My name's Bob. I'll be your fellow grinder today,' I say to break the ice with my American neighbour, a tall, greying, 40-something man with glasses. His name is Mike from Colorado ('I'm in plastics') and he seems to know an awful lot about boats already.

'I think we can count ourselves lucky,' he whispers as we prepare for action, nodding in the direction of the front grinders. 'The last place you want to be is on those. You watch.'

Sure enough, as the initial free-sailing session unfolds, the hapless souls allocated to the bow grinders are subjected to much more work than we are. Up front, cheeks are puffed, eyebrows are raised and arms are stretched in pain while I do the odd bit of grinding – nothing too strenuous – and Nick sits cockily at the side of the boat having managed somehow to evade any hint of hard work. It's okay, though. The captain tells us if we're in trouble or fancy a break just to raise a hand and he'll put someone else in place. Mike from Colorado takes this option after 20 minutes ('I'm here for the view. I can do this stuff back home if I want.') which means Nick has to step up to the plate and we become a grinding team, for a while at least. However, five minutes later I can't resist the thought of watching him suffer so I stick my hand up to be replaced by Mike's wife. All's fair in love and sailing, especially now it's time for the race proper against *NZL40*.

After much tacking and gybing to enter the starting box on time, the captain's synchronised stopwatch counts down and we're off down the course at 15 knots. There's only a light wind and it's currently behind us. For the first stretch we're neck and neck with the other boat, drifting along in a fairly leisurely fashion although the professionals on both boats are rampant with the desire to win what for them must be an inconsequential race. Maybe the end-of-the-day beers are being wagered as I grind; who knows, but it seems they'll stop at nothing to gain a few extra metres. Our first turn completed, the order goes out on our boat to let loose the spinnaker, the big flappy sail at the front, and disaster strikes. It won't unfurl. The other boat steams ahead. Our crew is fuming quietly, cursing their luck, when a voice comes over the walkie-talkie from *NZL40*.

'Do you like what we did there?'

It turns out our boat has been sabotaged by the other boat's crew. Our guys don't know whether to laugh or swear. In the end they choose both options and demand a restart.

The practical joke seems to have galvanised our spirit. Even Nick and I, not renowned for our competitive attitudes, now want to beat the other boat like a ginger stepchild. Fortunately that's exactly what we proceed to do, by about a length and a half in the end. Honour is restored.

As an added bonus I even get to take the helm and play Cap'n Bob for a few minutes as we sail back towards the harbour. It's a glorious evening with a vivid orange sunset, and for the first time since the race began I get to appreciate the stunning spread of Auckland, with Nick har-harring beside me.

The fresh wind is shivering me timbers by the time we pull back into the Viaduct and we quickly retire to a local hostelry. Over a beer in The Loaded Hog I ask Nick, as a strict fellow amateur, his first impressions of sailing.

'A lot more grinding and a lot fewer sea shanties than I thought,' he says, 'but a thoroughly enjoyable experience nonetheless.' We are still regaling ourselves with victories past – that is, today – when Nick points excitedly towards the glass cabinet behind me.

'Wait there,' he says, and disappears to talk to the two guys who are in the process of removing the replica of the America's Cup for the evening. He returns a few seconds later.

'Come on. This'll be the icing on the cake.'

And so it is that I am photographed holding the America's Cup aloft in triumph having just won my first (and probably last) yacht race. A fitting end to a great day.

I'm sure to upset some people here, for which I apologise, but after much consultation, with Aucklanders I might add, it has been decided that Manukau, Drury and even Runciman are all now considered suburbs of the sprawling metropolis. Thus in an effort to dispel as soon as possible the popular Jafa myth that life does not exist south of the Bombay Hills, the following day I wave goodbye to New Zealand's largest city and drive as fast as is legally possible to those hills. As luck would have it I also farewell the Electric Cow, which means I can drive as fast as legally possible, and with a good deal less mooing.

It took me a while to discover that the town of **Bombay**, nestling comfortably at the foot of said hills, isn't named after a duck or a curry dish at all, but after a boat which came to these shores from England in 1865. Its passengers mostly settled in this vicinity, and thus the name of the new town was born. Seems perfectly reasonable – maybe they enjoyed the trip across so much they didn't want to forget it, or more likely were simply referred to by everyone else as 'that Bombay lot'. Either works for me.

My quest here today is to locate a cairn which our old friend A.H. Reed mentions in his book:

> The cairn was built of stone taken from Bishop Selwyn's original St Stephen's School at Parnell, Auckland. It also marks the spot where Selwyn slept at the close of his first day on foot when journeying from Auckland on his southern visitation tours.

Bishop Selwyn was the first official Bishop of New Zealand. Having arrived here in 1842 he then travelled around the country preaching the gospel. He obviously meant business too, as he started learning Maori on the boat over.

I'm delighted to relate that the cairn is visible on the left from SH1, about a kilometre before exit 471, just before the end of the Southern Motorway. I turn off and double back up the old Great Southern Road to get a closer look and fire off a few shots; ironic really, as shots of a different kind were what Governor Grey had in mind when he ordered the Great South Road to be built in the first place. To aid his invasion of the Waikato he also set up the Queen's Redoubt, a large army camp, at my next stop, JenniferAnn.com. Did I say JenniferAnn.com? Sorry, I meant **Pokeno**.

It says in the *Reed Dictionary of New Zealand Place Names* that Pokeno means 'night of the underworld'. These days 'day of the underpants' would seem a better fit. Struggling economically to maintain its claim as the centre of Bacon Country, in 2000 Pokeno agreed a deal with a certain lingerie company to be renamed, for a year, JenniferAnn.com. The aim at the time was mutual publicity, creating cyberspace in a real place and bringing prosperity to both. I'm here with Nick to see if it actually worked, and if any memories of those heady days remain.

There's certainly no clue as we drive in – 'WELCOME TO POKENO VILLAGE,' reads a particularly battle-scarred sign, followed by 'EXCITING COUNTRY FARE'. We soon discover that this refers mainly to two ice cream shops, one boasting 'big' ice creams, the other 'huge'. It's obviously a cut-throat industry. However, I am put off buying a cone full stop by the fact that the young guy behind the counter is wearing a 'McShit' T-shirt. Some words just don't mix with hospitality.

Barbara in Jewels of Time and Present, a second-hand shop on Main Street, tells us 'it went down very well,' when I mention the change of name. 'Local businesses thrived and I think the company did okay out of it too.'

'Did you change the town signs?' asks Nick.

'Oh yes. We even changed our postal address legally, just for a year, to, um, Sally-whatever-it-was-dotcom.'

This tickles me and I laugh. Fancy not remembering where you lived for a whole year; a form of geographical amnesia. Barbara doesn't think I'm very funny, though. She darts a frown in my direction, so I decide to retire into the depths of her shop, eager to retain her approval by buying something.

'Do you know what Pokeno means?' she asks as I slink away, daring me to answer. I don't want to appear even more of a smartarse, so I shake my head.

'Deep, dark valley,' she says, with an air of finality.

'But Bob thought—' starts Nick, before I tread on his foot. 'Ow!'

We decide on a candle holder, to light the darkness of the valley, although I'm not telling Barbara that. Boy, am I glad I didn't try and get in the joke about renaming your town after a pair of pants. We pay up and leave. On the way out of town we see the remains of the Queen's Redoubt, now just a hole in the ground shored up by sandbags, but once the mustering point for what was to become the Second New Zealand War.

Mercer, too, takes its title from that period of unrest, named after a British officer, Captain Henry Mercer of the Royal Artillery, who died at the Battle of Rangiriri in 1863. Today it is a town of two sides: a picturesque scattering of buildings on the hill to our left, and towards the river on our right a collection of gaudy commercial ugliness including a McDonald's and the obligatory Irish pub complete with leprechaun sign. Thankfully, hidden among the neon gloom there is one oasis and it is based on cheese.

Albert Alferink is a Dutchman who makes, sells, lives and probably sleeps cheese, and a damn fine job he does of it too. To recap, then, Albert is passionate about cheese. He must be. His shop, Mercer Cheese, is open seven days a week and he personally creates over 14 different flavours, most of which are proudly stacked up on the shelves behind his counter.

'Please try some before you buy,' he suggests, slicing off a decent wedge, so we do: a Blue Vein which has a kick as hefty as any top Stilton. It's wonderful stuff, but it's not Albert's favourite. That honour lies with his Extra Mature Gouda with Cumin, and I cannot argue. At room temperature it is exceptionally tasty, but as I discover later a combination of age and refrigeration transforms it into a very decent rival to fresh Parmesan.

On learning that he is my '1 Thing' for Mercer, Albert modestly suggests I try other attractions, too.

'The town has a lot of history,' he tells me as I munch through some more Extra Mature. 'My shop is relatively new.' I think, however, I have achieved my goal here. It's so refreshing to see how much Albert loves what he does that I can allow myself to move on. As Nick comments when we're back on SH1, 'Blessed are the cheesemakers.' Blessed indeed.

We leave Mercer and follow the river around. 'The mighty Waikato, a taniwha at every bend.' Indeed, we are now approaching the spot where one of them famously halted construction on widening the road. Fortunately it is rumoured that this taniwha also proved highly susceptible to large amounts of hard cash, and work now continues. In fact, the roadworks are still in place here as we pass the old derelict power station at **Meremere** on our way to a rather auspicious event for which we have felt the need to dress up: Winter Dragwars. No, I'm not talking stockings and suspenders, but T-shirts appropriate for racing at the Champion Dragway. Nick is resplendent in a black number which has a picture of a car on the front (good start) coupled with the immortal line 'Burned Out'. I, however, have made a serious error. God alone knows what I was thinking but I am now sporting a cream T-shirt with a picture of a trout on the front and the message 'Fishing is Life (the rest is mere detail)'. I soon realise that you can't get much further away from revving engines and burning rubber than fishing, and that judging from the odd looks being thrown my way I must look a right pillock. I console myself that there is a fish connection here this morning – the proliferation of mullets among our fellow racegoers.

This is one of those meetings where you turn up in your own car and, well, just race. 'Windows up, seatbelts on and no singlets,' screams the voice on the speaker system as the drivers rev their engines for the qualifying rounds and everyone else scrabbles for a seat in the small grandstand. A succession of semi-souped-up vehicles lines up two by two on the starting grid before squealing off into the distance. Some, like the obligatory V8s and the restored Ford Capri with super-wide wheels, give off a tremendous amount of smoke from their tyres in a show of bravado before their 12 seconds of glory. Others, such as the orange VW Scirocco, look rather as though they are out for a Sunday drive, even after the green light has flicked on, to hoots of good-natured derision from the crowd. Testosterone levels rise even more when a real-life hot rod, the only one of the day, pulls up to the starting grid in a haze of burning rubber only to reveal that the driver is a young woman with long, blonde hair. The motto on the back of her car, named *Gumdrop*, reads 'A hot rod without flames is like sex without a tongue.'

In an attempt to make sense of the qualifying rounds we approach Kevin, on duty in the pits. 'Oh, yeah,' he says, tolerant of our ignorance. 'This is just to get your DYO. There'll be a burnout later on. All sorts of fun and games.' We have no idea what he is talking about and tell him so. 'Oh, sorry,' he adds, 'you looked like you'd been here before.' Maybe my T-shirt isn't such a dead loss after all. 'The burnout is just cars messing about at the end of the meeting. Burning rubber, that kind of thing.'

'Donuts?' ventures Nick.

'Yeah. And more besides. All sorts of fun and games,' repeats Kevin. 'Big business for Jack, usually.'

Jack, it turns out, is the owner of the local breakdown truck. He lives in a solitary house on the hill overlooking the dragway. His driveway actually leads down to the track so that when a car, any car, blows a tyre, a gasket or whatever, he can race down and pick up some easy business. Sure enough, a couple of races into the afternoon session a cloud of smoke appears in the distance at the end of the track. Jack's truck comes storming down the hill. Sniffing disaster, another pick-up and an ambulance join in. It's the closest race all day, but it looks to be in vain as all three return empty-handed not long afterwards.

It's time to go, unfortunately before the burnout. As we sneak out to the car park to avoid the rush, we pass a disgruntled young man sulkily scraping the white paint off his windscreen, and a seemingly never-ending array of personalised number plates: DVOST8, HLLRZR, URA1AB. The last one takes me a while to translate, although as far as I'm concerned any personalised plate should really read IMATWT.

Back on SH1 we're soon cruising along through the beautiful rolling countryside of the Hampton Downs to the turn-off for **Te Kauwhata**. Meaning 'the empty storehouse', the name harks back to a time when the local iwi was caught with no provisions for a visiting tribe. Fortunately for us, the town is now home to the Rongopai Winery, which means they should be pretty well stocked. The winery owes its existence to an Italian, Romeo Bragato, who came here in 1895 at the request of the New Zealand government to head up a viticultural research station. Whatever he did was obviously a success as he is credited with being the pioneer of the entire New Zealand wine industry.

'History in every glass' promises the sign outside as Nick and I crunch up the gravel to the front door of the attractive main building. We are greeted by Vivianne who engages us in a tasting session of both the seasonal and reserve wines on offer. I'm particularly keen on the Chardonnay as it gives me an excuse to drop the word 'buttery' into the conversation. Vivianne agrees. 'Matured properly in oak barrels, you see. Not just chippings added,' she adds, sagely. This leads to a general discussion on how best to describe the different characters of the wines we have tasted so far. Nick is convinced that if you want to sound as if you know what you are talking about, it is imperative that the adjectives you use should in no way be descriptive of flavour. Instead, use 'robust', 'leathery', 'educated', or even 'rotund'. And if you can get away with 'irksome' then I salute you. I don't think I ever have.

'Have you ever thought about teaming up with Albert, the cheesemaker from Mercer?' I ask, feeling quite smug at making the connection. Cheese and wine, see? Geddit? Vivianne wrinkles her brow.

'We have mentioned it to him,' she remarks, 'but he says he doesn't want to expand his business too much.' I suppose you can't blame Albert. He works flat out seven days a week as it is. Imagine if he landed a massive contract. There'd be no mercy in Mercer.

Before we leave we taste the Noble Late Harvest, the original dessert wine that started everything rolling here, and Nick buys the huge bottle of port he has been eyeing up since we arrived. I take a couple of Chardonnays (buttery, obviously) and the signature wine. Vivianne kindly helps us carry our stash out to the car. What a very civilised afternoon this is turning out to be. I wonder what my next scheduled stop will be. Oh.

By the 1860s, there was huge pressure on the colonial government to provide the ever-increasing numbers of European immigrants with land. Maori quite reasonably feared that their birthright was being taken from them, and so elected a king at **Rangiriri** to spearhead their resistance to a complete

Pakeha takeover, but it served only to strengthen the colonial resolve. Despite severe warnings not to do so the British under Governor Grey invaded the Waikato. And so began the next phase of the New Zealand Wars.

Stalling tactics at Meremere and harassment of the British lines in the area gave the Maori, under the direction of Te Wharepu, time to construct yet another ingenious pa. More of a line of defence than a fortress, the earthworks at Rangiriri stretched about a kilometre from water to water, from the Waikato river in the west to Lake Waikare in the east. They were both deceptively defendable and strategically superbly situated. When the British advanced under General Cameron and attacked by both land and river gunboat on 20 November 1863, each wave was successfully repulsed by a comparatively small force within the pa. Indeed, by nightfall very little ground had been gained by the British and as they dug in, the Maori chiefs actioned their inevitable escape plan. It rained heavily that night, soaking the Maori gunpowder. By morning, those left inside the pa offered the white flag as a sign of willingness to negotiate. The British, inexplicably for the etiquette of the time, took it as acceptance of defeat, and despite protests merely walked into the pa and declared themselves the victors, a sneaky trick for sure. So after the initial fearful bangs the Battle of Rangiriri ended with a whimper.

The first time I approached Rangiriri from the north, the cloud formations seemed more something you might see in Tornado Alley USA than over the green pastures of the Waikato. Grey, scudding masses filled with sweeping rain and atmospheric foreboding. Later I discover the name of the town translates as 'angry sky'. Today, too, the weather seems to have taken a turn for the worse and I'm certainly taking my life in my hands attempting to turn right across the traffic flow to all that remains of the Rangiriri pa, directly beside SH1 at the northern end of town.

The earthworks are much depleted now, naturally, but you can still appreciate the scale and ingenuity of their construction. Standing here in the gathering dusk I can see both the river and the lake in opposite directions – what a massive undertaking it was for the Maori to build a complete line of defence here and then defend it so bravely. Unfortunately the undertaking didn't end there. After the battle the bodies of some 35 Maori defenders and an incredible 130 British soldiers littered the battlefield. Those of British officers were taken to Auckland for burial, but the rest were interred right here in Rangiriri, in the graveyard near the tavern, where I go next.

There are individual unnamed plots for the British troops who died and a mass grave for the fallen Maori marked by a small grassy knoll. It is a neat, well-tended place, yet bleak. I sympathise with both sides, but as an Englishman I can't help wondering what must have been going through these poor young British guys' minds, dying in a meaningless war against a fearsome enemy in a land about as far from home as it was possible to get. The rain intensifies so I dart across the road to the Battle Site Heritage Centre, where it looks like the ladies running the café are preparing to close for the day.

'We could do you a pot of tea,' says one.

'No. Thank you. I'm just here to see the film.'

'Ah. You want Pat, then.'

Pat Gaitely, an elderly man with piercing eyes, shuffles through a few seconds later. I ask him if I can see his renowned film of the battle.

'Hmmm,' he snorts. 'I don't usually show it just for one,' but nevertheless leads me through to his mini cinema. Posters are displayed on the walls, but I only catch glimpses as Pat pulls the curtains, turns the lights out and sets the film rolling.

Ten or so minutes later, after an entertaining and informative documentary on the whos, whys and whats of the Battle of Rangiriri, I find my way back to the café where Pat is in conversation with the only remaining café lady. I tell him how much I enjoyed the film, and he seems pleased. He must be, because he thaws a little and offers me some very helpful pointers on other aspects of local interest, including a lowdown on the local taniwha ordeal. The café lady nods behind him, affirming his local knowledge and stacking away the teacups as she does so. I get the feeling they're eager to shut down, so I make my excuses.

'Where are you off to?' she asks.

'South.'

'Ah,' she says. 'Watch out going that way.'

'Why?' I ask. 'There's not another taniwha on the loose, is there?'

'No,' she laughs. 'Speed cops. They're buggers round here.'

We don't have much luck with lakes, Nick and I. At Okaihau we had fish dropped on our heads and talked ourselves into getting lost. This time we're wondering if we've even found the lake in question. It's **Lake Ohinewai** and the map shows two areas of water in the vicinity. I'm pretty sure the lake we want is the one right in front of us, with the twin chimneys of Huntly power station poking up over the hill behind. Nick thinks that lake is the smaller of the two and there must be another one behind the rise. It's not until we drive back towards SH1 that we notice a small swamp on our left-hand side. There is supposed to be a hot spring around here somewhere, too, or there was once upon a time, but I'm thinking we should maybe quit while we're ahead. After a quick recce of the town, including a beautiful little orange grove surrounded by olive trees, we're back on the road.

The Topp Twins may well be the town's most famous export, but ever since 1842 the history of **Huntly** has for the most part lain in coal. Still one of the main coal-mining centres of New Zealand, the area produces over 10,000 tonnes of the stuff per day with an estimated 300 million tonnes still buried in the vicinity. Do the maths and it should be good for another 80 years or so at least – plenty of time to convert totally to a more environmentally friendly solution. I say totally because the process has already started.

If I wanted to find out more about the black stuff I would no doubt visit the Waikato Coalfield Museum here. But to me coal means only one thing, and that is being sent out in the freezing cold with a bucket and scuttle to fetch some fuel for Mum and Dad's ancient boiler. So no offence, but no. Besides, anyone who has ever even passed through the town will remember it for the twin chimneys of the Huntly Power Station that dominate the skyline.

Commissioned in 1983 and now run by Genesis Energy, Huntly is the country's largest thermal power station, generating about 20 per cent of the nation's electricity requirements. No coincidence, then, that it's a massive coal-powered complex, although it can burn natural gas, too, and will do so increasingly as soon as the Huntly Energy Efficiency Enhancement Project (or Huntly e3p) is up and running. Good news for the environment, not so great for my purposes. As soon as work started on expanding the plant, tours of the station became a no-no, or at least that's what they say. Conspiracy theorists would have it that the power station only became too big for its boots after sampling the glamour of Hollywood. The movie *Atomic Twister* was filmed here, strangely concerning tornadoes wreaking havoc on a nuclear power station. Yes, nuclear. I guess Huntly power station didn't want to get typecast.

Anyway, you used to be able to just turn up and have a whiz around inside, but I've heard it may be difficult on spec. Still, nothing ventured, nothing gained, so no sooner have I passed the 'Switch on to Huntly' sign which cunningly embraces the chimneys as carved wooden Maori pouwhenua, than I find myself crossing the sublime steel arches of the Tainui Bridge on my way to the station.

I park and approach the gate. Although helpful in trying to locate the person I need to organise an impromptu tour, I can tell the woman in the kiosk doesn't rate my chances.

'Are they there?' I ask, as she waits patiently on the phone.

'Somewhere. Probably hiding.' She laughs, shrugs, then hangs up.

I've not made an appointment, I'm certainly not a potential client and I think we both know I'm on a loser. I guess I'll just have to appreciate the view instead, so it's back over the bridge I go to River Haven, a strange shop-cum-café beside the Info Site on the bank opposite the power station. I try to buy a Huntly postcard but they are sold out.

'We had a run on them last week,' says the guy behind the counter in explanation. 'Students.'

I am forced to sate my hunger for local goods with a Huntly thimble instead (complete with a picture of the power station, naturally), then it's down to the lookout for one last photo. On the way back to the car I hear a rustling in the car park bushes and bend down to see what it is, imagining I will spot some cheeky blackbird cracking open a snail shell. It is a rat.

Rarely have I seen quite such a yellow yellow as that adorning the River Mill Bakeries building on the way out of Huntly. The relative gloom of a rare overcast day accentuates its glare and the colour is emblazoned on my retina as Nick and I follow the river towards the Hakarimata Range in the near distance. Directly to our left though, another range seems almost to overhang the road south.

Taupiri nestles at the foot of its eponymous mountain, a village with strong cultural ties for Waikato Maori. The lower slopes are also home to a sacred burial ground, final resting place of all the Maori kings: Potatau, the original figurehead of the King movement; his son Tawhiao whose reign coincided with Rangiriri and the Waikato War; Mahuta, Te Rate and Koroki, too, all noble leaders of their time.

It has been our intention, if permitted, to visit the burial ground, or at least to survey it from a respectful distance. However, it soon becomes apparent that there is a funeral taking place today so we drive slowly past, noticing that to reach the graves the mourners must first take their lives in their hands by negotiating the train track which hugs the base of the hill.

We're soon on our way again, past Candyland and the 1B alternative route turn-off where SH1 cuts west again to follow the Waikato River. The frog on the sign for the Hopin Stopin Café looks distinctly disgruntled in the knowledge that he is 'open' before we say 'Haere ra' to Taupiri and 'Haere mai' to **Hopuhopu**. Ah, I see. Frogs ... hopping ... it all starts to become clear when suddenly Nick shouts for me to stop the car. He then gets out and frogmarches himself 100 metres in the direction we have just come. I look in my rear-view mirror and he is soon returning with something in his hand. A single, discarded gumboot. In Hopuhopu. You couldn't make this stuff up, could you? He throws the gumboot in the boot of the car. As he well knows, I'll be needing that later in my journey.

Just as Taupiri provides the resting place for Maori royalty, so **Ngaruawahia** houses the reigning Maori monarch, at present Te Arikinui Dame Te Atairangikaahu, at the Turangawaewae Marae. As you would expect, access to the marae is strictly limited and if a pleb like me has trouble getting into Huntly Power Station then I'm certainly not going to waste anyone's time trying to purloin an invitation into the most revered Maori site in the country. Instead I make do with an outside glimpse of Turangawaewae House just off the grassy town square. Originally built to be the Maori parliament building in 1919 by Mahuta, son of Tawhiao, it became largely redundant when the marae was constructed soon after. During World War Two it was converted into a health clinic, and also housed the Maori Land Court during the 1950s and 1960s. I'm not sure what purpose it serves today, but for a lowly foreigner it offers an interesting blend of European and Maori architecture with its carved wooden entranceway and brightly decorated door.

After the invasion of the Waikato in the 1860s, Ngaruawahia was renamed Newcastle by the British ('Na-what? Call it bloody Newcastle.') but only briefly. Granted the iron bridge over the river here is slightly reminiscent of the old Tyne Bridge, and I'm sure there are plenty of towns around New Zealand whose Maori names have disappeared since the advent of Pakeha, yet few surely can have a more interesting translation than 'Break open the food pits.' Apparently this refers to a time around the 1660s when the local chief found himself host to some important guests and was forced to pull out all the stops to ensure they were well fed. The feast he laid on was said to cover over 1.5 kilometres of table space. Nice recovery.

There's certainly an aura to the town as I pass through, a clash of past and present, custom and history sitting uncomfortably next to takeaway outlets and second-hand shops. Then again, it might just be me. I look over to the vast expanse of green on my right and see an array of green poles sticking up out of the ground at regular intervals. Travelling through here previously I have assumed them to be of some Maori significance. It is only recently I have learnt from my friend Jason that they are in fact gas vents to prevent expansion or even explosion from a previous landfill site. How wrong can you be? But you see what I mean? Ngaruawahia strikes me as a town still coming to grips with its past yet already burdened with the trappings of modern culture.

I'm past the golf course and heading for **Horotiu**, which means 'swiftly flowing'. The name referred originally to the river, although nowadays it serves equally well for the traffic.

Splashy™ studio is housed in what used to be the old Horotiu Village Hall. It promises ceramicware that is 'unique, funky and colourful' and they're not joking. Compared with the relatively drab scenery outside, the colour inside is almost deafening. Crossing the threshold of Splashy™ is the closest I'll ever get to feeling like Dorothy in *The Wizard of Oz*, venturing outside for the first time after her house has crash-landed. There, however, the Oz metaphor must end (that's okay, blue gingham and bunches never suited me, anyway). The rainbow effect here comes not from artificial flowers, a yellow brick road and some highly entertaining midgets, but from a huge array of tiles, plates, bowls, cups, mugs, saucers, etc, vividly painted with fish, sheep, cats, cows and, if I'm not mistaken, the odd pukeko. There's no getting over it, Splashy™ is a cheerful place and the atmosphere has certainly rubbed off on Jane Martindale (or vice versa), who approaches us to offer help.

After a quick lowdown from Jane about what's on display, I ask the question Nick knows only too well.

'Do you have anything that especially represents Horotiu?'

Jane wrinkles her forehead, not usually a good sign in my experience. 'No,' she says, troubled. 'But you can always make one up for yourself.'

It turns out that at Splashy™ you can paint your own design on a plate and they will fire it and send it on to you later. Brilliant. Jane takes us through the basics and we soon have our sleeves rolled up in readiness to ruin a perfectly good piece of pottery. Not being an artistic sort I choose to paint a SH1 shield with a Horotiu emblem and Nick, equally challenged in the realm of visual creativity, accompanies me with a similar theme on a mug. A backwash of green, a couple of familiar red delta shapes and a few raised outlines (and eyebrows) later we are standing back to admire our unhandiwork. I even attempt a personalised thumb print in one corner of my plate, although it later transforms into an indistinct smudge.

'Not bad for a first go,' says Jane diplomatically, or maybe trying to ensure we actually cough up for the messes we've just created. 'Where would you like them to be sent?' Nick kindly allows me to pay for both items, remarkably inexpensive considering, and after a friendly chat we wave goodbye to Jane and say hello to a couple of New Zealand monsters. No, not taniwha this time, but the big Fonterra plant at the south end of town, and then the place where everyone gets a bargain.

It's hardly surprising, as employee Clinton confirms, that **Te Rapa** currently hosts the country's second-largest branch of The Warehouse. The whole town has now been swallowed up by the northward commercial sprawl of **Hamilton**, and although undoubtedly good for business there appears to have been little or no planning in how this infestation has spread.

Drive straight for the heart of the nation's fastest-growing city and you pass kilometre after kilometre of brash signage leaping out at you from every angle. Yes, Hamilton starts early these days, and it's definitely not pretty at first, which is a shame because as you draw closer to the hub of activity it's really not that bad. In fact I bet most of the bad press that Hamilton receives (one poster for Tui beer specifically springs to mind) is rooted in this rather ugly approach to what is reputedly a young and vibrant city. Then again, betting really isn't my forte, as I am about to confirm with a night out at the Sky Casino.

'Wall to wall entertainment'. That's what Sky City has to say for itself, and it may just have a point. Certainly the thematic photos which cover the walls all show people being entertained, and why the hell not, with the Riverside Complex housing a wide selection of bars, clubs, pubs and even tenpin bowling. Nick and I, however, are here for one thing and one thing only: to break the bank.

Carried on a wave of post-All Black victory euphoria, we enter the gaming floor at about 9.45 pm. The casino is alive with lights from the pokie machines and already bustling with boozy punters like us, all willingly volunteering to lose potfuls of cash to our own distinctive poisons. The card and roulette games at the back are particularly full, so being virgin gamblers, we grab a drink from the bar and loiter at various tables in an attempt to pick up the general rules of the house. Nick disappears and five minutes later I locate him, the only player at a $10 minimum bet Blackjack table. Ah well, in for a penny. I cash in $50 for five red discs and we're away.

Paul, our dealer, seems a good guy, professional but always willing to explain the rules without patronising us.

'If you want another card just tap the table,' he says.

'And if I don't want another card?' I ask, stupidly.

'Then don't.'

Things start poorly. Despite a voice somewhere in the back of my brain telling me I should always force the house to play, in the first hand I twist on 15 and get a king. Bugger. Nick sticks on 17, but dealer draws two picture cards and he's stuffed as well. Never mind. Early days yet. On the second hand I stick on 19 and Nick on 17. Dealer gets Blackjack. What's going on? This isn't what it's like in James Bond movies.

The third hand brings a change of luck, albeit fleeting. Dealer must twist on 13, and busts. He then toys with us over the next couple of hands with varying success. I'm back up to $30, but after little more than five minutes Nick's $50 is gone. I give him one of my remaining three chips and we go again. And again. And again. Hang on, this is more like it. All of a sudden we're on a roll. Now it's us getting Blackjacks and Paul foundering on a combination of ugly low numbers and picture cards at exactly the wrong time. Before I know it I'm $20 up on the night, and Nick has broken even. Eat your heart out, David Niven, who's the daddy now?

Unfortunately the answer to that question is only too forthcoming. A dozen or so more hands and it's all over, money gone. I look at my watch. The whole adventure has taken less than half an hour. We thank Paul for his hospitality – a bit like complimenting the executioner on his shiny new blade – and retire to the roulette tables to watch some other poor mugs lose their money. And then a thought occurs to me. I have set myself a limit of $100 gambling funds for tonight. So far I have lost half of that, which still leaves me $50. I cash in my $50 at the roulette table and immediately stick it all on black. It comes up red. *Rien ne va plus*, as I believe the saying goes.

A good few drinks later, on recommendation of Joao, our hotel barman, we find ourselves at a bar called The Bank on the main drag. In between feeling very old and observing a succession of extremely attractive, busty young girls attempting to pull polo-shirted rugby players, Nick and I come to the startlingly intelligent conclusions that 1) this gambling lark really is all down to luck; 2) no matter how you look at it the odds are stacked against you; and 3) he's one of my best mates in the whole world, he is. Alcohol. It's a wonderful invention, isn't it? Especially for casino managers.

Hamilton to Taupo.

There being no lakes in the immediate vicinity over which to disagree, it is time for Nick and I to part company, for the time being at least. Our night's festivities have inevitably given way to a morning of hangovers and grumblings which, combined with a fairly lethal checkout time of 10 am, has left us both in a sad state of repair. So while I press on southwards, Nick is off back to Auckland. 'Don't forget,' he groans through his headache, 'if you bypass Taupo on your way back home you'll cut about an hour off your journey time.'

I point out that such a shortcut would necessarily take me off SH1, the sole reason for my trip in the first place.

'Oh,' he replies. 'Oh, yes. Well ... fuck you, then.'

'Safe journey, Mr Ward.'

Getting out of Hamilton takes a while, even after several Nurofen. My first stop of the day is **Tamahere**, which has turned out to be an enigma in terms of research. I see that the name translates as 'son tied up' (not to be confused with Tamihere which comes out as 'tongue tied up', or is that just wishful thinking?), but apart from this rather startling revelation it has offered me little. So I accost a local man in his garden studying trees. As he firmly shepherds me away from his property he tells me he is originally from Bath Spa in the UK. I tell him I'm from just up the road in Worcestershire.

'Ah,' he says, relaxing his iron steer just a little. 'Graeme Hick country.'

'Something like that,' I say. (To mention that cricketer Graeme Hick is in fact Zimbabwean seems flippant at a time like this.)

'He came here once, you know. Played for Hamilton Old Boys when I was Treasurer. I invited him back here for tea, in this very garden.'

It is clear that the same courtesy will not be offered to me, so I push on to **Pukeroro**, which continues the general idyllic Waikato theme by offering cattle standing aimlessly in fields, one select herd rather splendidly contained in a rectangular pen whose posts are trees with their heads severely chopped off. This novel approach to livestock control is followed by one, two, three places to PYO strawberries. I note that one is disturbingly situated right next to a Genetics Centre. Not long afterwards the road curves around to the left, past St Peter's School and officially into the Waipa District where SH1B rejoins its more stately sibling on the outskirts of **Cambridge**.

'You've put me on the spot there.'

I seem to have upset the girl at the Info Site. All I asked was what the one thing to do in Cambridge was and she was overcome with indecision. I even apologised and offered her two simple options, horses or antiques, but now she's looking worriedly at her mate, entreating her to come to the rescue. I'm on the verge of suggesting maybe I should trek around every antique shop in town to see if they have any statues of horses for sale when all of a sudden an answer is forthcoming.

'Mmmm. It's got to be horses, eh?' she says, sounding utterly unconvinced. Her mate nods in encouragement. Sold. But my options are immediately reduced by the fact that I've not arrived here on a race night so the trots are definitely out. My next best bet would seem then to be something called 'NZ Horse Magic' on the far side of town. It sounds intriguing, although I'm guessing it won't involve geldings doing card tricks or stallions in glittery costumes sawing the thoroughbred in half. And indeed it doesn't. The leaflet does mention something about costumes, but it seems more of a hands-on 'meet the breeds and feed the horses' type affair. However, when I arrive at the Cambridge Thoroughbred Lodge it is shut. Off season, you see. There are plenty of horses in the neighbouring paddocks, but definitely not much magic. I curse my lack of horse sense and canter back into town where, not wanting to upset the girl at the Info Site again, I sneak in and whip away another leaflet with a horse on the front. 'Equine Statue and Equine Stars Walk of Fame' it says. So there's my thing.

Despite the inevitable onslaught of consumerism, which seems to threaten every historic town these days, Cambridge, 'town of trees and champions', has retained the greater part of its dignity thus far. The centre is a delight to walk around, especially on a sunny day like today, and it's not at all difficult to imagine a more pastoral yesteryear as you stroll past the tree-lined cricket pitch, especially if you turn a blind eye to the garish Briscoes and KFC signs. Surely the local council should shoot someone in the knees for allowing those. Still, the people of Cambridge remain very proud that they don't yet have a McDonald's, although it can only be a matter of time. Maybe they think it would be in poor taste to open a burger joint next-door to a racecourse, if you get my meaning.

The only dead horses tolerated in Cambridge seem to be those commemorated by the statue and pavement mosaics at the Equine Statue and Equine Stars Walk of Fame on Victoria Street. Octagonal, winner of the Australian derby is here, as is Mainbrace, victor in the NZ Derby and St Leger, and Mark Todd's Charisma, double gold medallist at the 1984 and 1988 Olympic Games, along with many other racing stars. They add character to this quaint little shopping street, as does the resplendent clock tower on the grassy island which scares the living bejesus out of me by chiming right beside me as I walk back to the car.

On the road out of Cambridge for the second time today, I pass the golf club again and finally realise the meaning of its sign: 'The Waikato River 15,000 years ago'. I remember reading somewhere that the river has changed course many times over the centuries and now the channel it once carved has been employed by people in Pringle jumpers who enjoy 'a good walk spoiled'.

Since the middle of the last century **Karapiro** has been famous for a rather different kind of alteration in the flow of the river, namely one of the series of massive dams built for harnessing hydro electric power. I know this huge manmade construction can't be far away as I've been following the river for the last few kilometres, but true to form when I arrive in the town I can't seem to find the bloody place. I'm muttering a few dams of my own by the Karapiro turn off. Serendipitously I stop and ask directions at the Hydro Road Art Gallery and B&B, and boy am I glad I do, or I might never have met Gavin and Judy Smith.

Gavin waves cheerily as I pull up the drive narrowly missing his small pet dog. 'Don't worry about her,' he says, 'she knows when to get out the way.'

He shows me into his gallery, hung with beautiful water-colours of rural scenes. The guy's got talent. Until fairly recently he was a farmer in Gisborne, but when he retired and sold up he decided to follow his other passion, painting. He and his wife Judy have lived a rather enviable lifestyle ever since.

'We moved to Provence for a year,' he says without a hint of pretension, 'then the UK. I was butler to a Lord for a while would you believe, and Judy played the lady-in-waiting. Wasn't much fun though. All my mates thought we were mad to go in the first place, but you've got to do these things, haven't you?'

I try to draw him out on his painting style. I've got him down as a bit of an impressionist, but he's not buying it. 'I just paint the way I like. Some people tried to get me to change a few years back. I didn't reckon it much.' You can't blame him. He paints beautiful landscapes and townscapes, country scenes, the odd few dotted with almost Lowry-esque people and horses. I joke that he's in the right area for those.

'Yeah,' he says, furrowing his brow. 'The trouble is I'm not really a fan of the colour green.' It's an odd statement from someone who's retired to paint in the middle of the Waikato.

'So which of these paintings are local?' I ask.

'About half of them, I suppose, but then I could tell you they all were and you wouldn't be any the wiser, would you?' he grins.

I choose one and offer him my EFTPOS card, which disconcerts him for the first time today.

'I better get Judy,' he says, 'she does the old zip zap.'

Having narrowly avoided Gavin and Judy's dog for the second time, I find I just can't leave Karapiro without a quick look at the dam. As I arrive at the base of Hydro Road another British guy joins me. We stare through the wire mesh at the impressive dam and the spectacular Lake Karapiro beyond, now venue for many a gala rowing event.

'It's not right, is it?' he ventures, nodding down at the power station. 'They've painted it pink. I mean, a power station, I ask you. Still, maybe it was trendy in nineteen-forty-six.'

You can actually drive over the Karapiro Dam if you want to, although I don't recommend jumping the lights if you do – it's single lane only. Me, I'm heading back out to SH1 and more of the vivid green countryside that so typifies this part of the country, even if Gavin doesn't like painting it. The river is still prominent on my right as I leave the Waipa District and head into the hobbit-like hills near the Waitoa Stream on the road to **Tirau**.

Tirau literally means 'many cabbage trees' or 'many sticks', but I would say a more apt name today would probably be 'many pieces of corrugated iron'. The town is humming with them. The two most famous examples are the dog-shaped Info Site and its partner the sheep-shaped wool and craft shop next door, and I have to say I think it all works very well. What would otherwise be a pleasant but fairly nondescript town on the main highway between Hamilton and Taupo has now become a favourite stop-off, especially with families. I join some of them taking a good nose around the sheep-shaped craft shop, the building that started it all, and then cast a quick eye inside the Info Site dog, originally an idea for a public toilet. One more thing about Tirau before I leave: it used to be called Oxford. Surely, with Cambridge just up the road and a first-class rowing venue in between, some kind of annual challenge has got to be on the cards. Or is that just me being English again?

Striking south alongside the Oraka Stream, I soon hit **Putaruru**, a place I mispronounce so badly I make it sound like some kind of marsupial with a gas problem. Ron at the Info Site doesn't seem to mind. He's far too alarmed at my questions, and points me instead in the direction of Megan who kindly sets me straight on my pronunciation then very professionally furnishes me with all the information I need for the Te Waihou Walk.

'You've got a fabulous day for it,' she says. 'It looks different every time you go there. I hadn't been there for about six months until recently, then I took the family the other Sunday and it blew me away.'

She's talking about the famous Blue Spring, home to Pump and Kiwi Blue water among others (including Pam's, so don't believe the hype), source of over 60 per cent of New Zealand's bottled water and God knows how much more exported all around the world. Before this, the town of Putaruru was known mainly for its farming and timber trade, and maybe also for Grant Fox, the All Black kicking machine of the 1980s. Maybe there is something in the water after all.

The increased demand for bottled water has been the making of this little town, so much so that they now hold a Water Festival every year and recently have even developed a new, award-winning water park through the centre which pays homage to the traditions of the area. It's well worth a look, but personally I prefer to get to the heart of the matter, so I'm soon heading off down Whites Road to find the track to the Blue Spring. As Megan at the Info Site said, it is indeed a beautiful day and I couldn't wish for a more picturesque setting. Native bush, overhanging trees and the bright blue water gurgling and splashing right beside me make this possibly the most delightful stroll I have ever taken. Before I reach the spring, however, a weird and wonderful thing happens. It's late afternoon and I can see my shadow in front of me on the grass as I walk. But there is another faint shadow, dancing just above my head. I turn to see a fantail a couple of metres away. What a friendly little fellow. Even my direct attention doesn't scare him off, and at one point he comes close to landing on my outstretched finger before he flits off into the bush. It is a magical moment of the zippedy-doodah variety.

Now there's only one thing left to do. I bend down beside the spring, cup my hand and take a sip. It tastes cool and dark, beautiful. I'm thirsty again by the time I get back to the car so I reach inside the passenger door for my bottle of Pump water and take a long swig. Ugh. Lukewarm. Not that it would really make any difference. After the past half an hour, I don't think water will ever taste as good again.

Back on the road, I pass **Lichfield**, which boasts the biggest cheese plant in the southern hemisphere, and hit **Tokoroa**.

It probably wouldn't be right to talk about Tokoroa without mentioning **Kinleith** in the same breath, and vice versa, for the two are mutually dependent: one the place of work, the other the living quarters. In other words, without the Kinleith pulp and paper mill 10 kilometres to the south, the town of Tokoroa wouldn't exist, and without the people of Tokoroa the mills at Kinleith couldn't function.

Tokoroa grew up from around 1948 purely to service the timber industry, and then some. With the promise of constant work in the thousands of hectares of surrounding forest, people flocked to the area from all over. The beacon of employment not only created jobs for millers, drivers, tree planters, thinners, pruners, bushmen and a multitude of other roles in and around the mill, it also brought together a truly eclectic mix of creeds and ethnicities – the New York of South Waikato, if you will. Today, over 25 nationalities are represented in a town of just 15,000 people: New Zealand Maori, Cook Islanders, Samoans, people from Nuie, Tonga and Fiji, New

Zealand Pakeha, Brits, Dutch, Swiss, Swedes, Danes, Finns, Canadians, Yugoslavs ... they're all here. And it's because they're all here, I'm presuming, that the town has recently launched its 'Talking Poles' venture.

No, we're not talking conversationalists from Warsaw, rather a town centre initiative to celebrate the diversity of cultures on which Tokoroa, literally 'Long pole', is built. The project has so far been driven by Gary Brunton, manager of the Info Site on SH1 as you drive through town, but wouldn't you just know that he isn't here today. Mary is here though, and her warmth and helpfulness make her an equally admirable ambassador for the town.

'Yes, you should take a look at our Talking Poles,' she says, hunting for a newspaper article on the subject. 'We've got thirteen so far, but the plan is for over fifty eventually. Now where is it?'

The article has gone astray but it really doesn't matter. Mary takes me through some of the poles, what they are and what they represent. Some such as Tu, Maori God of War, are about tradition, others more contemporary like the Sports pole with its distinctive Waikato rugby jersey on one of the figures. Most are carved wood, but I notice one is mosaic tiled and in future other ceramic and steel efforts are on the cards.

'It's really just to give us a "thing",' says Mary, 'an angle based on our heritage. So that people will want to stop and find out about the town. We're very friendly and tolerant people, you know,' she adds.

I can sense a slight defence mechanism at work here, and I think I know why.

'Brian Tamaki's from Tokoroa, isn't he?'

Mary smiles. 'Yes,' she says.

'What do people here think of him now? Did you know him ... before?'

'No,' she says. 'I've lived here thirty years but I'm not from here. My husband grew up with him, though. The Tamaki boys were always very normal as far as he was concerned, and then, I don't know, something must have happened.'

I stay silent in the hope that Mary might fill me in on the gossip, but she remains the soul of discretion.

'Let's just say that Brian Tamaki didn't get those views by growing up here.'

It's obvious she doesn't want to be drawn any futher on the subject. Shame. I was hoping for some dark revelation, but Mary's back on to the lighter side of Tokoroa.

'We also get called V-eight town. People here just like them,' she says.

In the twilight I take a brief tour of the poles in the now deserted main shopping area, an equally brief gander at the Kinleith Mill, and push on to my last stop of the day. I pass the Bullroom Tavern & Tearooms, the last pub in Waikato, before the run into the Taupo area. It's not long before the yellow sign I've been searching for shines out in front of me, and I pull into the lay-by for the Hatupatu Wishing Rock in **Atiamuri**.

Legend has it that here a young Maori chief, Hatupatu, having just escaped the clutches of an evil Birdwoman, asked the rock to open up and hide him from her pursuit. Kurangaituku, the ogress in question, searched for him in vain and then crash-landed in the mud near Rotorua, hence the constant bubbling from her wrath. The rock itself is quite bizarre, about my height and perfectly conical with a convenient hole in the side, almost like a teepee. With no cars passing the atmosphere here is eerie, especially with those tall cliffs looming behind it in the half light. I feel very cold all of a sudden. After firing off a couple of blurry shots I'm happy to be back in the car again, zipping through Te Pouwhakatutu to Taupo, where I park the car, and myself, overnight.

Definitely one of my better ideas. Following a fantastic night's rest at the Tui Oaks on the lakefront, I wake up to a fine morning, fully refreshed for the return to **Wairakei**. Indeed my only quandary now is what to choose from the multiple attractions on offer. I'm rather spoilt for choice compared with some of the places I have visited. Should I take the Huka Jet up to the Falls, for example, or wander around the Craters the Moon? Maybe even drop in at Wairakei Village to see what's going on there? There's really only one way to decide in situations such as this, I find, and that is to study the name itself. Wairakei means 'pools of adornment', so called for the reflective qualities of the water. No contest, then. Besides, a spot of geothermal activity is good for the soul.

Wairakei Terraces are built on a reclaimed part of the thermal power plant next-door, a positive addition to an area where there has been much criticism of man harnessing nature's bounty and destroying natural wonders.

The reverse is true here. Nature destroyed the original Pink and White Terraces at Tarawera, so-called eighth wonder of the world, with the huge eruption that devastated the area in 1886 and wiped out whole villages overnight.

The new site is just off the main highway north of Taupo. It doesn't appear anything special from the road, but enter the main complex and it's clear that a lot of time, thought and effort has gone into this modern manufactured 'wonder'. I amble past the beautifully carved pole outside the Weaving House towards the steamy promise that lies beyond. An amazing heat rises from the stream as I walk down the steps and then up to the Waiora Pool and Waterfall. Some of the surroundings here may appear deliberately sculpted, but there's nothing artificial about the colour or other properties of the water. Leaning over the edge I'm struck by just how reflective the vivid blue surface of the pool actually is, all thanks to the minerals it contains. On this evidence it's no wonder Maori used them as mirrors.

The star attraction is already billowing steam in my direction, rendering an otherwise clear morning misty. From the viewing platform I catch glimpses of the manmade sculpted terraces through the mist. It is an awesome sight in the true sense of the word. Water from the extremely vocal geyser at the top gushes down over the steps in incessant torrents as steam billows across the hillside. I can't actually see the geyser itself, but I can hear it thumping and splashing and I see the occasional globule of boiling water flung across the garden and sometimes even on to the path, which I find a little worrying. My mind is eased somewhat by the presence of a rather well-built member of staff gardening inside the fenced area. Surely the big geezer wouldn't stand next to the big geyser if it were lethal.

'Did you enjoy it?' asks the ticket lady as I return.

'Fantastic,' I say. 'Inspiring stuff. It must get a little hairy if there's any wind, mind.' I resist using the phrase 'boiled tourists' even though I'm itching to.

'Mmmm, sometimes,' she laughs, 'but we don't let people through that way when it is.'

It makes me wonder how on earth they built it in the first place. Hardly reassuring to have working conditions where the soil just below you is 130°C and there's a six-metre geyser right next to you in an area renowned for massive and unexpected thermal activity. I hope they got danger money.

I love **Taupo**. I think that first glimpse of the lake as you roll down the hill is one of my favourite views in New Zealand. On a clear day it never fails to gladden the heart: the random groups of buildings sweeping down to the shore and the great, calm expanse of the lake itself with Tongariro, Ngauruhoe and the mighty Ruapehu brooding in the background. If ever there were a case for explosions being good, this is surely it. And what a bloody big explosion it was to create a lake this size.

The crater lake of Taupo, as we know, was formed by a series of volcanic eruptions, the most violent of which occurred about 1800 years ago and is thought to be the largest ever recorded. It felled forests, burned trees 30 kilometres away and covered 20,000 square kilometres of land with up to 200 metres of pumice. Its effects were seen as far away as China and even Rome, where literature tells of the sun in the east being blood-like, lacking in light and giving the appearance of the heavens being ablaze. I guess that's what happens when mountains blow themselves apart.

The result of course is the beautiful lake we know today – 40 kilometres long, 30 kilometres wide and 90 fathoms deep in places, with an area of over 616 square kilometres. Twenty-eight rivers flow into Lake Taupo, with only one, the mighty Waikato, flowing out. Being a volcanic crater, and a relatively recent one in geological terms, little of anything actually lived in the lake until 1886, when English brown trout were released here, followed by North American rainbow trout 11 years later. These days, keen fisher folk catch over 500 tonnes of rainbow trout here a year. So I'm thinking, surely just a few extra kilos by a non-fisherman wouldn't be too much to ask? Doug doesn't seem to think so.

'No worries,' he tells me on the phone. He obviously hasn't seen me fish.

I found Doug's 'His Nibs' Charters after leafing through a pile of leaflets of landfill proportions at the Taupo Info Site. Doug's looked the most honest: 'Hi. I'm Doug. I've been fishing Lake Taupo for over 26 years. Come fishing with me and try for that "big one". You catch 'em. I'll clean 'em. You eat 'em!' Doug himself is merely a silhouette in the photograph, which I find even more humble. Either that or he's hideously deformed and doesn't want to put people off by appearing in promotional material. He gives me directions to the marina and the next morning I am out the door by 4.50 am and rolling into the marina car park bang on time.

Doug is just as I imagined and hoped: a greying, affable, good old boy, not hideously deformed at all, who looks like he knows exactly what he is doing. After 26 years working the lake, he must know a thing or two. As we chug out of the marina, I am determined not to ask the usual bullshit questions I imagine he gets all the time from tourists, so I try a different tack.

'So, Doug, what was it like when the mountain erupted?'

'I dunno, mate. That was nearly two thousand years ago.'

Actually I am referring to the 1996 Ruapehu eruption which threw up tonnes of volcanic ash, and probably spume (what a good word that is) into the air.

'No, I meant Ruapehu.'

He laughs heartily. 'Oh, sorry, mate. I wondered what you were on about. No, it was fine here. All the ash blew over to Napier apart from one day, I think. The boat was covered. Didn't seem to upset the fish, though.'

How civilised this all is, two grown men chatting as we cruise along with the lights of Taupo on our left in the perfect calm of darkness. Peaceful. Sedate. Then Doug opens her up.

'You might want to hold on to that rail.'

Holy cow. He isn't joking. As we pass the outer buoy the darkness around us erupts in a whirl of white water. Doug shouts that we are heading for a spot about 25 minutes away and I revert to nodding again. It's too noisy for conversation so I hold on and hope Doug can't see the mild terror in my eyes.

The lights of Taupo retreat into the distance and after what seems like a very long 20 minutes we slow to a gentle crawl, whereupon Doug shows me the ropes.

'There's nothing to it, really,' he says. 'You just give it a quick flick every few seconds, like this.' He flicks. He's right. This is dead easy.

It's still a little breezy and choppy out in the middle of the lake, which I'm assured are ideal conditions for catching trout. 'The light's just about to show too, they should start biting any minute now, you'll see.'

Ten minutes pass, biteless. I can sense Doug's reassured demeanour dwindling. It's his constant repetition of the words 'I don't understand it' that gives him away. He tells me that the trout don't like all the extra activity on the water during the holidays. Their peace shattered by teenagers on jetskis, they tend to retreat down under the reefs and show little interest in unrealistic yellow-bellied green flies, or whatever kind of lure we are using.

Then it happens.

'Here we go!' shouts Doug. 'Got one.' He hands the rod to me. 'You get to land every fish that comes in on this boat. I just help you hook them,' he explains, and scoots off to the cabin to fetch a tray. 'Just reel him in steady, don't pull too much on the line or you'll pull the hook through. We should see him jumping any time now.'

Sure enough, there's a silver gleam looping out of the water about 10 metres away. I do exactly as Doug tells me, reeling steadily, while he gets the net ready. Ten seconds later he's scooped a beautiful rainbow trout onto the deck. He puts it down on the tray and bludgeons it. I hadn't been expecting that. Doug can tell.

'You have to, or they'd be jumping all over the boat,' he says. Then he weighs the prize.

'Nice fish. Just under five pounds. Not bad for a first go,' he says, suggesting it isn't really that impressive. But the fish looks huge to me and anyway, I am too chuffed to care. What is important is that I, Bob Moore, the most unsuccessful angler I know, have finally landed a fish. Have that, Joe Bullman.

I should explain here that Joe is a mate of mine back in London, one of the keenest anglers I know. Much to the irritation of Julie, his wife, he uses up half his holiday allowance on fishing trips with the boys, after which he returns home, to work, wherever, and talks incessantly about his fishing exploits. We had a standing joke about it, in fact. Every time one of his mates would ring to discuss sticklebacks, eels or some such nonsense, I would interrupt and ask him whether he used a swimfeeder, practically the only advanced item of fishing tackle I know. He would then tell me to piss off. It was hilarious.

Joe always told me the only reason I didn't like fishing was because I didn't understand it. Either that or I was crap at it. I think possibly he was correct on both counts. In an attempt to dispel this theory, however, I resolve to take a photo of my catch to send him. But not now. Now I am fishin'. And, like the poor little bugger that just got hit on the head, I am hooked.

'They should start coming in thick and fast now,' says Doug.

I can't wait, and luckily I don't have to. No sooner has he put his rod back into the water than 'twang', off it goes again. I struggle manfully with the line, bringing another fish alongside while Doug scoops it up with his net. This one is smaller.

The last catch of the day is a beauty and all my own work. I struggle manfully for, oh, at least a minute to bring her in. And when I do it is another five-pounder. Bloody marvellous. I am aglow with pride as Doug suggests we clean up the catch and head back to shore. Has it really been three and a half hours? I must have been enjoying myself.

Doug guts the fish on our journey back in, much to the approval of the birds which seem to swoop from nowhere as he chucks the innards out into the lake. Back in the marina I take a quick photo of the three fabulous trophies with the aid of my mobile phone. Doug then bags up the biggest fish for me, and I let him keep the other two. I thank him for a great trip. He seems to have enjoyed it, too.

'It was nice not to have any pressure,' he says. 'Sometimes you go out with these groups of businessmen and they literally demand to catch fish. It makes me very uncomfortable.'

I hop off the boat and back to the car with my prize fish. Doug waves me off. I am a happy man, and even happier to be heading back to town just in time for a well-earned hearty breakfast. I am tempted to order kippers, but sanity thankfully wins the day and I order a full English instead, which reminds me, I still have one duty left to perform. I pxt the shot of my three fish to Joe in London, accompanied by the words 'I caught these'. His reply comes the next day.

'Did you use a swimfeeder?'

Taupo to Bulls.

Driving out past hotels, motels, apartments and holiday homes it strikes me just how far the main township of Taupo stretches, right up past **Wharewaka** Point nearly to the turn-off to the airport in fact, or so it seems. After an overcast morning the sun is finally poking through the clouds, and by the time I cut inland slightly at **Waitahanui** the pine trees on either side of the road have definite shadows. After **Hatepe**, the extent of my fishing trip with Doug, I'm soon into **Hallett's Bay**, white cliffs on my left in a perfect arc, like a big Pacman poised to swallow Motutaiko Island out there.

The road hugs the cliffs perilously close to the lake around some fairly hairy corners and climbs to reveal glimpses of blue water below. Here, the lake views dominate the journey, through **Motutere**, **Mission Bay**, **Waitetoko**, **Te Rangiita** and **Tauranga-Taupo**. In **Motuoapa** my focus is finally distracted by Parikarengarenga, the Echo Cliffs. It has been my intention to test this echo theory, but at the reserve I discover there are burial grounds in front of the cliffs. 'Climbing up the cliffs is not permitted', reads a notice beside them, although I may be tempted if that huge dog in the garden next-door manages to get out.

Safely back in the car I'm soon crossing the bridge into **Turangi** over the world-famous Tongariro River, world famous for one thing. Trout fishing. Now, quite apart from not having a rod or a guide, I think flyfishing here would probably be pushing my luck, and very definitely pushing my ability. So instead I shall visit the Tongariro National Trout Centre on the far side of town. The Trout Centre turns out to be much less commercial than I feared. I'm not really sure what I was expecting, a petting zoo for fish perhaps, but certainly not such a natural and peaceful stroll beside the water. It's a working wild fishery, a place where wild trout spawn, hatch and grow with a little human help. This not only safeguards the fish that swim here from Lake Taupo, but also ensures that should ash from an eruption of Ruapehu or one of its neighbours wipe out the trout in the lake, they could restock the streams and rivers with fish from here. Brilliant.

I walk along the bank of the Waihukahuka Stream, past the stripping pens where they separate the male and female fish to harvest eggs for spawning, and through the hatchery which is far from busy today. A sign informs me that koi carp are 'a noxious and unwanted pest species'. If this is so then I wonder why they're worth so bloody much.

Back at the River Walk Visitor Centre a man accosts me.

'I've just put the video on. Go on in,' he says. 'Mind you wait for your eyes to adjust before you try and sit down,' he adds, as I walk into a wall.

The short movie gives a little background on the life cycle of a trout; those swimming upstream to spawn are aggressive and territorial, which is why they snatch so readily at fishing flies. Of course while so much aggression ultimately leads to them being hooked, reeling one in also becomes more of a proposition. The film shows one poor angler chasing his catch halfway down the river, stumbling over rocks and weed before finally securing his prey. And then letting it go. Well, honestly. If I'd gone to all that trouble I'd have whacked the bugger and gutted him ready for the grill. Or maybe let Doug do it for me.

An hour later I'm back on the road. If they'd had an 'I got waylaid at the National Trout Centre' T-shirt I would surely have bought it. After all, I'm rather partial to shirts with pictures of fish on them, as we know. As it is I'm now feeling rather peckish and I still have over 60 kilometres to go – the longest stretch without a single town on SH1 – before sustenance awaits. There must be worse journeys you can make on a growling belly, though. I'm 15 kilometres out of Turangi by the Rangipo prison gates when the mountain views come into their own. And after the initial twists and turns, the **Desert Road** opens out into a vulcanologist's dream and what must surely be one of the finest views in the country: the stubby peak of Tongariro, the classic cone of Ngauruhoe dusted with snow, and the sprawling mass of Ruapehu dominating all. Today the starkness of the orangey-brown grass is offset perfectly by the true blue blueness of the sky, clear except for three tiny clouds off to the south, and I begin to skirt Ruapehu in absolute awe.

It's a fast stretch of road, too, the Desert Road. A cop car swoops ahead of me at the halfway point, and a couple of kilometres further on I see he has booked a guy in a Lancer. Not so lucky, lucky, today then. The rough terrain here is also used for military exercises, as I'm reminded by both a sign at the Tokino access road and a fleeting glimpse of an Army truck moving at speed down desolate on the desolate plains. The evidence of military presence builds, however, once I'm through the southern gates and entering **Waiouru**.

With thousands of troops stationed here at any one time, I guess it makes sense that Waiouru also plays host to the National Army Museum. Down the fairly barren commercial main street I soon find myself staring down the barrel of a tank turret or two outside the fortress-like museum building. Inside the main foyer it is relatively deserted. After a quick cup of tea and a pie at the café I nose around the museum shop.

'If those panels showed tanks rather than servicemen, do you think you'd be more likely to buy a poster?' asks the woman behind the counter.

'Ummm ...'

She looks down at my purchase. It is a postcard to send to my son. A postcard of a big tank.

'Ah,' she says.

'If you're selling to boys, I think tanks would definitely be better,' I offer in consolation. 'Boys love tanks.'

'Yes,' she says. 'We get mostly boys here.'

I buy my ticket and hastily sound the retreat to the exhibits.

The two floors of memorabilia deliver an honest and often brutal tribute to the full scope of Kiwi military history, from the New Zealand Wars right through to the modern day. Familiar paintings and sketches from Okaihau and Ohaeawai. A photo of the Queen's Redoubt at Pokeno in its prime – so that's what that big hole used to contain. The two world wars, Korea, Vietnam. And an impressive display of weapons and medals.

Most striking for me, however, is the large Gallipoli exhibit, complete with eyewitness accounts and a landscape recreating those sobering scenes. The horror those young men had to endure underlines both the futility of war and the fragility of human life. Whenever I read stories such as these, about World War One especially, I am thankful for being born in an age where, thus far at least, I have been spared the enforced involvement in senseless and gruesome bloodshed.

Back outside the museum I take one last look at majestic Ruapehu through the flagpoles that are whipping in the breeze, and head south again. Before long the grass returns to a more customary green and I'm entering the unspoilt Rangitikei district, and more specifically **Hihitahi**. In 1961 a train, the Ka945, derailed here after it hit a boulder that had slipped down on to the track. Today the track still hugs the hill above, and workmen are busy building a new road bridge to iron out what is a markedly meandering stretch of the highway.

The roadworks continue to **Turangerere**, or at least I think so. Short of one farmhouse there are no other tangible signs of life in the area, and I'm soon past the Napier turn-off and heading for **Ngawaka** when I see the sign: 'Taihape Golf Course,' it reads, 'NZ's finest 12th hole'. Now who could resist a challenge like that?

Amazingly I've timed everything right today – there's a man putting studiously on the practice green as I park the car.

'Yeah, good as gold, mate,' he says, when I explain I only want to play the one hole. 'It's just over there. Go for it.'

I even have my clubs and golf shoes in the boot, so it's not long before I'm kitted out and trundling over to the twelfth hole to see what all the fuss is about. And I do. The rest of the golf course is picturesque, nestled as it is in this undulating valley, but the par three twelfth hole is especially superb. Standing at the top I'm looking down on the flag which today sits towards the front of the elevated circular green. As if this weren't enough, the perfect shot takes you over bush through a natural gap between the trees, and the out-of-bounds on the right-hand side is marked by the Hautapu River which can also come into play if you drop too short. So basically, it's a great hole but if you don't get it right first time you're in big trouble.

I'm limbering up with a 9 iron when I catch my friend from the putting green gesticulating wildly. Ah. It appears I'm on the ladies' tee. The men's tee is further up the hill. This is getting harder by the minute. I tramp uphill and change to a 7 iron. A touch more limbering up and I can't put it off any longer. I line up, jiggle a few times for good measure, and *thwack*. Hmmm. A surprisingly good connection for someone who hasn't played for two years. Pretty straight, too. In fact, blimey, straight at the flag. Go on, you little git, go on, I don't believe it, it's going to hit, it's … *thud*. My ball hits the near bank of the green, five metres short of the hole, and rolls gently down the slope. I'm slightly disappointed but at the same time elated at the thought of what could have been. There's a lot to do to save my par. With not much green to play with, the best I can do is chip and hope I don't go too far past. I do, though, and end up about five metres beyond the hole. This for my par. I don't know what it is but everything seems to be going dreadfully right today. I judge the weight of my putt amazingly well. It rolls up, rims the hole, and stops a hand's span past. It's a simple tap in for a bogey. A bogey. Ah well. I suppose I should be delighted, and I am really as I trudge back up to the clubhouse.

Two new arrivals are busy sorting out their gear for a round. They turn out to be Gary Thomas, the Club Treasurer, and his wife. Gary tells me that the great Arnold Palmer once played here in the 1970s, indeed it may even have been he who dubbed the hole I've just played New Zealand's finest twelfth.

'He didn't play a full round,' says Gary. 'Flew down in his helicopter for a few swings, then buggered off back to his fishing in Taupo. There's some more bumf in the clubhouse if you're interested … '

Gary gives me a quick tour inside, and shows me a frightening shot of the twelfth hole during a flood – the green has become an island. 'Yeah, that made it interesting. We've got new drainage in now, mind,' he adds.

I don't want to hold up his round, and I tell him so.

'Nah, good as gold. We're waiting for another couple anyway. It's just there's a race on about now and I'd quite like to …' He kindly promises to send me some articles on the club (which he subsequently does – what a nice chap) and I leave him to his radio. Thanks, Gary. I hope you picked a winner.

I'm continuing my journey south in the direction of the snow-capped Ruahine, past **Bennett's Siding** where the Hautapu Timber Mill puffs two plumes of white steam energetically into the sky, and on through the Oraukura Gorge into official gumboot territory.

When the big 1980s agriculture slump hit New Zealand many rural communities faced extreme hardship, even extinction. **Taihape** was perhaps the first town in the Rangitikei to re-invent itself, the first to hit on an angle for enticing through-travellers to stop en route between Wellington and Taupo, and thus give a much-needed boost to the local economy. The plan? A load of old boots, and some new ones, too. Yes, they say the best brands are based on truth, and for Taihape that means gumboots. In 1985 some rather clever inhabitants decided to put their best feet forward and stage their very own Gumboot Day for the town. It turned into a festival the following year, and has since grown into an internationally renowned date on the calendar.

The World Gumboot Festival is now a three-day celebration of all things rubber and boot-like, with attractions including gumboot racing, gumboot decorating, gumboot carving, and of course gumboot throwing. Nowadays they even have a dedicated and beautifully kept throwing lane up behind the main street, next to the infamous Jeff Thompson corrugated iron gumboot sculpture (infamous because his use of Australian corrugated iron caused a furore at the time). There are really no prizes for guessing the nature of my mission in Taihape. I have timed it all wrong to attend the festival – that goes without saying – but I can still perform the ritual. I am delighted to see that a few people walking around the streets on this lovely sunny day are indeed wearing gumboots. Clean gumboots, too, or there'd be a riot at the local Electrical/Post Shop. 'Please remove muddy footwear and leave at door. Thank you.' says the sign. Lucky I've got my city folk shoes on.

I've nipped in here to ask if they think it would be okay to use the hallowed turf, explaining that I'm on a pilgrimage.

'Ooh, I should think so,' says the lady behind the counter.

'If anyone says anything, tell them to bugger off,' adds a passing customer.

Good enough for me. I stroll up a side street to the sculpture and survey the throwing lane, which resembles a very small fenced grass tennis court, without the ends, the net or the markings. To my horror I realise that I'm actually limbering up.

'Ah, but you've forgotten something haven't you, Mooron,' I hear you sneer smugly. 'You don't have a gumboot.'

That's just where you're wrong. Remember Hopuhopu? Apologies if you were asleep at that stage of the journey, but I believe it was Nick who spotted a solitary gumboot by the side of the road and forced me to stop the car so that he could pick it up. Well, I could kiss him now were he here (and possibly a little less unshaven) because I am clutching that very boot in my hand. Okay, it may not be regulation size and weight for competition purposes but it's close enough for mine. And as per the rules I shall be allowing myself three throws, possibly with a discus-style spin to launch. So here we go.

Throw 1: Disaster. The boot clips the top of the wire mesh on the left of the lane and cartwheels over the top. I am lucky not to lose it completely in the garden next-door. Saved by a stone wall.

Throw 2: That's more like it. A nice, straight trajectory, the boot thumps down at a distance two poles from the end of the mesh. I don't have a tape measure but I'd say about 20 metres. Come on.

Throw 3: Yes! My boot reaches the penultimate pole, 22 metres possibly, 25 metres tops. A little honour is restored.

Or at least I think it is until I realise from my information sheet that the New Zealand record is a very respectable 38.66 metres, and the world record set by a Finn is an incredible 63.98 metres!

Quite drained after all that activity, I wolf down a steak pie from the Taihape bakery and then regret it on the way out of town as the road rollercoasters queasily on towards **Winiata** where the countryside really opens up again. At **Ohotu** the large shell of a disused building on my left is the only evidence of previous human habitation. Wait, there's the odd farmhouse dotted here and there too. They're really not joking about this 'unspoilt Rangitikei' thing.

'What's your excuse?' demands the sign for the Gravity Canyon Flying Fox just before **Utiku**. I suppose I could say I don't have the time to stop, or I don't have the money, or the energy, or that adrenalin sports are so last century, darling. But like a small boy left to get ready for bed on his own, it's not going to wash, is it? The truth is I have no excuse, except that I've seen the video on the website and I'm a limping, steaming coward who hates heights. So no thanks. In fact, give me a choice between Gravity Canyon and a Wool Shop and despite being allergic to wool I'll choose the Wool Shop every time. And as luck would have it, there's a wool shop right here.

One baby beanie hat purchase later (for Arthur, my youngest), I'm travelling through some serious 'after the event' lumber country, flanked by rolling, grassy hobbit hills to the west and mountains to the east. From the road, **Manui** marks the first evidence of the steep sandstone river gorges, as seen in *The*

Fellowship of the Ring masquerading as the River Anduin. For me these gorges also represent a chance to regain a sliver of my manliness, and it is this prospect I am contemplating (as well as that pie still sitting in my stomach) as I drop down over the hill into **Mangaweka**.

You might not be able to place Mangaweka in your mind, but if I tell you it's that place with the DC3 café between Taupo and Bulls I think at least half of the New Zealand population will know where I'm talking about.

Some of you may also have spotted the 'BEWARE LOW FLYING TEAROOMS' sign that trumpets its presence. I could have severely wimped out here and simply had a cup of tea. I can only hope that the fact I am now preparing myself for a whitewater kayaking experience redeems me a little.

'Good on ya,' says Tricia, co-owner of the Mangaweka Adventure Company, when I tell her I don't want to take the easy option.

I sit down and half introduce myself to a young English couple who also appear to be waiting. Chris seems keen on kayaking, but girlfriend Kerrie is busy making excuses. Honestly, some people. I think she's trying to say she's hungover but it's taking her a long time to say it.

I'm just polishing off my tea when Paul arrives – matey, confident and looking every inch the outdoors type. 'You're a big guy, aren't you,' he observes, the polite Kiwi equivalent of 'You're a fat bastard, eh,' as I stand there squeezed into my wetsuit, fleece and boots. 'Right, let's get going.'

Down by the river, he takes us through some safety information which basically amounts to 'don't panic if you capsize' and 'don't let go of your kayak or paddle'.

'Are we likely to fall in, then?' I ask casually.

'The bigger you are, the higher your chances,' he replies.

I can almost feel the chill of the icy water already.

Our short practice session in the shallows reveals a great deal wanting in my technique, paddling straight for one thing, but hell, we can't muck around here all day, especially as I think an hour sitting in this position will prove more than adequate for bringing on a bout of lumbago. It's nothing to what Paul appears to be attempting, mind, kneeling down in his stubby little pro kayak.

'You have to be pretty fit just to get into one of these,' he says without a trace of superiority, and I believe him. In fact, I believe everything Paul says from now on because Paul is the man who's going to be keeping me alive over the next two kilometres or so of river, which is quite high and fast at present due to the recent rain.

'You guys go first and I'll tag on behind,' he says, as Chris eases out into the faster water and I somehow scuttle out sideways, bouncing off Paul's kayak. 'Let's head for those first rapids.' Is he sure?

Chris certainly seems to be, paddling firmly ahead of me as the water turns choppier. The waves splash with white, currents collide around me, and then the world turns at an odd angle and I'm in. Rapids 1, Moore 0. Thanks to the wetsuit the water isn't as cold as I feared, and as I splutter to the edge to remount I'm actually quite glad to have gotten that over with so soon. At least that's what I'm telling myself. The good news is I managed to hold on to my equipment.

'Let's have another go,' smirks Paul, holding my kayak steady as I climb in. 'You'll soon get the hang of it.' And before we know it we're nearing the next rapids, possibly a little more treacherous in appearance than the first. This time I'm at the head of the three-man convoy. I am barely over the initial swell when my balance goes again and I end up in the drink for the second time in as many minutes, the water stinging my cheeks with shame. Both sets.

'You just need to be more aggressive, Bob,' Paul says patiently as I clamber back into my kayak with all the grace of a beached whale. 'Attack the current and keep paddling.'

On the next rapids I grit my teeth, push through with as much fury as I can muster and hey, it works. Somehow I stay upright. At the next frothy patch I am treated to the sight of

Chris going arse-up, although I think Paul has purposely sent him on a more difficult route in an attempt to humble him.

And so our journey continues, patches of whitewater mayhem punctuated by calmer stretches of gentle paddling and plenty of opportunity to appreciate the incredible scenery: huge sandstone cliffs looming on either side, and the occasional waterfall gently cascading in a soothing patter. Some of the Anduin river scenes in the 'Rings' movies were shot around here, a little further upstream from where we are today. Paul worked as river security on the set.

'We've done a few movies here, actually. Bloody hard work, too, especially with the hobbits,' he says. 'But awesome,' he adds. Or possibly 'oarsome'.

I ask him if he gets a lot of business from Tolkien fans. 'Nah. "Lord of the Rings" types don't normally like kayaking. It's not a good fit, so we don't really advertise it. Besides, the whole bloody country's got some angle on the movie.'

Time flows past as quickly as the river, and before I know it there is Tricia waving from the bridge ahead. My brain can't quite believe we've been on (or in) the water for an hour, although some of my lesser-used muscles are readily convincing it. Unlike Tricia, I am not fit. She has dropped the 4WD off for us, walking the two kilometres back to HQ while we take our time lumping our gear into the trailer and sinking gratefully into the padded seats of the truck.

On the way back Paul points to the sheer cliffs retreating into the distance. 'I saw a sheep fall off the top of those the other day. Stupid bloody animal. Bounced all the way down.'

Ohingaiti translates roughly as 'little place of childhood' so a visit to Porky's Bits & Pieces antique shop seems appropriate. The town once had high hopes of burgeoning into an important centre for the district, but it has grown hardly a jot since first being established. Indeed its main feature today is its chicane rail crossing, so I'm wondering whether I will be able to buy some item to reflect this landmark. Porky's yields plenty of old tins, bottles, china, farming gear and even an old Austin motor car out the back, but little that's railway related, so I ask the lady behind the counter if Ohingaiti is renowned for anything else, or if anything else exciting has ever happened here.

'Not a lot,' she smiles. What about trains?

'Mmmm, not really … oh, hang on.'

She opens a display cabinet I have missed, inside of which sits a beautiful framed schematic of an old steam engine much like the one that derailed at Hihitahi. Sold to the man with the stiff calf muscles. Perusing the postcard rack, I note that, bizarrely, one card depicts a small town in Gloucestershire, UK, near my birthplace, and another a Spanish hotel on the Costa Brava. Very confusing. I plump for a view of the sandstone cliffs with a glimpse of the famous Makohine viaduct, built from locally produced steel and spanning the hills just before **Mangaonoho**, which I pass a little way down the road.

From here it is a pleasant valley drive to **Vinegar Hill**, the place to camp it up quite literally as it boasts a well-known gay and lesbian campsite.

The **Hunterville** district owes much to the Huntaway dog, a recognised breed of canine that barks as it gathers and moves sheep. Not only has it been instrumental in the successful farming of the area – in the steep and broken hill country around here the dog must be heard by the sheep to have any effect – it now also provides Hunterville's 'thing'. Yes, just as Taihape has its gumboots, Hunterville has its dogs. And, according to the posters up all around town today, its Shemozzle. I just have one question. What the hell is a Shemozzle?

Jude Lampp at the Window Box Gift Shop is more than happy to fill me in.

'It's like a kind of Fear Factor race for shepherds and their dogs, I suppose,' she says, glancing upwards as if picturing the weary contestants in her mind's eye. 'During the town festival anyone who enters has to run a course, and both they and their dog have to perform all kinds of funny stuff on the way – slide down mud banks, drink vinegar, eat raw lambs' testicles, that kind of thing.'

'And it's, um, a popular attraction?' I ask.

'Ooh, yes!' Jude replies. 'It started out as a bit of a giggle, but it's gradually got bigger and bigger. Sponsors, all that. The winner gets two thousand dollars this year, and we get huge crowds for the weekend. It's on the twenty-ninth. You should come along. Bring the family.'

And, do you know, such is her enthusiasm for the occasion that I really would love to, but I'll be somewhere in the middle of the South Island by then, and I tell her so. Unperturbed, Jude recruits husband Barry, himself a past organiser of the event, to lend me his DVD of last year's contest.

'That should give you a giggle,' Jude says.

(I watch the organised chaos of the race in the comfort of my own home later that evening. I learn that all the contestants are forced to wear sacks, and that only owners of Huntaway dogs can enter – if any doubt exists judges can force entrants to make their dogs bark on command. Also that everyone competing is barking mad, too. Jude is utterly wrong. I'm not so much giggling as snorting with laughter at the sight of around 40 good keen Kiwi men and women careering down a hillside with a dog somewhere in tow. It's a good job Huntaways are loyal. Shemozzle, a confused situation, is about right. But at least when it's over the owners get to down a beer or two, not least to rid themselves of the taste of testicles.)

Clutching my future viewing pleasure under my arm, I wave a hearty goodbye to Jude and Barry and cruise on out of town past a little shop with the delightful name of Wee Crafty Pea.

A local winemaker in Marton has named a wine after **Silverhope**, and much as I'd appreciate a glass right now, I'm kicking on to **Rata** where it seems the butter factory has closed down. I may be wrong, though; it's hard to tell with some of these old buildings. Then I'm passing a lone taxidermist's shop on the way to **Porewa**, after which lies one of the famous Amazing Maze 'n Maizes. Impeccable Moore timing means it's off-season and the maze is closed, but I can tell you that this one boasts over eight kilometres of maze. In maize. I would attempt a pun here but I think they already did them all. So instead I'll reserve it for **Greatford** which these days appears neither great nor ford-like. It can, however, lay claim to the cute, grey-painted St Martin's church built in 1882 when I'm guessing there were more houses in the vicinity. Nowadays I imagine congregations are rather a challenge, there being only two homes and an electricity substation nearby.

Now then, at the risk of upsetting the local population and in no way an attempt to denigrate its founder, **Bulls** must be one of the few towns in the world to be named after a shop. Originally called Rangitikei (the eponymous river forms the southern boundary of the settlement), one James Bull leased land here in 1862 and opened a general store. Naturally, 'I'm just going to Bull's' became a catchphrase in the area. In 1872, in recognition of the store and its proprietor's other contributions to the town, the courthouse and sawmill for example, it was decided to drop the apostrophe and call the town Bulls in his honour. The name has remained ever since, despite one scare during a 1901 royal visit. In Wellington (no doubt on his way to Tinwald as we shall find out), the then Duke of York apparently asked a member of the crowd where he was from, and on hearing the reply 'Bulls' quipped that he had heard of Cowes on the Isle of Wight, but not Bulls. This casual remark offended some townsfolk who promptly lodged a spirited yet ultimately short-lived appeal to change the town's name back to Rangitikei. So unlike a royal to put his foot in it.

Today Bulls is renowned for its antique and curio stores, which normally would seem an open invitation to insert a 'bull/china shop' joke. However, on the subject of puns the town is doing very nicely all by itself.

It all started in 1991 when the Bulls & Districts Enterprise Committee introduced the 'A-Bull' register, an initiative to promote local business through the joy of punning. 'Unforget-a-bull', now the town's official website (www.unforgetabull.

co.nz), began the punfest, and Bulls now boasts over 100 wordplay signs that continue to delight tourists.

I'm here today to play a game, and for once I'm not alone. TVNZ is sending a *Close Up* reporter and camera crew to record me as I am-bull around Bulls attempting to find as many bull-related puns as possible in half an hour. Rawdon Christie, the reporter, seems especially enthused by the prospect. Cameraman Rich is keen, too, despite his heavy kit.

Producer Laurna clicks the stopwatch, and off we go. I start in the main shopping street. Immediately we have 'Befriend-a-bull' for the Friends Society, 'Construct-a-bull' for what looks like a workshop, and litter bins carrying hopeful 'Respons-a-bull' stickers. Three in 10 seconds. Not bad. 'Veget-a-bull' comes next for a fruit and veg shop, raising the bar somewhat, followed by the pharmacy ('Indispens-a-bull'), the post shop ('Post-a-bull') and the Medical Centre ('Cure-a-bull') which also risks overkill by having the town's huge wooden 'Trojan' bull standing outside. This is all going brilliantly, I think. At this rate I'll be up to 50 in no time.

'That's great, Bob,' says Rich, bursting my bubble. 'Can you just do that bit again? I need to get a shot of your feet.'

Bullocks. I should have known. We do the shot a further three times and it's a similar story all the way round. Through retakes of 'Comest-a-bull' (Four Square), 'Const-a-bull' (police station) and 'Relieve-a-bull' (public toilet) the clock is eating into my allotted hunting time, but I'm going to be on telly so I'm not complaining. At 'Bank-a-bull' (no prizes for guessing the whereabouts of this sign) we also manage to scare some poor local woman insensi-bull. She thinks she's about to get mugged at the cashpoint.

'Sorry,' I say. 'We're just after the sign.'

In the end I manage a respect-a-bull 25 bull puns in half an hour. Not great, but not bad considering.

'Right,' says Rawdon, eyeing up the painted SH1 sign on the road. 'There's one more shot we'd like, Bob. If you could just get back in your car …'

Bulls to Wellington.

A helicopter patrols the sky ahead as I cross the Rangitikei River to the south of Bulls and turn right towards **Ohakea** Air Force base. There was a crash landing here yesterday; some fans aboard a charter flight bound for the Wellington Rugby Sevens had the fright of their lives when they ended up ditched on the runway. Nobody was injured, thankfully, but it was apparently a close call. As I pull into the Air Force Museum car park there are still a few official looking vans in the distance, presumably parked at the section of landing strip where the plane ended up. The story and accompanying photo of the old Devon aircraft, covered in firefighting foam, is plastered over the front page of the newspapers today, and understandably the hot topic of conversation at the museum.

'Seen this?' asks the old guy behind the counter. He holds the *Dominion Post* aloft almost proudly.

'A lucky escape,' I say, for want of a better comment.

'You betcha.'

I buy my ticket.

'Yes. You've got an airshow coming up here soon too, haven't you?' I say.

'Oh, I wouldn't know about that,' he replies, resuming his study of the article for probably the umpteenth time that morning. 'We haven't been informed.'

If knowledge of future events is sketchy around here, information on the past certainly isn't. The place is rife with memorabilia, a mish-mash of photos, models and other pieces of aviation history. If I wanted to I could get inside an Armstrong Whitworth gun turret, or step inside a fuselage to watch an airshow video. Instead I try my hand at the flight simulator. 'See if you can do a lap of the airfield and land again,' it says. I take off, machine-gun some innocent civilian housing, become disorientated in all the excitement and conclude my flight by crashing into a beacon. Still, it beats doing it for real on the tarmac outside.

One wall bears testimony to the New Zealand 'can do' attitude gone slightly awry. A series of posters lists would-be inventions from keen civilians during World War Two. One man is obsessed with ejecting substances from the back of aircraft into the path of any unsuspecting enemy: paint to obscure their cockpit vision, a sugar mixture to make their engine stall; both suggestions magnificently fail to acknowledge the risk factor in positively encouraging an enemy fighter to set you in its sights before you deploy your rudimentary, hit-and-miss contraption. To my delight another prototype suggests protecting airfields with homemade barrage balloons – standard party balloons inflated with hydrogen and held in position over the area with number eight wire. Never mind that the weight of 1500 metres of wire would have kept the balloons grounded, just like his idea. Not even this monument to Heath Robinson-ism, however, can trump my favourite exhibit. Behind the flight simulator sits a scale model of Ohakea airfield itself. There is a button beside it. 'Press here for a night view,' it says. I do. The lights go off, leaving the model in darkness. No landing lights, nothing. Where's that number eight wire when you really need it?

My thirst for knowledge sated for the time being, I saunter through to the other side of the building where, over a cup of tea and a cheese scone in the Crew Room café, I muse upon what the future will hold for this base, and the museum, too. Within the next 10 years or so Ohakea is set to expand dramatically, possibly quadrupling in size as all other RNZAF squadrons transfer here. I imagine the powers that be may choose to upgrade the museum somewhat, bringing it up to a standard to rival the Army Museum up the road at Waiouru. To the fiscally minded it might also seem a good time to invest in property in Bulls. Who knows? My tea leaves don't have the answer (probably because they're still in a bag). And certainly the two decommissioned jets sitting out there on the tarmac at the back of the café aren't giving much away. Sadly, they're also two jets more than the Air Force currently has in operation after being phased out in 2005.

The planned expansion of Ohakea could also be good news just down the road in **Sanson**, home to sleepy antique shops and tea rooms. With luck, the new boost in population may lead to the renaissance of the local rugby club and, by natural progression, provide a crowd to sit inside the object of my attention today – the iconic Sanson RFU 'A' stand.

If you've ever travelled south from Bulls to Wellington you cannot have failed to notice this loveable blue building which sits forlornly by the highway as you leave town. It has even starred in its own TV commercial, playing comic relief to the nation's other more famous rugby venues. Until recently its future was in serious doubt. Vandalised and dilapidated, the stand was saved only by an initiative from local residents and the council who felt it was part of their past well worth preserving, and possibly a hope for the future. I know how they feel. Certainly I've always passed it with a secret yearning that one day I would see the flags flying and the car park overflowing with vehicles, and hear a familiar roar from the rafters.

Much of that would of course depend on there being a set of rugby posts erected once again on the domain. A roller on the grass wouldn't go amiss either, and some of the gravel on this car park has more in common with boulders than pebbles. Trying to avoid the larger of these, I pull up beside the stand for my brief brush with Manawatu rugby history. The eight banks of seats inside might fit 30 to 40 people across, so you'd definitely get a decent crowd in here. You might want to bring your own cushion, mind. After 80 minutes these wooden benches would play havoc with your gluteus maximus, no matter how well padded.

Regretfully moving on, I pass Woodlands Lodge with its

sizeable garden statues – two giant moa, possibly to scale, and a kiwi that dwarfs both of them, so probably not then. I wonder if I've hit the outskirts of **Carnarvon** yet, claimed by locals to be one of the world's largest townships at some 100,000 acres. This is news to Kevin at the Waireka Honey Centre, however, and he should know.

'I'm the only thing in Carnarvon these days,' he says adamantly. 'Apart from the Scout hut.'

Kevin's been an apiarist here for about 11 years, collecting from his hives to produce a variety of honeys and many other delicious goodies besides. He sells a wide selection of meads, all brewed from his own stock, and even makes his own honey-flavoured ice cream from only natural ingredients.

'It's a big seller,' he comments, 'especially in this weather.'

As if to prove his point two ladies enter the shop.

'Ice cream o'clock,' says one, flushed and panting from the scorching conditions outside.

'And make it quick,' adds the other, good-naturedly.

Thinking it seldom advisable to come between a lady and her ice cream, I quickly buy a bottle of Gary's top mead and melt away.

The road continues flat and straight. To my left the Tararua Ranges nose into view as I reach **Oroua Downs**, famous for two reasons as far as I can tell: the Sheepskin Tannery, and the Manawatu Outdoor Leisure Club Incorporated, for which read nudist colony. Much as I'd like to get my kit off in today's heat, their literature makes me doubt they'd appreciate an impromptu visit from a guy intent on humorous anecdotes, so it's the tannery shop for me, I'm afraid.

'It's not really sheepskin weather,' I say to Andrew, the owner, having passed on buying woolly slippers given the temperature is in the high 20s.

'It's nice stuff, though,' I add as I leave. And it would be too, if I weren't allergic to it. Perhaps I should have gone *au naturel* after all.

By **Himatangi** I'm regretting that choice even more. The

car is baking, even with the windows wide open, so I decide on a stroll by the ocean to cool me down. I turn right by the Realistic Computers store (what would an unrealistic computer look like?) and cruise down to the Himatangi Beach settlement, a popular seasonal destination for over 500 years now. Whereas Maori used to camp here specifically to catch and eat fish and shellfish, part of the attraction these days seems to lie in less relaxing pursuits such as quad biking and blokarting, although there are also plenty of families here enjoying the archetypal Kiwi summer holiday.

Unfortunately I'm not here to sunbathe, nude or otherwise. No, my quarry today is a large buoy that floated across the Tasman Sea from Australia and has now been adopted by Himatangi Beach as its icon. It's been set in permanent place near the sea front by all accounts, yet typically I succeed in missing it completely on the way down to the beach and have to ask at the local dairy.

'It's right over there,' says my informant with a suitably incredulous look. Her husband also raises his eyebrows at my stupidity. As I'm inspecting the buoy outside, they walk past me and I hear the husband whisper something under his breath, presumably a joke at my expense.

'You're as funny as a fart, boy,' she tells him, laughing. So possibly not very funny at all, then, depending on the seriousness of the fart, I suppose.

The approach to **Foxton** marks the start of Horowhenua, the Nature Coast, as opposed to the Naturist Coast of Manawatu. By the time I reach the racecourse the traffic has built up and I find myself following a car with a yellow Labrador poking its head out of the back window, barking futilely at every vehicle that passes, taking an especial dislike to a builder's lorry.

I can see the famous Mushroom Tower in front of me as I drive up Foxton Beach Road, but today I'm looking for another tall structure, one more commonly seen on the windswept fields of Holland. A windmill, if you hadn't already guessed.

De Molens (literally 'the mill') was originally conceived in

1992 after an initial scheme to grow tulips here went belly-up. The planning and funding stage seems to have taken an age, however, as work on its construction didn't start until 2003 and the whole thing was finished a year later.

An impressive sight it is, too, and even more so as I walk up to the entrance and sense the power of the sails as they whoosh around above my head. The interior of the structure only serves to amplify this effect, which grows in intensity the higher up the windmill you go. First, though, I have to buy my ticket at the counter on the ground floor, a tasteful souvenir area with a definite hint of Holland, although I'm relieved to see they haven't gone full-on Dutch with pigtails, clogs and the like.

Up the steep steps I am lucky enough to bump into Jan. Who is Jan? Jan is the man who quite literally set all this in motion. He's Dutch, naturally, but came over here in 1952 and has stayed ever since. My opening question to him is simple. Why?

He laughs. 'Why not? It is a nice attraction for the town.'

'So you didn't grow up in a windmill, then?'

'No, I knew nothing about windmills until we started this project,' he says, 'but it doesn't take long to pick it up, as long as you have some expert guidance.'

Jan tells me many of the working parts of the mill such as the stones and gear system came from Holland, although the building itself is mostly Kiwi, including the wooden sails. I comment on the noise.

'Ah,' he says, dismissively, 'you should hear it when we really get going.'

'And what do you do on excessively windy days?' I ask, knowing only too well that this stretch of coastline can some-times make you check that your eyebrows are still attached.

'We just shut it down,' he replies. 'Follow me, I'll show you.'

He takes me outside to explain the stop mechanism and sail direction changer. Then we go back inside and up the stairs to the milling area on the third floor, where he explains the grain feeder, the rope and pulley system and the grooves required for maximum performance on the millstones.

'So how long do the stones last?' I ask.

'I've no idea,' he answers with refreshing honesty. 'We've only been open two years and I've never done this before. These ones will outlast me, though.'

Back downstairs, having thanked Jan for his personal guided tour and congratulated him on a fine windmill, I think it only right to buy some authentic de Molens flour, complete with free recipe.

'Jan told me this was the easiest one to follow,' I tell the lady behind the counter.

'Jan?' she says. 'You're not Dutch are you?'

'No. My English isn't good enough to be Dutch.'

'Sorry,' she says, 'it's just that you called him Jan and not John. Not many people do. We have some free Dutch recipe books here if you'd like one.'

When she says Dutch recipe books she means Dutch recipe books in Dutch. I politely decline and head back outside. I didn't notice it on the way in, but en route to the car I see the Flax Stripper Museum opposite the windmill. I bet those costumes must chafe.

A long, low bridge helps me across the Moutoa floodway, followed by a shorter one over the Manawatu River, and before long I am driving through **Poroutawhao**, erstwhile home pa site of Te Rangihaeata, nephew to the great Te Rauparaha. We'll be meeting both of these gentlemen later on, but for now let me just tell you that somewhere around here was where Te Rangihaeata spent his latter, calmer years during the 1850s, directing the construction of roads for the government. In fact he probably had a hand in the very one beneath my wheels.

Disappointingly there are no visible clues as to the location of his pa these days and my map isn't any help, either. So I continue on to **Levin**, the heart of Horowhenua, and source of another personal quandary.

For no specific reason, I've always quite liked Levin. Once you get past the tackier, prefabricated north end of town the main street (Oxford Street) transforms into a lively, bustling centre, a picturesque tree-lined thoroughfare with awnings over the shops on either side of the road in the archetypal Kiwi fashion. In fact whenever I try to picture a typical New Zealand main street it's Levin that comes to mind, and whenever I visit here it always seems to be sunny.

But I've no idea what the hell to do here. I've already asked two people I know who grew up here, Helen and Mike, for guidance on choosing my 'thing' for Levin and the results were very similar: a faint frown followed by a look of confusion and an assertive 'I really don't know'. To make matters worse the old grey matter isn't exactly working overtime today as it's still boiling hot in this car. The clock tower on the ANZ building in the town centre says it's 26 degrees out there, but that's from a bank so it's bound to be a stingy estimate. As I'm watching, the gauge pops up to 27 degrees quicker than a home loan rate change. Spooky.

So, anyway, Levin. I'm hoping someone at the Info Site may have an agenda for me, until I pull into the car park and realise it shut five minutes ago. Bugger. I am scanning the noticeboard outside the entrance in desperation when I hear a key in the door followed by a kindly voice.

'Are you hopelessly lost?' it says.

I duck inside gratefully to ask my new-found lady friend the sixty-four million dollar question: "If you had to choose one thing to do in Levin, what would it be?"

There's the usual frown followed by faint confusion. It only requires the 'I really don't know' and I'll have a hat trick.

'Hmmm,' she says, bucking the trend, 'I'd probably go for a walk.' And with that she hands me a leaflet on the Papaitonga Scenic Reserve and kindly but firmly ushers me out.

Three kilometres further down SH1 I turn right into Buller Road and soon find myself in the Reserve Walkway car park. Like the lady at the Info Site, a sign advises me not to leave any valuables in my car. I'm not entirely sure I've ever had any valuables in my car, so carefree I set out on what I am promised will be nothing more than a 10-minute walk to the lookout over the lake. Immediately I am plunged into the cool, shady canopy of bush, a welcome respite from the heat of the day. I can hear the lone cooing of a wood pigeon or kuku above me, and then much sooner than expected I arrive at the lookout, a tranquil vista over the lake and its protected wetlands.

It's not always been this peaceful around here. In 1822 Te Rauparaha and his Ngati Toa drove out the Muaupoko people who had settled here, having narrowly escaped death at their hands, an incident which claimed the lives of his son and daughter. All that seems an age away today. The small Motukiwi and Motungarara islands float dreamily in the calm waters of the lake as I stand and survey the serenity, breathing in the fresh, earthy smells of the forest.

Ohau, it appears, is shut. I receive no answer at either the candlemakers or the antique-cum-post shop, and I can't say I blame them. If they have any sense they'll be down at the beach, so I cross the Ohau river and move on to **Kuku**, a recently familiar name meaning wood pigeon, and proof positive were it needed that onomatopoeia is equally prevalent in Maori as it is in English.

By **Manakau** I'm in need of refreshment, which is handy as I'm due to call in at the Kirk Wood Café. What the name of the premises doesn't prepare you for is that it has a small steeple and some beautiful stained-glass windows. Until 1970 it was a Methodist church, only closing as a religious establishment due to falling numbers in the congregation. David and Diane bought the place, then pretty much an empty shell, in 1998, Diane with the idea of converting the church into a café and David using the residence at the back to continue his business of manufacturing fine furniture. No prizes for guessing where the tables and chairs in the café come from then, although David has other tricks up his sleeve, as I am about to discover.

'Pet coffins,' he says, proudly, grooming his moustache. 'Made to order. Any size from rats up to humans.'

I ask him if they're much in demand.

'Oh, yes,' he continues. 'We've even been on TV with them. They did a story on us.'

We're about to swap stories on our respective 15 minutes of TV celebrity when Diane approaches with what will turn out to be the best toasted sandwich I have ever tasted – perfectly melted cheese and tender ham off the bone. With prompting from Diane, David thinks it better to leave me to eat my sandwich in peace. Either that or now he's gauged my height he's off out the back to begin work on my very own wooden overcoat.

'So, coffins and cafés,' I say before they wander off to carry on with their work. 'It's a great set-up you have here.'

'Yep,' smiles David. 'And if times ever get hard Diane can always drum up a bit of business for me.'

We're going to die
We're going to die
We're going to live
We're going to live
This is the man, so hairy
Who fetched and made the sun shine.
Step upwards, another
Step upwards, another
The sun shines.

Somehow the words of the famous haka lose something in the translation, especially when compared to the rendition in Maori by an impassioned All Black team before a test match. Although traditionally haka has been the generic name for all Maori dance, for this particular version we have arguably the nation's greatest chief to thank: Te Rauparaha of the Ngati Toa. He is said to have created his new lyrics around 1810 after hiding from Ngati Te Hou warriors in a kumara pit, his inspiration stemming from the sunshine flooding in when it was opened up, thankfully for him, by a friendly local chief with hairy legs. And since hairiness represents strength, it's good news indeed for my mate Blair, among others, who looks like he has a busted carpet down his front every time he wears an open-collar shirt. Or even when he doesn't, for that matter.

I mention Te Rauparaha because I'm now approaching the Kapiti Coast, his old stamping ground, and if anyone was partial to the odd stamp here and there it was the great man himself. By modern standards it would be easy to describe him as a bit of a ruffian, since in his time he led war parties on the rampage through much of the North and South Islands. And yet it would be unfair to impose such contemporary values on someone who was a boy at the time of Cook's first visit to these shores. Despite his relatively minuscule stature (5'3" by all accounts) Te Rauparaha was a strong man, a powerful leader who commanded respect, a skilled orator and tactician. He obviously retained an air of nobility throughout his life, especially for missionary the Reverend Octavius Hadfield who, when the great warrior was 60 years old, described him as 'more like a chief than any man I had seen.'

Te Rauparaha's exploits have become almost legendary nationwide, but particularly in this part of the country. Kapiti Island, which became his main base, is a name synonymous with this fierce warrior chief. Wairau in the South Island, too. And yet it's in **Otaki** (or 'Sunny Otaki' as it appears to have been rebranded) that I find what is possibly his most lasting contribution to this area: Rangiatea, considered by many to be the most sacred Maori church in New Zealand.

'I seek no more honour on earth. I seek honour in heaven. Go and build us a church.'

Such were Te Rauparaha's reported words to the Ngati Raukawa, Ngati Toa and Te Ati Awa tribes on returning to his homeland from imprisonment in 1848. And build they did. Pillars were hewn from selected totara just up the road in Ohau, floated down the river to the sea, then across to Otaki Beach where they were dragged up through the surf and hauled two miles inland to the chosen site. Te Rauparaha himself oversaw the project, issuing instructions as he watched his wish come to life over three years, resulting in what has been called New Zealand's equivalent to St Paul's Cathedral.

Even more incredible is the revelation that this church has in fact been built twice, the original having been tragically gutted by fire in 1995. Not that you'd ever know. From the outside Rangiatea looks impressive, but it is inside that it really comes to life. Enter through its portals and immediately you're captivated by the three giant central pillars, and by the incredible brightness and vibrancy of the décor. All around me is the kowhaiwhai pattern of the hammerhead shark, symbol of power and prestige and a link to the fish of Christianity. The rafters, the crossbeams, even the kneelers continue the theme. The whole project heaps huge praise on André Baker and his team of hand-picked locals involved in the reconstruction, many of whom are descendants of the original builders.

Apparently in the restoration they tried to use as much of the previous building as possible. One of the huge pillars is original, the two others are new, although cut from 600-year-old trees. But what makes this story even more incredible is that no plans of the previous church existed, so the rebuild had to be gauged purely from photos. The height of the pews, the width of the floorboards, the size and depth of the lights – nobody had recorded these figures, and why would they? As a result the new church is six inches higher and two inches wider and longer than the previous one. I think we can forgive them that.

To the rear of the church, nestled at the foot of a shaded slope, stands a cluster of modest headstones. I can just about make out the name of Te Rauparaha on one of them, beside those of Tamihana his son, and Matene te Whiwhi. The grave itself is in a surprising state of disrepair for such a great man. I wonder whether this is because, as he said, he now seeks 'no more honour on earth', and thus his descendants have decided to allow time to take its course, or whether they know something that other people merely suspect. It is said that after

Te Rauparaha's funeral in 1849 his body was disinterred and taken at night by waka to be reburied on Kapiti Island. Somehow I don't think we'll ever know.

I cross what my son refers to as the Screaming Bridge on the way out of Otaki (the screeching of the tyres echoes eerily back at you from the raised parapets) and take a hard left up Otaki Gorge Road for another slice of local history at **Te Horo**.

Bill Jenkins, originally a whaler, was one of the first Pakeha to settle in this area around the 1830s, marrying Pae Roke of the Te Ati Awa tribe and thereafter farming the family land and running an accommodation house. In 1878 he further established his local legendary status by rescuing passengers from the stricken *City of Auckland* ship when it ran aground off Otaki Beach. Waste not, want not, he then stripped the timber from the wreck to build himself another abode, Jenkin's Cottage, which, if my research is worth the paper it's written on, should be just up here on the right.

I find the cottage easily, thanks to a brightly painted sign. It's a cute little dwelling, newly painted cream with a corrugated iron roof that's red all over except for one patch which has clear plastic corrugations, presumably to show the angular, tooth-like slates of the original roof. A well-worn plaque on the front door, hard to read in the bright sunlight, says: 'Built in 1879 by Mr Miller. Constructed in timber from the *City of Auckland*, October 1878. Cottage built for William Jenkins 1815-1902, the first white whaler to settle on Kapiti Island.' Well, fancy that. He must have made sure he was on the right side of Te Rauparaha, then.

The continuing existence of Jenkins' Cottage owes much, if not all, to Graham Atmore and his wife who have lovingly restored it to its full glory and even housed a small museum inside. You can also actually rent it out for the night. Were I further from home I would probably do just that, for no other reason than the novelty of spending a night in a shipwreck. I only live up the road, though, which reminds me I have a date with my family in **Waikanae**.

I steam past the two red sheds, remnants of the area's last surviving flax mill on the northern stretch of town, and then once inside the settlement duck down Te Moana and Ngarara Roads until I find the Nga Manu Nature Reserve where in the car park some little hands are busy waving to attract my attention.

'You're late, Daddy,' says George, my five-year-old. 'We don't want to miss the eel feeding.'

Well, quite.

Much as watching a seething, serpentine mass devour dead rats may appeal, we're also here today, aren't we George, because Nga Manu offers a rare opportunity to get up close and personal with the defining icon of this nation. So after the 2 pm daily spectacle of feeding time in the Eel Area, we wind our way back through some splendid native flora to the Kiwi House, where we are plunged into darkness. Now, I'm not expecting great things from kiwi spotting, given that they spend a lot of time in their burrows and are very timid creatures, easily spooked by loud noises or sudden movements, such as you'd expect from an over-excited young boy, for example.

As it turns out my prediction couldn't be further from the truth. One of the North Island brown kiwi is right up close to the window, scrabbling enthusiastically. Even George's nose pressed up to the glass does nothing to deter its purpose, and it walks nonchalantly past on its hunt for bugs. Boy, that must be some thick glass.

George is impressed by the kiwi's staying power nearly as much as I am, and it surpasses even the eels as number one topic of conversation on the journey home. That is until we drop in at the impressive Southward Car Museum, where his imagination is understandably captured by, among others, an original De Lorean, a Bond Bug and a real gangster's car from 1930s Chicago, complete with bullet holes in the windscreen.

'I'm going to drive a fast car when I grow up,' says George.

'Good for you, mate,' I reply, visions of boy racers flashing uneasily across my mind.

'Cars are awesome, aren't they, Daddy?' he adds, dreamy-eyed. If only, as I shall soon be lamenting not for the first time, small children were equally enthusiastic about walking.

The woman from the Department of Conservation steps up to the shoreline as our boat cruises into Rangatira Point.

'Welcome to Kapiti Island,' she says, in a manner of which even Ricardo Montalban would be proud, and beckons our little group of 15 or so to the meeting shelter for a briefing.

We're a motley bunch, mostly foreigners, kitted out with varying degrees of professionalism as far as tramping goes. Boots, trainers, shorts, waterproofs, and some of the more serious walkers among us have even brought their own hiking poles. However practical, it gives them the slightly ludicrous appearance of skiers who have lost their skis.

My choice of activity here in **Paraparaumu** is a straight-forward decision, wholeheartedly endorsed by my own fellow travellers today: George, because he gets to ride in a boat, and my mother, over here from the UK on her first trip to New Zealand, because, well, just because. It has, however, taken a degree of planning and several phone calls to DOC before we have been able to book our berths on one of the two dedicated charters to service the tourist trade at Kapiti Island.

Kapiti Island is a constant companion and inspiration to all who make this wonderful stretch of coastline their home. Its dense, rugged features are dark and brooding by day, yet dramatically well-defined in the evening light (and at dawn by all accounts, but I'm not really a morning person). Artists, sculptors, cheesemakers, councils – give anyone a chance and they'll do their utmost to incorporate the distinctive profile into their logos and their lives. I suppose there's just something deeply satisfying about the way Kapiti sits there, isolated and captivating, accessible yet just out of reach. The ideal quali-ties, in fact, for anyone considering it as a stronghold.

Te Rauparaha used it as a safe haven from which to initiate

his many empire-building raids. Whalers, too, saw its location as the perfect launch-pad for their bloody deeds; indeed two of their trypots used for boiling down blubber remain. These days, however, Kapiti Island has an altogether greener purpose. It is now a protected nature reserve for endangered and indigenous species, including the kakariki (red-crowned parakeet), the saddleback and the lesser-spotted kiwi, which very nearly became the never-spotted kiwi before being moved here. Even then it apparently took trappers an age to eradicate all potential predatory vermin on the island, such as rats and possums. Before this someone seems to have had it in for goats, too. As a sign says, 'Over 2000 goats were removed from the island. The last goat was shot in 1928.' Maybe they called Goatbusters.

It's funny, you wouldn't think clearing an area approximately 10 kilometres by 2 kilometres would cause so many problems, until you see the lay of the land here. Don't be fooled by Kapiti's smooth appearance from a distance; once you cut inland and uphill from the pleasant grassy strolls along the front you immediately hit rugged and exhausting native bush, with literally millions of hiding places for any creatures possessing a keen sense of survival. Our merry band of three (generations), Mum, George and myself, has wisely plumped for the 'less demanding' Wilkinson Track to the island's 521 metre summit, Tuteremoana, but it's not long before even this route begins to tax a certain member of the group.

'I'm tired,' says George. 'Can you carry me?'

Barely 20 minutes past the whare we decide to stop for a sandwich break and immediately a large kaka appears, Hitchcock-like, on the branches above our heads. You're not supposed to feed the birds here, not least because they might also take a chunk out of your finger, so we do our best to ignore its advances which inevitably means only one thing: carrying on up the track, carrying George. Ah, the joys of parenthood.

An hour and a half of gruelling ascent through increasingly damp undergrowth later, the weka, fantails, pigeons and even a very friendly little North Island tomtit are losing their appeal.

We stop for the umpteenth time, next to a picnic table, and a cheerful, booming female voice comes from behind us.

'Having fun?' it asks, issuing from an upright, elderly woman in khakis. 'Seen any birds? That's what it's all about.'

'Yes,' says George. 'And wasps.' Two have just divebombed us from the birdfeeder laden with fruit 10 metres away.

'Are we nearly at the top?' I pant hopefully.

'Oh, no,' she replies. 'You're about a third of the way there.'

George is walking again by now, but we all know we're not going to make it. The boat leaves at 3 pm and it's 12.30 pm now. With an air of resignation and not a little relief, we retrace our steps. By the time we reach the beach again our legs are jellified in places we never knew muscles existed, Mum looks whacked, and George has overcome his testiness by consuming everything left in the lunchbox. It's time for me to move on to another climb, alone this time and, thankfully, in the car.

Just before the petrol station at **Paekakariki** I turn left up the hill. The road twists and turns quite alarmingly as I climb up and up until gradually traffic jams fade into a distant memory and the view takes over. And what a view it is from the lookout here. To my right the Paraparaumu promontory points gently out to sea where Kapiti Island, until so recently unconquered, sits sedately amid the blue. To my left the northernmost fronds of the South Island reach out into the Cook Strait. And below, the constant stream of cars on the Centennial Highway pass through like so many links on a chainsaw. Alas, I must soon rejoin them. But not just yet. Let's stay here a while longer. A week or so would be good.

Back down to earth, I'm soon another link in that dreaded chainsaw, grinding my way on to **Pukerua Bay**, originally named after two hills although no-one these days is quite sure which. Whatever their location, they've probably made it into the movies in some shape or form. The great Peter Jackson grew up in Pukerua Bay, you see, and shot his very first movie on location here, mostly at weekends. He doesn't live here any more, of course, but I've heard that another of Pukerua's famous sons, author Alistair Campbell, still does. To confirm as much I drop into Archway Books, pick up a copy of *Tia*, and approach the lady behind the counter.

'Is he still … erm … here?' I ask, pointing at my book.

'Oh yes,' she says, 'he's still alive. Lives just up the road.'

I would ask where but I don't want to come across as a stalker, so it's back into the four-lane traffic and on to my next destination.

What do I know about **Plimmerton**? Not a lot. Just that the bay here is a firm favourite for family outings, that some of New Zealand's oldest-known relics from the time of the moa hunters have been recovered locally, and that Te Rauparaha once had a pa here. In fact it was at this pa in 1846 that Governor Grey arrested the great man, seizing him unawares from his whare while he was sleeping and, by all accounts, having him ignobly led out by the testicles just in case he decided to turn nasty. He was a charmer, that George Grey. Even more so when you consider Te Rauparaha was only released once the land sales in the Porirua area were done and dusted.

There's supposed to be a plaque here to mark the event, but can I find it? Fat chance, even with the help of a local information board. Luckily, an elderly couple soon put me right.

'If you go back down the way you've come you'll see a tiki by the side of the road,' the husband explains, 'next to a couple of new flats. The plaque's actually in their driveway,'

'But you can go in. There's a right of way,' adds his wife, helpfully.

I do so, waved in by one of the new flat dwellers to a small, unprepossessing patch of concrete where a cabbage tree used to grow. Here now is a simple Historic Places Trust plinth:

THIS RESERVE OVERLOOKS TAUPO PA
FROM WHICH TE RAUPARAHA WAS TAKEN BY
GOVERNMENT FORCES ON 23 JULY 1846.

No mention of his testicles, I note to my disappointment, and retreat to the car.

The new **Mana** transit lanes are in full swing as I head up the Esplanade towards Paremata, the fifth 'P' in a row if you'll pardon the omission of Mana, and to be honest I'm really not sure where Plimmerton ends and Mana begins. What I do know without doubt is what I intend to do next, and it's a good job I've brought my togs.

Anyone driving through **Paremata** during evening rush hour in the summertime cannot fail to have noticed a little buzz of activity on the new bridge before the roundabout. On any sunny day, you'll usually see a group of at least four or five teenagers laughing and egging each other on as they prepare to jump into the water below. It always looks like such fun that I thought I would give it a go. So, unsure as to whether I'm breaking the law, here I am.

I park around the back, ironically next to the New Zealand Institute of Sport, and walking to the bridge find a solitary teenager already standing at the usual position. He looks me up and down, then turns away.

'Have you jumped off here before?' I ask.

'Heaps,' he replies.

'What's the secret?'

'Nike.'

'I beg your pardon?'

'Just do it.'

Fair enough. These one-syllable conversations bore the hell out of me anyway, so I climb over the barrier and after a cursory check for boats, I jump. It's a bigger drop than I imagine. Jesus, colder than I thought, too. And wetter. I swim as fast as I can over towards the car park where luckily I've had the foresight to leave my towel tucked in behind a rear wheel. I dry off and wave goodbye to my bridge partner. He nods coolly.

Porirua has been officially classified as a city for over 40 years now. 'It's amazing,' so the advertising slogan goes. It certainly is. Porirua doesn't look much like a city to me, although to give it its due it does possess the North City Shopping Centre, a mall of which any decent-sized town in the area would be envious, not least for the size of its McDonald's – the smallest in New Zealand. I'm not here to supersize myself though, nor to shop. I'm getting ready to rumble.

At the age of 33 my friend Jason, a car dealer by trade, decided he wanted to try his hand (and possibly his fists, feet, knees and anything else legally charged to clobber people) at Thai kickboxing. Now, just three months later, he finds himself third on the bill at 'Rumble 6' in Porirua for his first-ever public fight. Why the hell he's putting himself through this I can't begin to imagine, but like a good few of his friends and workmates sitting here in the VIP area of the Kennel Club tonight, I'm keen to support his endeavours. And praying that he doesn't do himself a mischief.

While Jason no doubt paces and sweats in the dressing room, we at least have two fights and half an hour's booze time to help settle the nerves … or so we think. The first fight between Bayden Reid and BJ Bland is over in five seconds when the former falls before even throwing a punch. Bland indeed.

'Let's give them both a big round of applause,' shouts compère for the night Kevin Sinnott of TV3 Sports. The crowd jeers. It wants blood.

Next up is some poor guy who has his leg kicked repeatedly in the exact same spot for nearly three rounds, resulting in a great reddish-blue welt the size of a football on the outside of his thigh. Never mind wincing at the slightest contact, he can hardly walk by the end of it, and he's forced to retire.

So much for the warm-ups, then. This is the main event. I ask the hirsute Blair what he thinks Jason's chances are.

'How the hell should I know? I've never seen him box before either,' he says, and nips off nervously to the toilet.

It's a fair point. We none of us really know. Jason is quite tall and wiry. Nimble, I guess you'd call him. Even as a late starter he could be a natural. But what will his opponent be like?

'A muscly twenty-two-year-old kid from the Army, by all

accounts,' says the guy facing me at the table. 'Saw him on the way in.'

I was afraid he'd say that. Still, he could have got it wrong. It could be a case of mistaken identity. It could be that …

'Ladies and gentlemen,' booms Kevin, 'please welcome, in the blue corner, weighing in at seventy-two kilograms, Kane 'The Pain' Wilson!'

Music starts. Lights flash. The crowd cheers as a muscly, mohawked 22-year-old full of bravado struts his way to the ring, vaults over the ropes with all the confidence of a pro and bows to the judges. Bloody hell.

'And now,' booms Kevin, 'in the red corner, weighing in at seventy-three kilograms, make way for Jason 'White Thunder' Willis!'

The crowd goes wild, especially at our table, as Jase and his crew bob and weave their way to the ringside. Somehow it all seems surreal. I can't quite believe someone I know is about to risk life and limb in the name of the noble art, yet there he is. And before there's time to catch my breath, the bell sounds and they're off.

The first round is predictably on the side of youth. Kane comes out like a tiger, launching blow after blow in an attack that fortunately is more about energy than precision. On instructions from his corner, Jase weathers it well and not only manages to survive the barrage but also gets in a few telling shots of his own.

By the second round Kane appears to have blown himself out a bit. Despite giving Jase a bloody nose early on, his youthful enthusiasm is waning and Jase starts to pick him off with increasing ease. It's still a fairly even fight, mind, and by the third round both of them are giving it all they've got, almost out on their feet by the end from the constant battering they're giving each other. After a gruelling final two minutes, the bell goes and we await the result.

'By a unanimous points decision …' Kevin's voice silences the hum of the expectant crowd, 'in the red corner …' We don't need to hear any more. He's only gone and done it! His first fight at the age of 33 and he's pulled it off! What a bloody hero! Much drinking ensues as Jase trots off to the dressing room glowing with pride, and rightly so.

Our main event over, we can now sit back as neutrals and enjoy the rest of tonight's bill including lightweight, middleweight, heavyweight and, in a couple of cases, overweight. I quickly discover that shape and build are not necessarily an accurate guide to the outcome. Despite looking tougher, thickset, stocky guys do not always beat lanky beanpoles. I imagine this is even more the case in kickboxing as one decent whiplash kick at close range is always going to send a short guy bandy.

'Blair Sayer to the burger stand, please. Blair Sayer … oh, I see he's already been,' shouts Kevin, cruelly, over the mike.

The fights continue. A young slip of a girl performs admirably against a chunkier local favourite, losing narrowly. Two teenagers give it all they've got and get the crowd whooping with encouragement. A man built like a brick dunny lays his opponent out cold with one single, massive punch. By the time the top fight on the bill happens, Jase and erstwhile opponent Kane are out ringside swapping stories, which is good to see. Me, I'm simply in awe of anyone who's got the guts to step inside a ring.

Until very recently the last place you'd go for a beer was **Tawa**. Not that there's anything particularly wrong with the place; it's simply that up to the 1999 election it was legally, officially and categorically dry. What a terrible state of affairs.

To confirm this is no longer the case, I'm here today with my brother-in-law Paul in search of a pub, bar or anywhere we can happily relax with a tumbler of finest ale. Fortunately once we've turned off SH1 we don't have far to go. Down Boscobel Lane there's a sign for the Bucket Tree Restaurant, Brasserie & Bar, which sounds promising.

'What the hell is a bucket tree?' asks Paul as we swing into the car park, and his question is answered almost as soon as it's left his lips. In front of us stands a large tree, about 50 feet high, its copious branches lovingly pruned into the shape of an upside-down bucket.

'Ah,' he says. 'That'll be it, then.'

'It's actually five to seven trees all intertwined,' says Murray, the owner. 'Macrocarpa, and over a hundred and twenty years old. The guy who first cut it that way back in the eighteen eighties was a young Pom called Frederick Westbury. His grandson still comes in here occasionally. Lives in Upper Hutt now.'

I ask Murray if there are many other pubs in Tawa these days since the ban was lifted.

'Maybe two or three. Don't be calling this place a pub, mind,' he adds sternly. 'We're a restaurant, really, although some of the locals enjoy popping in early evening for a swift one. I'll just get my son to open up.'

He does so, and we enjoy a cool lager on a bench outside, the evening breeze nudging the fronds of the Bucket Tree which, we're told, is pruned at the council's expense once a year.

I've already quizzed a few friends who live in **Johnsonville**, or J-ville to the initiated, on what I should do here. For the most part the suggestions I've received have been polite, although bars and clubs would seem to be out of the picture considering my accompanying travellers for this stage of the journey. Not only my wife Claire, but two boys this time, five year-old George and Arthur (10 months), as well as my sister Val and brother-in-law Steve, over here on a breathtakingly active three-week jaunt around both islands. This should be right up their respective alleys, then.

Mount Kaukau is the most visible high point in the Wellington landscape, further accentuated by the TV transmitter mast sitting atop. The fantastic views from the summit can be accessed via a number of tracks within Wellington itself, and by parking up at the end of Truscott Avenue here in Johnsonville. My sources describe it as 'an easy climb, about 40 minutes to the average Joe'. They obviously never brought the average Arthur into the equation.

What starts off as a pleasant climb on a gentle gradient through the greenery at the base of the hill soon turns into a distinctly more testing exercise, especially with 11 kilos of Arthur strapped to my front. A quarter of an hour in and I'm lagging badly behind. Luckily, today I have Steve to come to the rescue and share the burden. We are all enjoying a healthy stroll on what is a beautiful day, all of us, that is, except George. By the time we reach the signpost indicating a further half hour to the top, he is having a Kapiti Island moment. The decision is made. He will turn back with his Mum, while Val, Steve, a contented Arthur and I carry on.

Mountain bikers and joggers pass us in both directions as we walk on, up hill and down dale towards the TV mast, now tantalisingly visible ahead of us. Occasionally we stop to admire glimpses of Wellington on our left, or the top of the South Island beyond the steep drop to our right. One final push and we make it to the mast itself. The purpose-built viewing podium offers spectacular views across the harbour, taking in the stadium and CBD below us, sweeping round to the airport and Seatoun, and right across to Eastbourne and the Hutt Valley. Breathtaking.

Our journey back down is smooth, punctuated once by a wrong turn and sporadically by Arthur's flatulence. He's done very well for a little 'un considering the windy conditions (not just his), but even he turns gripey in the final stages, and with the exception of Steve who looks like he could do this kind of thing all day, we're all relieved when his mum and a rejuvenated George appear on the horizon bearing yoghurt. It's been loin-girding stuff – just the preparation I need for the significant final destination in the North Island leg of my journey.

There's something intrinsically endearing about the small, understated green sign that greets you as you sweep around the corner at the bottom of the Ngauranga Gorge (mind that speed camera) towards the capital. '**Wellington**' it reads, plain and simple, and sure enough there it is, full of promise, laid out before me again. I rather enjoy that, which is lucky because it's a sign that I've clocked many, many times.

Working in Wellington on a daily basis I'm probably better informed about this windy city than any other place in New Zealand. I've wandered its lively central streets, sat quietly steaming outside its countless cafes, and been blown hither and thither by unerringly powerful gusts in the process. This being the case you'd think choosing an activity for what is ostensibly my adopted home town would be a relatively simple affair. Don't you believe it. They say a little knowledge is a dangerous thing, and on this occasion they are absolutely correct.

Most of the obvious touristy things have a big tick next to them already. Freezing my extremities at the Westpac Stadium, creaking uphill on the Kelburn Cable Car, making a beeline for the Beehive, touring Te Papa in search of, well, anything really. I've considered and subsequently rejected them all. I'm not going to get Konged at the Embassy Cinema either, or entrench myself in a 'Lord of the Rings' marathon until I have orcs bursting out of my ears. The truth is I'm just not a tourist here any more, so it seems only right to find something a little less fleeting, something that will really allow me to get under the skin of this bounteous city. Or possibly vice versa.

Having just dismissed hobbits as transient, I do now have to admit that the solution to my quest has materialised via a magazine article on Peter Jackson's Wellywood, and LOTR specifically. During the filming of the trilogy, it tells me, the nine actor members of the Fellowship decided they would like to mark their time together in a more permanent fashion. So, with the exception of John Rhys-Davies, who sent his stunt double instead, the start to a fictional joke was born when four hobbits, two men, a dwarf, an elf and a wizard walked into a tattoo parlour in the centre of Wellington. All nine then had the number '9' etched in Elvish onto various relevant parts of their body. I'm sure you can see where this is going.

The artist they chose was Roger, a renowned tattooist in Cuba Street, the Bohemian area of town. As it turns out he's a friendly, fatherly kind of guy with a greying beard, and recently I've been in discussion with him over the nature of my very own commemorative tattoo, a State Highway 1 shield.

'Sure this is what you want?' he asked at our first meeting.

'Yes, please.'

'Hmmm. Okay then. Should take about an hour.'

At the first scent of blood you can usually count on a camera crew to appear, so I have the *Close Up* team in tow for this one, too. Roger wasn't keen on them coming to begin with ('They always want to move stuff around, including me') but I talked him round by pleading it would be good publicity.

We turn up at the appointed time and Rawdon, the reporter, is the first to notice the sign: 'Roger's TatooArt', it reads.

'Are you sure you want to get a tattoo from a man who can't spell the word?' he asks.

'Shut up,' I tell him. 'I doubt he can go wrong with a "1".'

'Hmmm, yes, that was a friend of mine,' muses Roger on the subject of the sign, once we've passed the cordon of tattoo groupies (tatoupies?) gathered in his front office. 'He offered to do it and I didn't have the heart to change it afterwards.' That's typical of the man who still has a post-tattoo photograph of himself with Peter Jackson and the nine Fellowship cast members that he's never really shown to anyone, much less thought about selling.

'I suppose it might be worth something to someone,' he says, modestly. 'One day this guy walked in wearing rags and asked if it would be okay if nine people turned up for a tattoo on the Sunday. I asked him if he was one of the extras and he said no, he was a main character. Turns out I was speaking to Viggo Mortensen. Shall we get started, then?'

There was plenty of discussion as to which part of my body should receive the tattoo. The LOTR guys chose parts relevant to their roles in the film – a hobbit's foot, a sword arm. Certain of my unkinder friends suggested perhaps I should have mine on my backside, but I was thinking more my accelerator foot, until I found out the pain there would likely be worse. I'm not a brave man, so in the end I plumped for a nice fleshy left arm, my gear-changing arm.

I ask Roger whether he minds if we chat while he works. 'As long as you don't put me off my stroke,' he replies. I decide to remain quiet while he does the outline.

The needle gun starts, and I grimace as directed for the camera although the pain is minimal, like a series of wasp stings without the lasting ache.

'You're not going to faint, then?' Roger asks.

'No,' I say, 'I'm okay with needles. You must laugh at people who aren't.'

'Not at all,' he says. 'I'm okay with these needles. These ones are fine because they're only skin deep. Show me a hypodermic and I'm keeling over.'

Five minutes of surprisingly little pain later, Roger moves on to filling in the colour, this time with a seven-needle brush. His task is made marginally harder by the red of the shield merging with the crimson of my blood, which he wipes away occasionally with expert dexterity. The basic design completed, I now feel brave enough to quiz Roger further about his art. I can't help noticing that both of his arms are covered in various designs. Practice, he calls it.

'Do you let other people work on you then, or are you ambidextrous?'

'Nah,' replies Roger, 'I'm just good with my left hand.'

And then, almost before I know it, I'm all done. Roger fetches the mirror. An excellent job, and I thank him.

'Welcome to the club,' he says, and shakes my hand as I leave, delighted. Is it just me or do the *Close Up* crew appear a little disappointed?

Anyway, plaster firmly in place over my newly delicate area, I have just one more task to perform here. I return to the car and drive out through town to the official end of State Highway 1 on the North Island at Wellington Airport. Quite handy, you might think, for someone about to cross the Cook Strait. Me, I'm off to catch the ferry.

Picton See the hull of the *Edwin Fox*. *Mount Pleasant* Admire the view (if you can). *Koromiko* Visit Totara Grove Alpaca Farm. *Para* Spot the swamp. *Tuamarina* Visit the site of the Wairau Affray. *Spring Creek* Spot the creek. *Grovetown* Do anything you can. *Blenheim* Take your pick of wineries (and olive oil). *Riverlands* Enter Cobb Cottage. *Dashwood* Sample Dashwood wine at the Vavasour winery. *Seddon* Cross the famous Awatere Bridge. *Lake Grassmere* See the Solar Salt Works. *Taimate* See Lake Elterwater. *Ward* Visit the East Coast Inn. *Mirza* Spot the Flying Pig. *Wharanui* Visit St Oswald's Church. *Kekerengu* Stop off at The Store. *Clarence* Visit Clarence Woodcraft/ River Rafting. *Rakautara* See the seals at Ohau Point. *Mangamaunu* Go surfing. *Hapuku* Visit the deer farm. *Kaikoura* Go dolphin watching/swimming. *Kowhai* Visit the Maori Leap Cave. *Oaro* Take the Omihi Scenic Reserve walk. *Hundalee* Find Hundalee. *Ferniehurst* See New Zealand's longest railway cutting. *Hawkswood* Find the Staging Post. *Parnassus* See the old store. *Spotswood* See the farm buildings. *Cheviot* Play the twelfth hole. *Domett* Visit the Mainline Station Café. *Greta Valley* Call in at Junk & Funk. *Spye* Spot the farmhouse. *Omihi* Sample the excellent wines at Daniel Schuster. *Waipara* Take a trip on the Weka Pass railway, or sleep in a converted carriage. *Amberley* Call in at the Nor'Wester café. *Leithfield* Visit the Old Leithfield pub. *Saltwater Creek* Taste the salt water, possibly. *Waikuku* Take a walk on the beach. *Woodend* See St Barnabus Anglican Church. *Kaiapoi* Take a trip on the MV *Tuhoe* clipper. *Belfast* Cross the River Styx. *Christchurch* Visit the new Art Gallery. *Templeton* Eat cookies. *Weedons* Find the oldest cricket club in New Zealand. *Rolleston* Eat the food of the future. *Burnham* Spot the Military Camp. *Norwood* Don't lose your camera. *Selwyn* Visit the White House Café. *Dunsandel* Visit the Dunsandel Café. *Bankside* See the old railway sign. *Rakaia* Try to hold your breath across New Zealand's longest bridge. *Overdale* Don't start a fire. *Chertsey* Come for the NZ Woollymunchers, or see the school. *Dromore* Spot a Crozier's turkey … *Fairton* … before it goes to the Food Processing Unit. *Ashburton* Find Turton's plaque. *Tinwald* Locate the two royal oak trees. *Winslow* See the Winslow Feeds factory. *Windermere* See the old train station sign. *Hinds* Visit the 'Shake Hands' gallery. *Ealing* Find the space balls (go back to Ashburton). *Rangitata* Go whitewater rafting, or visit the Outside Inn. *Orari* Spot the Moo-seum. *Winchester* See the War Memorial. *Temuka* Buy some pottery. *Arowhenua* Visit the hotel. *Washdyke* See the Phar Lap raceway. *Timaru* Go on a sporting pilgrimage. *Normanby* Visit the Tuhawaiki monument. *Pareora* Find the L&P link. This may take some time. *St Andrews* See the Old

Grain Store. *Otaio* See the cemetery, testament to the town's grander past. *Makikihi* Visit Country Crafts. *Hook* Take a break at The Cup & Saucer. *Willowbridge* See the site of the first NZ Grand National. *Glenavy* Drop in at the Carriage Restaurant. *Hilderthorpe & Richmond* Stop at the 45° parallel. *Pukeuri* See the Freezer Works. *Oamaru* Visit the blue penguin colony. *Waitaki* Go fishin'. *Alma* Stop at the veg stall. *Totara* Visit the Totara Estate. *Maheno* Visit the Maheno Tavern. *Herbert* Spot a Herbert sheep. *Waianakarua* Drive over the oldest SH1 bridge. *Hampden* Stop at the Hampden Beach Reserve. *Kilgrove* Find the historic bridge. *Moeraki* Walk down to the famous Moeraki Boulders. *Katiki* Visit the lighthouse. *Shag Point* Spot at least two different species of shag. *Bushey* Spot the McKenzie monument on Puketapu hill. *Palmerston* Visit Appleby's Store. *Wairunga* Find Wairunga! *Jumai* Walk to the Matanaka settlement. *Waikouaiti* Check out the moa bones at the museum. *Merton* Visit Evansdale Cheese ...*Evansdale* ... which isn't here after all. *Waitati* Spot the blue duck mural. *Pigeon Flat* Spot a flat pigeon. *Dunedin* Walk/run up Baldwyn Street, then visit the Speight's Brewery. *Green Island* Find the island. *Fairfield* Climb Saddle Hill. *East Taieri* Visit the fish and chip shop. *Allanton* See the Honey Shoppe. *Otokia* Don't miss the first Henley turn. *Henley* See the last remaining part of the White Horse pub. *Titri* See the Motor Cross Track. *Waihola* Take in the beautiful lake views. *Waihola* Spot the old Ewing Phosphate Co. building. *Milburn* Go to the Whale Fossil Lookout. *Milton* Check out the Toko RFC stand. *Clarksville* Find out when the last train to Clarksville was. *Crichton* Find a Michael. *Lovells Flat* Visit Old Sod Cottage. *Stony Creek* Spot the chimneys of the old Benhar Pottery. *Balclutha* Revisit the three bridges. *Kaihiku* See the Kaihiku Hills. *Waiwera South* Don't look for hot pools. *Clinton* Drive on the Presidential Highway. *Wairuna* Spot Whiteside Road. *Waipahi* See the start of Southland. *Arthurton* Spot the railway. *Pukerau* See the Red Tussock Scientific Reserve. *Otikerama* Check out the soil. *McNab* Ditto. *Gore* Try a wee dram at the Hokonui Moonshine Museum. *Charlton* Spot the creek. *Mataura* Visit the Tuturau monument. *Brydone* See the freezing works. *Ota Creek* Spot a carrot. *Edendale* See the tulip fields. *Dacre* Spot Dacre Hall. *Woodlands* Visit the Woodlands Tavern. *Longbush* See another tulip field. *Kennington* Spot anything. *Invercargill* See a living fossil at the Southland Museum & Art Gallery. *Woodend* Spot a tree. *Awarua* See the wetlands. *Greenhills* Visit the restored church. *Greenpoint* Walk the track to the ship's graveyard and a glimpse ... *Ocean Beach* ... of the beach beyond. *Bluff* Go to Stirling Point.

Picton to Kaikoura.

Around 1994 some friends and I spent a holiday in France driving from place to place in a beat-up old Land Rover, pitching our tents in whatever town or resort took our fancy. The wine, the cheese, the topless beaches, the huge baguettes – it was a heady time for all of us. In fact all went swimmingly en vacances until, late one balmy French evening, we rolled up back at Le Havre for the Portsmouth ferry crossing. And there it was, in 10-inch high LED letters at the check-in:

> DELAYS EXPECTED ...
> ROUGH CROSSING ...
> WIND FORCE 5 to 6 ...
> WELCOME HOME, BOYS ...

Okay, so I might have made up that last line but if ever a sign struck terror into the very dew flaps of a young man, it was this one. Was this Blighty effecting her own nefarious revenge for our Continental infidelity, playing some dastardly trick to purge our systems of frivolity before returning to the motherland? Or was it just that it was choppy out there?

We sat there silently staring at the unchanging message on the board until a good three hours later when the ferry finally docked. Ghostly white, shellshocked faces were reflected in the orange streetlights as one by one the incoming cars drove down the ramp and back onto terra firma.

In the end, of course, our crossing was as calm as could be, but I've never forgotten the deathly pallor of those faces and the faint stench of vomit from that night. Nowadays I always check the countenances of the returning passengers whenever I set foot near a ferry. If they're not green it usually means you're okay. But if they are, or they're grimacing at you in a 'Ha ha, you'll soon be waving goodbye to your stomach lining' kind of way, you know you're in trouble.

Fortunately for me, this morning was a breeze in the pleasant sense of the phrase, and after an oddly misty crossing I now find myself out on deck and straining to focus on indistinct black shapes to starboard as we chug through the Marlborough Sounds. All the write-ups have told me what a beautiful panorama I will be treated to in the final two hours of the journey to the South Island: picturesque coves framed by majestic mountains and unsullied native bush extending towards their peaks. All I can see is fog. And a Spaniard smoking one of those pungent Ducados.

Picton is an outdoors town, or so the lady at the Info Site informs me, so it's a shame about the fog, now joined by a fine drizzle. I really want to start this leg with a bang, or at least a few phut phuts, so when I mention my desire to go jetskiing I'm a little crestfallen when she laughs in my face.

'Season hasn't started yet. Chap who does that is still off on his winter job. He'll be back in about a month, though. How long you here for?'

Somewhat deflated I cross the car park to the aquarium, where I'm greeted enthusiastically by the young Irishman behind the desk.

'Hello there. And where are you from?'

He sells me a ticket and I wander in to stare at some sedentary sea life. A notice warns me against dipping my hand in the shark pool. The octopus appears to have gone AWOL. One of the seahorses also seems distinctly unwell, unless he's practising his backstroke. There's no arguing with the impressive giant squid in a bottle though, until recently the closest we've ever been to seeing this kraken of the deep in all its glory. At five metres long, a tiddler in giant squid terms, this one would still have made a fairly decent calamari in its day.

There are plenty of other living marine fish on offer, including various types of ray and the magnificently named southern bastard cod ('Oi, did you just spill my krill?'), but I'm still more in the mood for skis than skates.

'No octopus at the moment, then?' I ask my Irish friend back out in reception.

'Sure there are two little ones in there. They're difficult to see.'

I bet he says that to all the tourists, along with the rest of his spiel. Just then two elderly persons trot in from out of the rain, energetically shaking their umbrellas.

'Hello there. And where are you from?' he singsongs in his melodic Irish brogue.

Told you.

In the greatest of Kiwi traditions you can't have fish without ships, so it seems perfect poetic justice that the Edwin Fox Museum should be found right next door to the aquarium.

Built near Calcutta in 1853, the *Edwin Fox* is officially the world's ninth oldest ship in existence today in its original state, preserved rather than restored. The origin of her name is unclear but we do know she was initially commissioned to carry cargo, and then chartered to the British Government as a troop transport in the Crimean War. In 1858 she was rewarded with an ignominious consignment of convicts destined for Fremantle in Western Australia, before returning to service as a cargo ship. Then she became an immigrant ship, and entered New Zealand waters, on one particular occasion with a Bob (well, Robert) Moore on board.

That's right. As I'm scanning down the passenger lists, noting a few convicts from my home county of Worcestershire, my name suddenly leaps out at me. Robert Moore. Well, shiver me timbers. And before you ask, no, he was not a convicted felon. He was in fact a fisherman from the Isle of Man emigrating to New Zealand, and by the sounds of it he had a rough time.

The *Edwin Fox* set sail from London on 28 January 1873 with our Robert Moore and around 190 other passengers on board, bound for these shores. Unusually (ahem) for Britain the weather was miserable and the ship had difficulty even getting out of the English Channel. Her progress may have been checked further by the fact that some of the crew had by now discovered a crate of alcohol in the cargo hold and were legless. Their timing couldn't have been worse. Entering the Bay of Biscay the ship immediately fell foul of violent storms, and with most of the crew incapacitated, many passengers were called upon to man the pumps. Being a nautical type I expect Robert was right in there … getting drunk with the other sailors. It wasn't a joke for many, though. As the vessel tossed about, the ship's doctor was impaled on a metal rod and died, along with another seaman who was trying to secure one of the lifeboats. A young girl was swept overboard, and then miraculously swept back on board and rescued.

The ship was towed by an American steamer into the French port of Brest to undergo a month of repairs, during which time 29 passengers decided to call it quits and return to Southampton. The remainder, undaunted or perhaps with little choice, continued their voyage. The rest of the journey was mostly uneventful – just an outbreak of scarlet fever which killed four, one man dead from consumption and a child from thrush – but as the ship approached Port Lyttelton bad weather hit again and she was forced to drop anchor outside the harbour for two whole weeks, waiting for the high seas to abate. And when the *Edwin Fox* finally docked on 27 June, 114 days out from Brest, she was placed in quarantine for 10 days because of the fever on board.

I will never again complain about 26 hours on a plane. Probably.

After several further world tours, the *Edwin Fox* was put to use as a stationary freeze ship, a landing stage and coal hulk, and then abandoned in Shakespeare Bay. Eventually, much battered and stripped down, she was moved to dry dock here in Picton. Just outside this back door in fact, so let's go and have a look at what's left of this gem of marine history.

The answer is a surprising amount, considering the ship's age and misuse over the years. Most of the hull and part of the top deck remain intact. This is largely due to the quality of the wood used in construction, and of course to the members of the Edwin Fox Society who have lovingly set about preserving rather than restoring the ship, the reason being that if too much were restored it would become a replica and lose its status of ninth oldest and, more importantly, any potential funding.

I must say I feel uncomfortable standing on this giant hulk. There's an eerie calm aboard her, an echo of horrors past which sends a shiver down the back of my neck. I'm not helped by the fact that I am the only person here, and as I descend past the 'tween deck where the convicts and passengers were berthed the hull seems to close in on me, as I'm sure it did them. I can hardly begin to imagine the sheer misery of spending over three months in such cramped, damp, disease-ridden surroundings, as so many did during her time. I'm glad to get out and back into the relative normality of the gift shop.

'Yes, it is creepy, isn't it?' says Andrea at the counter. 'A lot of people get spooked in there.'

I ask her whether anyone has ever reported seeing ghosts.

'No, but I wouldn't be surprised if they did. Restless spirits. It must have been hell on earth to travel like that.'

She then tells me a brief history of one of the convicts transported on board.

'He was sixteen years old, sentenced to fourteen years for sacrilege. His crime was urinating on a headstone. He served twelve years before being released, and drowned himself the very next day. Terrible.'

As I return to the car I can see the modern day ferry preparing to set sail again. No doubt on board chips are being fried, coffee machines warmed up and bars primed for action. We don't know how lucky we are.

It's great to be back on the road, even if the low cloud is obscuring my opportunities for soaking up some rather dramatic scenery as I start on the road south. I pass what must be one of the world's tinier cricket pitches in the square on the way out of Picton and then I'm into wild country, somehow rawer, fresher than anything I have encountered in the North Island. The road climbs to **Mount Pleasant** with its smattering of farm buildings before easing into **Koromiko** and another personal quandary.

The name Koromiko comes from *Hebe salicifolia*, a plant that grows here and which was used by Maori for a number of medicinal purposes, including a cure for stomach ache. It has been my intention merely to find one of these plants as my 'thing' and move on. The trouble is, I only have a black-and-white photo of it and I possess about as much botanical knowledge as Paris Hilton. I'm going to have to ask someone, and my eye is taken by a sign off to the right for Totara Grove Farm. Or rather, by the llama standing behind it.

I pull up in front of a small wooden building which professes to be a shop. All seems quiet as my shoes crunch up to the front porch.

'I'll just get the key!' shouts a voice somewhere behind me, and I see a checked shirt lope off towards the main house.

'How long have you had the llamas, then?' I ask Russell on his return.

'They're not llamas, they're alpacas,' he replies amiably, turning the lock and motioning me inside the shop. 'About 16 years now. We had some dropped off here by chance one year. They were due to be shipped out but the sea was too rough, and then my wife got attached to them, and, well …' Russell takes off his hat. 'Beautiful wool,' he adds. 'Much softer than mohair. You feel.'

The shop is decked out with a variety of beautifully knitted items, all manufactured on site by the fair hands of Marian, Russell's wife, and a team of local ladies she employs to help her. Russell concentrates more on the shearing side of things, and shows me the special shearing table he has invented, and now sells all over the world. He gives me a brief demonstration of how it works, using knowledge gained from years of practical experience, and just the kind of ingenuity you'd think would be praised and positively encouraged. Russell, however, has had run-ins with local authorities over his signs being a danger to traffic recently, despite every other club or retail outlet in Koromiko getting away without any hassle. It would be enough to rile a lesser man, but Russell is philosophical about the whole situation. Besides, he'd rather talk about alpacas.

'Do they ever spit at you?' I ask, wondering if the stories are true.

'Nah,' says Russell. 'They're very docile creatures unless they're provoked.' Like pushing them onto a shearing table, possibly, I suggest. He laughs. It may sound like the backing chorus from a Neil Sedaka song, but I don't think I'd really like to calm a llama down.

I buy a ball of alpaca wool and mention my previous intention with the koromiko plant.

'Right,' Russell says, enthusiastically. 'I'm sure there's one around here, actually. '

Beckoning me to follow on a tour of his garden, he zips from flowerbed to flowerbed without luck, and then all of a sudden he's off through the bush and into the totara grove after which the farm is named.

'Come on, there might be one through here.'

There isn't. Russell is crestfallen but it really doesn't matter to me. I wave goodbye and head for Picton airfield. By the time I reach the tiny runway amid the hills the sun is threatening to break through the clouds for the first time today. It looks like everything's brightening up. Now then, I wonder, what's next? Oh yes. A swamp. Is it me or did it just get darker again?

In colonial times **Para** was a large kahikatea and totara swamp prized by Maori for its abundant bird and fish life. The name comes from the word for kingfern which also thrived here and was considered a great delicacy to eat. Then most of the wood was felled and rafted down the river. Willow trees were planted to replace the native growth but have caused substantial damage to the habitat by choking waterways, and now there are plans to remove them and replant native forest.

Tuamarina is a corruption of Tuamarino or 'the calm beyond', so called because it marks the end of the swampy, hilly country at the north end of the South Island and the start of the more welcoming Wairau Plains. The area was anything but calm in 1843, however, as arguments over land here spilled over into the first conflict between Maori and Pakeha since the signing of the Treaty of Waitangi three years earlier.

The whole episode appears to be the perfect example of colonial English greed and bombast receiving justified, if brutal, come-uppance. A raucous group of settlers led by Captain Arthur Wakefield and a magistrate called Thompson, upset at the fact that they actually had to pay for land to own it, marched down here from Nelson to stake their claim and arrest the Maori obstructing their wishes. What they hadn't considered was that one of the Maori chiefs they were messing with was none other than Te Rauparaha who, as we already know, was not a man to be slighted and the other his nephew Te Rangihaeata, a much-feared warrior in his own right. 'I think we shall overcome these travelling bullies,' Wakefield is reported to have said. Boy, was he in for a shock.

The protagonists met right here in Tuamarina on 17 June 1843, Thompson and Wakefield with their band of around 50 armed settlers, the Maori and their group of 90 hardened warriors, along with numerous women and children. Thompson was allowed across the stream to talk, only to succeed in insulting Te Rauparaha by first refusing to shake hands and then brandishing a pair of handcuffs for the purpose of the chief's arrest. There followed what in sporting parlance today would be called a period of 'handbags' before someone on one side, it's not known which, suffered from itchy trigger finger. The consequences were disastrous. After a series of volleys from both sides the Maori were easily on top. The settlers started to flee but were soon surrounded and captured, including Thompson and Wakefield. Even then they may have been saved had not one of the Maori dead proved to be Rongo, Te Rauparaha's daughter and wife to Te Rangihaeata. Utu was swift and merciless. Thompson and Wakefield were struck down by the hand of the young nephew, it is said using Tuhiwai, Te Rauparaha's famous greenstone mere, which today sits in Te Papa Museum in Wellington. All in all, 22 Europeans died in the Wairau encounter, and it almost certainly would have been more had the Maori pursued those who retreated. The dead are buried in a mass grave on the hill overlooking the site.

Down here there is little to mark this gruesome affair save a small plaque which also suggests that the titoki tree I can see by the river is the one to which the Ngati Toa tied a waka so that Thompson could make his fateful crossing of the river. If only he had afforded them similar consideration he may well have lived to paddle it back. I'm also not entirely sure that this green, peaceful but otherwise nondescript spot should now be so lightheartedly referred to as the Wairau Affray Rest Area. What next? The Passchendaele Bloodbath Picnic Site?

A short drive on from Tuamarina and you really know you're out on the Wairau Plains. My next stop is **Spring Creek**, which sounds like the ideal destination for enthusiastic honeymooners but turns out to be home to little more than a lively backpackers, a particularly benign Jack Russell and a 4 Square, behind which lies the eponymous waterway. Having taken my life into my own hands by crossing the dangerous stretch of road here on foot, I ask the helpful chap in the shop what he knows about the creek.

'Oh, the spring's quite a way further up,' he says. 'When I was younger we used to feed the eels in the creek here by hand. They got to know you if you always went at the same time of day. It's still quite famous for trout fishing, though.'

He then tells me of a Danish tourist who came in here a few years ago clutching an angling book. Our friend here pointed him in the right direction for fishing spots upstream and he returned three hours later clutching a 9 lb trout. Not having a camera on him, my friend here took a photo of his prize for him and sent it on to Denmark. He's never heard back. There's Viking gratitude for you.

The rain is starting to fall heavily again as I approach **Grovetown**, which is a shame as I have earmarked a garden visit as a potential chance to chat with locals. Given the inclement weather however, it seems a much more attractive idea to stop for a pint at the Grovetown Country Hotel.

The bar is being renovated. 'Are you open?' I shout to a man in overalls, as he planes something or other on his workbench. He looks up, turns his head and repeats the question at someone else off stage left.

'No,' comes the distant reply.

Overalls looks back at me. 'No,' he shrugs.

Fair enough. I know when I'm not wanted.

The approach into **Blenheim** takes me past my first glimpse of the area's many vineyards, some kind of sculpted lake area and then a real buttock-clencher of a bridge – the lanes are fairly narrow and I just about manage to squeeze past a truck coming at speed in the opposite direction.

You wouldn't know it today as the rain is going horizontally, but the capital of Marlborough is also officially the sunshine capital of New Zealand with a long-term average of 2475 sunshine hours each year. That's nearly seven hours a day, followed by cool nights. It's for this very reason, and the rocky, alluvial soil of course, that Blenheim was perfectly poised to produce a wide selection of world-famous wines, particularly its definitive Sauvignons and Chardonnays. Even the briefest of tours around this area reveals some of the great names of modern winemaking – Montana, Villa Maria, Jackson Estate to name but three – yet oddly, and much as it bucks against my own philosophy, I'm not here to visit any of them. No.

Ask any Italian or Spaniard and they'll tell you that the exact same climate and soil conditions which help deliver such glorious wines are also ideal for producing outstanding olives. Olive oil is still strictly a boutique industry in Blenheim, yet the potential is undeniable. So I'm off to meet up with Paul and Jacqui, owners and proprietors of Antipode, at their property just a few kilometres west of town.

'Winemakers here see olive growers as something of a romantic myth, I'm afraid,' says Paul as he pours me a sample of his 2004 Extra Virgin oil. 'When we first bought the property here in nineteen ninety five it was a sheep and cattle farm. Since then the wine industry has spread out and beyond us.'

I ask him if there are many other olive stalwarts around.

'A few. We had a neighbour here who was also growing olives, but he sold up and they ripped up his trees.' Paul smiles and dips his bread. 'You could say we're an olive oasis.'

Paul and Jacqui's oil won a Gold Medal in their first-ever entry into an awards competition in 2004. It's purported to be a fresh, peppery and aromatic flavour in the true Tuscan tradition, so I've been looking forward to tasting it.

'What do you think?' asks Jacqui, but I think the fact that I'm already dipping my bread again is answer enough. It is superb.

'We cold press our olives within hours of harvesting. It helps keep our acidity low.'

The technicalities are a little beyond me, I admit, but I have done some layman's research into what makes a great olive oil. According to Italian folklore there are supposed to be five ingredients – sun, stone, drought, silence and solitude.

'Apart from the drone of the tractor, we must have it about right, then,' says Paul.

After dunking far more than is polite (hey, if they will keep pouring …) I bid farewell to Paul and Jacqui and head back into town past the Woodbourne Air Force base which reminds me of a story Paul has told me. Apparently, during the war and before he had so much as picked up a crampon, a young Edmund Hillary was stationed here. One day he looked out of his billet window and saw the white-capped peak of Mount Tapuaenuku in the distance. It so impressed him he decided to climb it there and then, and with no experience or equipment, eight hours later was struggling to the summit, nearly catching frostbite in the process. And that, as they say, was the start of all that.

There's no way I'm going to catch a glimpse of the mountain today, not in this weather, but I have just spotted a sign that's rather taken my fancy. Now, I've told myself that visiting a winery in Blenheim is just about as predictable as you can get, and there is no way I am going to succumb to their charms. But this place, which I wasn't even looking for (honest), just happens to produce probably my favourite wine of all time.

I first tasted a Cloudy Bay Chardonnay in the extremely exclusive I-Thai restaurant in London, part of the designer Hempel Hotel. The occasion was notable for two reasons: first, I'd never been to an extremely exclusive restaurant in London before, and second, I'd never drunk a bottle of £40 wine before. And certainly not two!

'Forty pounds!' exclaims Chris, while Rachel raises her eyebrows. They're two of Cloudy Bay's fantastic welcoming committee in the tasting room.

'We don't like it when people overcharge. It just gives us a bad name.'

Chris pours me a little of the 2005 Sauvignon, followed by its older cousin the 2002 Te Toko, matured in an oak barrel. I'm trying to remember my non-flavour adjectives to sound more knowledgeable but I'm not having much luck.

'Ooh, that is oaky,' I manage, unconvincingly. Chris smiles politely.

I'm nowhere near doing these amazing wines justice but I don't care right now because here comes the one I've been waiting for, the 2003 Chardonnay. The tasting notes refer to the various properties of the wine as 'the scent of pink grapefruit ... lemon blossom ... smoky, savoury aromatics ... chalky ... roasted cashews ... tightly structured and elegant.'

'Mmmm, buttery,' I say. Chris seems to approve. Thank God for that.

I buy two bottles for old times' sake and choose a postcard

depicting the team of girls, which Chris throws in for free.

It takes me a while to get out the other side of Blenheim as someone has kindly put a railway crossing on a roundabout in the middle of town, but I am soon back on SH1, passing a few motels before reaching **Riverlands** and its Cob Cottage. I'm not quite sure what to expect. The door of the cottage is wide open. I am about to knock and ask the occupier if it is okay if I take a photo when I see that the inside is set up in the form of a museum, and unmanned at that. The displays inside, complete with obligatory unlifelike dummies, reflect the early colonial life of the first settlers on the Wairau Plain. The whole building was originally saved from demolition and is now beautifully restored by the Marlborough Historical Society, and it's well worth a look if only to remind yourself of what a shock Maori culture must have been to the first Pakeha, and vice versa.

Down the road I'm disciplining myself to pass more top wineries – Montana, Matua, Villa Maria ... they all seem to be here, much closer to the geographical Cloudy Bay than its namesake. I can see the dark waters over there to my left as I drive south, and today it is sure living up to its name.

From here the road climbs through the hills, snaking around a now comparatively stark landscape of angular grass gorges. The lower gears come into play on the sharper bends. I cross the Seventeen Valley Stream, its name probably as good an indicator of the topography around here as anything I can add, before descending again into wine country, a vast plain surrounded by misty hills, and the vineyards of the Awatere Valley which can mean only one thing. Unfortunately it's now five o'clock, so the wineries will be shut.

I decide to stay the night in Blenheim.

'Aren't you going to join me?' I ask Anna.

'It's a bit early for me,' she says, and she has a point, but what else are you going to do in **Dashwood** at ten o'clock in the morning?

The Vavasour Winery is a quick turn left up Riverdale Road from SH1, past the fantastically named Ugbrooke Road and down a gravel track. I've had to cough loudly for anyone to know I am here – quite honestly who would be expecting visitors so early in the day – and now I'm about to practise my quaffing technique and exercise my limited wine vocabulary yet again. The Dashwood Chardonnay is wonderfully mellow. Anna seems more intent on having me sample the brand new 2005 Sauvignon though, with its trendily redesigned bottle aimed at the Auckland market.

'It's just been bottled so it's still quite lively,' she says, and she's not joking. A little too lively for this hour, she agrees, and brings me back down to earth with the much milder 2004. 'You see what a difference a year can make.' Nevertheless I buy a bottle of each (the 2005 will be perfect for spicing up a lazy lunchtime, I'm sure) and prepare to take my leave.

'Where are you off to next?' asks Anna.

'Seddon.'

'Be sure to go to the local store,' she says, mysteriously. 'You might just catch a glimpse of old New Zealand before it dies.'

If ever there were a case for a troll being found alive and well and living in New Zealand, he would surely be found underneath the Awatere Bridge just north of **Seddon**. When it was completed in 1902 it was an engineering marvel of its age, a unique double-decker system with trains crossing the river on the upper level and motor vehicles on the lower deck. Today it still serves both these forms of transport and retains all its charm and individuality, but unfortunately some of this is offset by the sheer ricketiness of the roadway. It's a haphazard, bumpy surface held together with asphalt and, yes, bare bolts and rivets, and as I cross I can actually see the wooden boards dancing under the weight of the tyres of the car in front. I find it hard to believe that not so very long ago there weren't even any traffic lights on this 325 metre-long, single-lane construction. And God only knows what it's like to be on the bridge when a train thunders over your head. I'm not hanging around to find out, that's for sure. A quick break to admire this incredible piece of heritage from the safety of the south bank and I'm off again, over Starborough Creek (Seddon was originally known as Starborough), and into the town centre.

Anna was right. I am just in time to see a dying piece of old New Zealand, but only just. Inside Seddon store half of the shopping area is cordoned off by huge tarpaulins hanging from the ceiling. Ownership changed hands only three days ago, yet most of the fixtures and fittings of the old-style Kiwi local store have already been ripped out. Only some of the sky-blue painted wooden shelving and backboards remain, along with the old window display area and hardware sign, but they too, are destined to be replaced by sleeker, brighter, franchised décor. It would be very easy to sentimentalise about a fading era of New Zealand history, but as Wendy behind the counter informs me, the simple fact is that the new shop will offer cheaper, more convenient goods for local people. And nostalgia, as well as not being what it used to be, won't pay for bread and smokes.

As it leads south through open countryside over Hog Swamp Bridge and out of the Awatere Valley, the road appears as though it is literally hewn from the landscape. I turn left up Kaparu Road to the Solar Salt Works at **Lake Grassmere**. Several huge white mounds are dotted around the complex and they become dazzlingly bright as the clouds clear briefly. The works here provide most of New Zealand's salt so it's no wonder the plant has its own rail link. It's also understandable that they don't exactly welcome visitors or encourage people to get too close to the massive evaporation ponds which stretch out across the natural lagoon. A sign states quite clearly 'No trespassers', so briefly skirting the west of the lake I continue on down to **Taimate**. 'Go All Blacks' is scrawled patriotically across a farm building but there are few other visible signs of life, and certainly no other cars before I reach Lake Elterwater, known to Maori as Lake Okainga ('place of plentiful food') for its supply of eels, freshwater mussels and birds. Unfortunately much of its flourishing wildlife has suffered in recent times as the lake dries up on a fairly regular basis, prompting some smart locals to rename it Lake Outtawater. From here it's a hop over the Flaxbourne River and Needles Creek into **Ward**.

At the heart of the Flaxbourne district, Ward had its beginnings in sheep farming. Indeed the station here was the first major sheep run in the South Island, established in 1847 by Charles Clifford and Frederick Weld with 3000 sheep imported from Sydney. By 1875 that figure had risen to over 60,000, but early in the 20th century the government bought much of the land and subdivided it, thus reducing flock sizes.

If Ward is the heart of the district, then the heart of Ward is either the pub or the church and I know which kind of heart I prefer. The needle doesn't exactly scratch off the record as I walk into the East Coast Inn – MTV is playing, so it can't – but there are certainly a few raised eyebrows as I stride up to the bar. Thankfully, they seem to be more curious than disapproving, and I'm soon talking to Nigel, a crayfisherman, and 'B' (who is talking to the barmaid and insists his name is just that), while Gordy looks on and listens in between throwing random darts at an equally random dartboard in the corner.

'Where you from, then?' asks Nigel.

'Originally? Worcestershire.'

Nigel's face lights up as he turns to the barmaid. 'Ah, you see. Here's a saucy feller for you.' He laughs like a drain, possibly too hard for the joke he's just cracked, until proceedings are halted by the Corrs appearing on screen. The lads seem to like the Corrs, for all sorts of testosterone-related reasons. They're fairly impressed by Sheryl Crow too, and she's up next.

'She's going out with that Lance Armstrong, the Tour de France guy, isn't she?' says 'B'.

'No wonder he finishes so quick,' Nigel replies.

Distraction over (Annie Lennox doesn't provoke quite the same reaction), I ask if anyone has any any travel tips for me. For example, what is their favourite place on the South Island, bearing in mind I have to stick to SH1. I receive a few suggestions in return from 'B' and Nigel: Kaikoura, the mountains, the West Coast ('Oh no, you can't go there, can you'). Then Gordy breaks his silence.

'Different eyes see different things,' he says sagely, before returning to his darts.

The guys try to get me to stop for something to eat, Nigel promoting some of the crayfish he has caught, but regretfully I must kick on through the rain.

As if to emphasise it's time for some food a hawk is eyeing up some lambs to my right as I go through **Mirza**, passing the Flying Pig Farm just before Mirza Creek. Nigel has told me there used to be a lot going on here in the old days, including a station and a flax mill. Apart from the farm there's no sign of life today, a state of affairs I'm beginning to become accustomed to in the South Island.

I drive between the peaks of Hungry Hill and Hollow Top and approach St Oswald's at **Wharanui**, and a more dramatic setting for a church you are unlikely to see.

Nestled underneath the hills of Ben More and Napoleon, St Oswald's Church was built in 1927 by Mr and Mrs Charles Murray in memory of their son, also called Charles. Constructed from local coloured stone it's a compact, honest-looking structure with a short castellated tower. It's also situated on a windswept stretch of coastline which looks almost tropical today, with a sea that changes colour from cobalt to aquamarine as it recedes to the drop off and the stormy grey, scudding clouds beyond. There's even a rainbow out there, arcing above the breakers as they smash into a rock shelf which juts out of the ocean. Such wild beauty forces me to stop, and I risk being run over just to fire off a couple of photos.

It's a little way on to **Kekerengu**, where the road heads out on to a promontory where I find The Store, recently judged best café in the Marlborough region. A plain, elegant white building, the outside looks welcoming enough. It takes me a while to locate the front door in the rain, however, so by the time I get inside I am dripping on the classic wooden floorboards. This doesn't seem to go down well with the lady behind the counter, whose expression has all the charm of a boxer dog chewing a wasp. Undaunted, I order a flat white and a pizza.

'You have to get the pizza yourself,' she barks, pointing at the self-serve hatches.

'Righto.'

I settle up and then settle down by the fire to wait for my order. It's a shame the weather is so lousy today as the back deck offers spectacular sea views. Still, I can at least eavesdrop on a particularly insightful conversation about whales at the next table.

'We looked around for ages,' says a gravelly male voice, 'the buggers never showed. Wrong time of year, the captain said. Better off with dolphins.'

My pizza arrives soon after the coffee. Both are excellent. By the time I'm finished my jeans have dried out too, which is a bonus. I give my thanks as I exit, to little response, and pass four elderly people on their way in. The contemporary feel of the café has already prompted confusion throughout the group, and I can see that 'We only came in for a cup of tea' expression forming on their faces as they approach the counter. It's not what they were expecting at all. In fact The Store is not what anyone without prior knowledge would expect out here all alone, but I can thoroughly recommend it, even more so with clement weather.

Clarence, I discover, has a gracefully curved bridge crossing its river. The water appears quite timid down below, although I know for a fact that further upstream it reaches white water grade five. What I didn't know is that by the time you cross the river you are pretty much on the south side of town, so I am forced to double back to find signs of life, or anyone who might consider taking me rafting.

I decide to try a woodworking place I saw signposted on the way in, so drop in and meet Nigel who up until now has been busy in his workshop. I ask him if he knows of anyone local who might do the honours on the white water front.

'Oh, yes,' he says. 'My brother-in-law Ben does all that.' Aha. A stroke of luck for a change. 'He's not here today though,' adds Nigel. 'Should be back tomorrow.'

Instead I chat with Nigel about his woodworking. The little shop he's opened on the side of his workshop carries all the standard gift fare such as bowls, place mats, picture frames. They're all beautifully crafted, but I can tell his real passion lies in the bespoke jobs he's often asked to undertake, and it's not long before he beckons me through to his lathe.

'Someone brought in this husk of gnarly wood the other day and asked me to do something with it. I'm trying to turn it into a bowl but I'm not sure it's going to work.'

He then points out another fantastic round of rimu that sits in the corner awaiting his attention.

'See that? That's going to be a table.'

Nigel's quite into wood, but he's sometimes disappointed in other people's conservatism when it comes to the things they ask for.

'People over forty want everything in rimu. It's only younger customers who'll try the more eco-friendly woods.'

I tell him about the kauri store I visited up in Northland.

'I'd love to get my hands on some of that,' he says.

It's time for Nigel's lunch break, or so he says, but I can see he's itching to have another go on that lathe. Sure enough, as I back out of the drive he's got his goggles on again and the wood chips are flying.

Past Waipapa Bay on the road south the scenery changes. All of a sudden the cliffs advance towards me and both road and rail hug the narrow shelf between solid rock and ocean. At one point the cliffs actually overhang the road and the stray stone remnants of previous minor landslides litter the asphalt beyond the white markings at the side of the highway. From time to time the train tracks disappear into tunnels on my right, as indeed I wish I could when I'm caught by possibly the slowest set of temporary traffic lights in the world. It takes an age to reach **Rakautara** where I have a chance to get up close

– but not too personal, thank you – with a colony of seals.

From the roadside car park at Ohau Point I descend the steps to see if any fur seals are going to play ball today. You can usually smell seals before you see them, so I'm not surprised when halfway down the path my nostrils are invaded by the pungent aroma of putrefied fish. From the viewing platform I count as many as 40 lounging around on the rocks below me. A few of the pups are playing in the surf, having mock fights, learning how to stink correctly, that kind of thing.

More seals line the shore as I scoot around Half Moon Bay to Rakautara proper, whereupon I pass the famous Nins Bin Crayfish stall, perfect if the stench of seals hasn't put you off seafood for life. More train tunnels precursor the tracks switching to the seaward side once again before I enter **Mangamaunu**, another popular surfing spot. To my surprise, a car with two boards on the roof rack has actually stopped here in this foul weather, two blokes surveying the not insubstantial waves and wondering whether to dip a toe in the water before potentially hanging ten. Blimey. You wouldn't get me to hang one today.

By **Hapuku** the rain is bucketing down again in the darkening late afternoon, and all the deer at the deer farm are lying down. I'm tempted to sound my horn in an effort to make them stand up, only I don't want to cause a stampede and upset the farmer before I book my tour. Except, of course, there are no tours today. This weather is ruining everything. I was hoping for a decent look at the Seaward Kaikoura Range on the way in, or even a UFO or two, but every potential view is shrouded in cloud. I think the sooner I get to Kaikoura the better.

Kaikoura to Christchurch.

It's fairly well known that the name **Kaikoura** means 'meal of crayfish', which in terms of global gastronomy puts it right up there with the towns of Lasagne in Umbria, Haggis in Aberdeenshire and Soggyfishandchips just north of Margate in Kent. Of course a decent supper is one thing – it's certainly a prized phenomenon in Margate – but it doesn't always make for great reading, which counts it out as my potential '1 Thing' here. Luckily, as far as other activities go in Kaikoura, I now find myself spoilt for choice, on land, sea and even in the air.

Now, about those UFOs. In 1978 stories were rife around here of strange lights in the sky accompanying various aircraft as they went about their business flying up and down the Kaikoura coast. The reports became so widespread that an Australian film crew was dispatched to New Zealand to shoot some background footage for a programme of interviews about the sightings. What they could scarcely have imagined was that they, too, would be caught up in one of the most astounding news stories of the decade.

Barely had they taken off, heading south from Wellington, when unexplained lights appeared in the sky around their Argosy aircraft, shifting about at great speeds and circling almost as if they were observing the plane. One of the lights tracked them almost to touchdown at Christchurch. As if this weren't enough of a scoop for the film crew, the return journey to Blenheim proved even more eventful. All those on board describe seeing 'a gigantic lighted orb' tracking off the wingtip of the Argosy for almost 15 minutes before shooting off north at terrific speed. Best of all, it was all caught on camera.

As a child at the time I can remember the grainy footage making the BBC News in the UK. I've watched it again since, and although the evidence isn't exactly cast-iron there can be little doubt that strange things were afoot that night. Five people on the flight deck of the Argosy supported the veracity of the Australian film and the objects were tracked on radar both from Wellington and on the plane. Yet a government inquiry dismissed all claims of the objects, concluding they must either have been fully lit squid boats or the planet Venus. The report failed to explain how and why squid boats should find themselves performing elaborately fast somersaults at an altitude of 5000 metres, or how Venus should be able to flip in and out of its usual orbit at will. Oh, and sporadically become larger than the moon.

I've got an explanation, though. Every aircrew that saw the mysterious lights in 1979 later agreed that whatever these 'craft' were, they behaved as if they were looking for something in a methodical and intelligent fashion. Now, I don't know if you've ever seen *Star Trek IV: The Voyage Home* but it seems perfectly logical to me that these objects were indeed UFOs piloted by extra-terrestrials searching for intelligent life forms on earth. Naturally they went for whales, which explains what they were doing in Kaikoura. It all makes sense, although if, as in the movie, they did succeed in speaking fluent humpback, I can only hope the whales didn't talk back.

Today of course, apart from spotting whales by plane (UFOs still refuse to conduct charter flights), Kaikoura is more renowned for its distinctly earth-based phenomena. Since the late 1980s eco-boom in watching marine life, tourism in the town has flourished. In addition to whale watching I could go albatross spotting, shark cage diving, or even seal kayaking, which I am relieved to hear does not involve hitting them over the head with a large canoe.

That said, with my patchy success rate in the South Island so far, I'm keen to find some activity where I'm near as dammit guaranteed to hit the jackpot. Also fresh in my mind is the conversation I overheard in Kekerengu about the unreliability of the whales at present. The girl at the Info Site agrees, and books me on the dolphin boat, watching only.

'Now, are you sure you don't want to go swimming with them, too?'

'No, thanks,' I say. 'Watching will be fine.'

'It's an awesome experience,' she adds.

'No, thanks.'

I suppose I could try to explain that I'm in the 'All Creatures Grunt and Smell' camp. Or that if the dolphins really wanted me turning up in their natural habitat, then I'm sure they'd ask. Happy as I am to watch them, I have no desire to bump into a dolphin down the pub.

'Well, you're booked in for eight thirty,' she says. 'And if you change your mind I'd let them know as early as you can. Swimming is very popular.'

Some days I feel I just don't get through to people. I'm sure she does, too.

Thus at 8.15 the next morning I find myself outside the Dolphin Encounter building, fully refreshed after a comfortable night at the exceptionally friendly White Morph Hotel nearby. Better still, gone is yesterday's gloom, replaced by beautiful blue skies and brilliant sunshine. I think there's time for a quick coffee before we push the boat out. Hell, let's push the boat out, a croissant too.

I sign in at the front desk and watch a string of people follow suit, some swimmers, some fellow watchers. Among the swimmers there's the American family – Mom, Dad and teenage daughter – the inevitable British backpacking couple who only ever really speak to each other, and a trio of Scandinavians, one of whom is constantly smiling and saying 'Wow' at any opportunity. My fellow watchers are an elderly couple and three Japanese teenagers.

Before long the swimmers are called out the back for wetsuit fitting, after which they squeak into the welcome room for a very brief briefing session and informational movie. The rules for swimmers seem simple. 1) The dolphins are wild so don't touch them. 2) Sing a lot through your snorkel and they might be interested in you. 3) Obey the hooter. For watchers they're even more basic. 1) Feel free to laugh at the swimmers singing. 2) If you feel sick, ask for a bucket.

A short bus ride later we're on the boat, chugging out of the harbour. The captain announces over the tannoy that he is rather excited as a pod of dusky dolphins has been spotted just over in Goose Bay this very morning. The other members of the crew introduce themselves: Sarah, giver of the pep talk earlier, and Leigh, whom I finally identify as my waitress at the restaurant from the night before, now cunningly disguised in shorts and a pair of shades. When I ask her where she finds the energy to do two three-hour dolphin trips a day and then work in the evenings, too, she tells me this is nothing. In summer she does three trips and starts at 5 am. I'm thinking maybe she enjoys it.

'Do dolphins and whales ever hang out together?' I ask in the vain hope of bagging a two-for-one bargain.

'No,' says Leigh. 'The whales are resident here, adolescent males having fun and building up their strength for migration in the years to come. The dolphins are transient. So, no.' She is spared further idiot questions by the roar of the engines.

It's not until then that I realise just what beauty the clouds were concealing yesterday. The view back to shore is breath-taking, the snow-bathed peaks of the Kaikoura mountains rising up out of nowhere just beyond the township. Just seeing them from out here is on its own worth the money, and I can tell some of my fellow watchers are feeling the same way. Not the swimmers, though. No. They're too busy nervously zipping each other up, disentangling flippers and spitting into their masks. Expectant and expectorating, with good reason.

Pretty soon the engines cut out and the hooter blasts for them to enter the water, close to a smattering of dorsal fins. Twenty seconds and a short burst of snorkel song later, the fins have disappeared and the hooter sounds again for the swimmers to get back in the boat. Round one to the dolphins.

'Wow,' says Scandinavian guy, followed by a word I imagine is the equivalent of 'awesome'.

The captain turns and we're off in hot pursuit, desperately trying to spot white plumes amid the cresting swell. And there they are, more dolphins this time, racing along beside the boat, some playfully crisscrossing the bow, one headbutting the water in what looks like an agitated fashion, and another performing a tail slap, which Leigh informs me is quite rare behaviour.

The hooter goes again and the swimmers are back in the water. By the look of it they're having more luck this time. Maybe their singing has improved, or maybe the Scandinavian guy has managed to translate 'wow' into Dolphinese. This time some of the dolphins stay for five minutes, circling their human counterparts as the latter dive down in ever more ridiculous and boisterous attempts to entertain their marine cousins. It's a bit like Seaworld in reverse.

One more hooter escapade and the dolphins appear to be losing interest, so the swimmers climb back on board and stick the warm hose down their wetsuits. Curiously, when the cookies and hot chocolate emerge most of them take it as a sign to begin vomiting into buckets. Sarah and Leigh are charged with the unenviable task of holding said receptacles for the afflicted. American Dad in particular comes over extremely ashen, although he seems more concerned at missing out on his photo opportunities. He's not helped, and neither am I, by the choppier waters further out to sea as we chase the dolphins. I don't know if you've ever tried to capture a dolphin on film with a shutter release of two seconds, but let me tell you you wouldn't want to try it without the aid of a digital camera.

'Okay, people, this pod is splitting up and heading for deeper water,' broadcasts the captain after a particularly steep wave has just sprayed all our lenses with salt water. I mention to Sarah that I can't help but feel we're partially responsible, but she assures me it's just what dolphins do sometimes, especially at this time of year. As we power back to shore she launches into what is essentially a Greenpeace rallying call to sign the petition back at HQ to help stop the slaughter of innocent dolphins in Japan, at which point my Asian friends assume a distinctly uncomfortable air.

'Wow,' says Scandinavian guy.

Before I get to **Kowhai**, but close enough for my purposes, I come across Caves Restaurant, quite logically the place to book a tour of the Maori Leap Cave. The tours are on the half hour, and sure enough, at 2.26 pm, up trundles Frank, a good old boy who hands me a hard hat. It turns out I'm the only one on the tour, so we chat about rugby and London as we head for the cave entrance, whereupon Frank assumes a more official tone.

'If I can just stop you there,' he says, not stopping me at all, 'I'd just like to point out that piece of corrugated iron up on the hill.' He motions to a patch of rusting metal at the base of the cliff. 'Make a note of that before we go in.' Frank then turns the power on, explaining that this area used to be a lime quarry until one day someone got over-eager with the dynamite. The resulting hole revealed the incredible sea-sculpted cave we're about to enter, which was great news for tourists but not so good for the fertiliser company, which had to relocate.

'I expect you're also wondering why it's called the Maori Leap Cave,' says Frank, 'if the Maori never knew it was here.' I wasn't, but I am now.

It turns out that when our old friend Te Rauparaha was down here doing a spot of marauding, one young local Maori warrior is said to have been pursued and left with little choice but to leap down the cliffside to save his skin. Miraculously he managed it relatively unscathed, enabling him to warn other tribes in the area of the impending danger.

'He did pretty well to survive that, don't you think?' asks Frank, urging me to look impressed and no doubt wishing I were more like that Scandinavian guy he showed around the other day. 'You need to mind your head,' he adds, disappearing into the cave mouth, and I realise he's back talking to me in the present day.

Once inside, Frank goes into full professional tour guide mode. I'm guessing, too, that he enjoys entertaining children more than adults on his tours.

'Do you see those rocks there?' he asks, shining his torch on our first small formation of perfectly aligned stalagmites. 'What do they remind you of?'

'Teeth?' I suggest tentatively.

'You've done this before, haven't you?' he says, and shuffles further up the path.

Where the cave rises into a natural entrance hall, Frank points up to the ceiling at the same patch of corrugated iron we saw before, only this time obviously from the inside.

'That hole,' he says, 'is where the dynamite went off to uncover this place. They left the hole open for a long time, but one day a cow fell through into here so they thought they'd better cover it over.'

'What about the cow?' I ask, fearing the worst.

'Oh, she was all right. A few bumps and bruises. Took them ages to coax her out the front door, mind.'

Stalagmites and stalactites may take millennia to form, but they're coming thick and fast now as we descend to the inner chamber of the cave, originally hollowed out by the sea. I've been trying to decide what colour best describes these incredible geological phenomena and so far I am plumping for earwax, a kind of yellowy orange. Frank also points out the black flint in the walls, the result of layers upon layers of fossilised marine life, and how the sediment has been twisted by earthquakes.

'Have you ever been down here in an earthquake?'

'No, thanks,' says Frank. He shines his torch at one shaped uncannily like the Empire State Building. 'If I say New York to you, can you tell me what that is?'

This proves to be the start in a succession of rock shape clues it is my duty to try to guess.

'We're not amused?'

'Queen Victoria.'

'Her son with a beard?'

'Edward the Seventh.'

'Copenhagen?'

'The Mermaid.'

I also decipher, with clues, the outlines of a bacon rasher, a submarine, a parrot and a whole menagerie of animals including a shark, a platypus, a group of seals (without the smell, thankfully) and, oddly, an adjustable spanner. Big tick, gold star for me.

'You see,' says Frank, obviously pleased. 'You're going like a one-track tram now.'

When we've reached as far as we can go, Frank introduces me to the fastest- and slowest-growing stalagmites in the cave, the former dripping regular as clockwork every five seconds, the latter not at all.

'Do you know, I've watched that one for hours and never seen it drip,' he says, incredulously, and then loses credibility by claiming another stalagmite resembles an upside-down St Paul's Cathedral. Even Frank can see how tenuous his link is on this one, and soon instigates our exit from the cave, but not before showing me a 10-million-year-old fossil of a sea urchin found down here recently.

'See you again,' he says, warmly, as we both squint against the invasive sunlight. 'Bring your kids next time.'

After Kaikoura golf course and airport I'm on past **Peketa** where people are surf-casting through the breakers on the beach. One guy looks like he's collecting paua just near Pinnacle Rock, and then I'm into the Parititahi and Raramai Tunnels in quick succession as they bore through solid rock to ensure the highway holds its southward course. Kie Kie Reserve is quickly followed by Paia Point (10 out of 10 for presentation) and then I'm into **Goose Bay** again, on land this time, before my last glimpse of the coast, for now, approaching **Oaro**, where I've decided to take the short Omihi Scenic Reserve walk. I pull over in the car park beside a lemon-yellow loo block. A man in a ute is just leaving, having planted some new saplings in the picnic area.

Once over the railway tracks, I put my head down and push on through the bush canopy. Actually, the gradient isn't too bad – not that I'd want it any steeper you understand – so although I'm soon huffing and puffing it doesn't take me long to reach the lookout, and boy, is it worth it! From up here I can see all the way from the Kaikoura peninsula in the north to Spy Glass Point away to the south. Fantastic. Now I think it's time for a celebratory cup of tea, which is handy as just further along the coast I find the Oceanview Tearooms.

Down by the settlement of Oaro the road cuts inland as it begins its dramatic climb south-westwards. To my right, bizarrely, as I cross the bridge sits a tennis court, tucked down seemingly in the middle of nowhere and ... whoops, I'd better watch the road. The turns are veritably alpine, so much so that I'm starting to feel queasy. Maybe it's a delayed reaction to the dolphin boat ride this morning. Who knows?

A road sign welcomes me to the Hurunui and before long I'm into serious yellow gorse country in an attempt to locate **Hundalee**, named after a place in Scotland. It's no good, though. The road is twisting so much that I'm not sure where the hell I am until I reach the turn-off to Conway Flat where a gorgeous mosaic of yellow covers the hill in front of me. Come to think of it, that's the Hundalee Railway Underpass crossing the road here. I wonder where the town went. **Ferniehurst** is also evasive. The only thing I do know is that somewhere around here, possibly down there to my right, is New Zealand's longest railway cutting at over a kilometre long. And, oh dear, I can't seem to find **Hawkswood** either, although I can see The Staging Post when I enter North Canterbury and turn up, ahem, Hawkswood Road. The Staging Post used to be an old sheep station, since converted into holiday accommodation and also marking the starting point of a three-day coastal walk. I don't think so somehow, not today.

The intriguingly named **Parnassus** is my next stop, so christened by Edward James Lee who owned the original sheep run here. A classical scholar, he believed the mountain away to my right resembled Mount Parnassus in Greece, and thus the town was born nearby. Prosperity soon followed as Parnassus became a bustling and lively town and the most northerly station on the main South Island railway system. As with many small towns from the pioneering era, bust soon followed boom and Parnassus fell into gentle decline. The 2001 Census states quite enthusiastically that exactly 900 people continue to live here. I'm not entirely sure how sweeping was their catchment area, but I'd be surprised if that were still the case, especially as a recent article in *New Zealand Geographic* magazine confirms 14 smiling little faces as the total number of pupils who attend the local school.

Certainly Parnassus seems a rather grand title today as I turn into the deserted main street and pull up opposite the old town railway sign beside the defunct local store. There being nowhere open I'm not sure what to do next, but I am saved by an elderly man in T-shirt and shorts, chewing earnestly on an orange. His name is John, and I ask him just what happened here, or didn't, over the last century.

'I don't know,' he replies, 'but I know a feller who does.' He looks furtively at his watch and pops the last piece of orange into his mouth. 'We might get a beer, too, if we're lucky.'

Twenty metres up the road we go through a gate, past two disinterested dogs and knock on Brian's door. We are beckoned into a chaotic, homely living room where Brian, his wife Jan and son Scott sit around a table. Sure enough, now the sun is definitely past the yard arm they are refreshing the parts other beers cannot reach with small green cans of Heineken.

'There's a chap here wants to ask you a few questions about the area,' says John. 'How much money has he got?' laughs Jan.

I assure her not much. 'I've got two children, you see,' I add.

'Oh, I don't want them,' says Jan.

I ask a few general questions about the history of Parnassus and the area where all three have spent the vast majority of their lives, but Brian doesn't have his hearing aid switched on and both John and Scott seem determined to remain silent. Fortunately Jan is very chatty, Brian, too, once he can hear me, and they both confirm that Parnassus used to be a big railway town. In fact, Jan seems quite put out that they didn't get a mention on the New Zealand train journeys programme recently, the one with 'that guy off the TV. Not Jeremy Wells, the other one.'

'We used to go on day trips to Christchurch from here when I was younger,' she says, smiling at the memory. 'It was a real adventure in those days, especially for a girl who grew up in Hundalee.'

Aha, so it definitely did exist, then. I tell Jan of my difficulties in locating her home town earlier today.

'I'm not surprised,' she says, wistfully. 'It's like Spotswood up the road. That place was a station stop, too. Used to have a real buzz about it. Now you'd hardly know it was there.'

We chat on for a while but sadly for me John's vague promise of a beer has not been forthcoming, although I notice that he is now sipping contentedly on a tinnie. I offer my thanks and leave them to it.

I can see the recent rains have swelled the fast-flowing Waiau river as I pass over the new SH1 bridge on the way into **Spotswood** which, as Jan confirmed not 10 minutes earlier, is now merely a small, sparse collection of houses. 'Blink and you'd miss it,' she said. I do, and I do.

Cheviot, on the other hand, is a veritable metropolis by comparison. It describes itself as 'a small, peaceful tourist stop between Christchurch and Kaikoura', but today the weather has brought people out in numbers, either to pootle around the smattering of gift shops or enjoy a coffee in the midday sun. I can't see any mad dogs around, but there's certainly one Englishman who's going to follow suit, with a pot of tea naturally, which I order at the counter, producing much hilarity from my young waitress in the process. At first I think she is laughing at having poured way too much milk in my little jug, but then I catch her eyes peering at my trouser area and I realise to my horror that I have a large hot chocolate stain down the front of my jeans from the dolphin boat trip in Kaikoura. Worse still, I have been walking around like this for the past day. No wonder I wasn't offered a beer in Parnassus.

I ask directions to the local golf course. Yes, it's twelfth hole time again, only on this occasion the twelfth hole is actually both the sixth and the eighteenth. Confused?

'G'day. How's it going?' Ian keeps the greens of the 12-hole course here, set picturesquely on the plain with the distant mountains forming a spectacular backdrop. He says he used to be a keen pig hunter before he got 'fed up with all the palaver', so he took up golf instead and now enjoys actually being able to advise people on how his course plays. The Golf Club is funded by the keeping of livestock on Club grounds, although Ian assures me the sheep are never used in place of his trusty lawnmower to keep the grass shorn. I ask him the burning question: why only 12 holes?

'We've got room for a full eighteen-hole golf course and maybe one day we'll do that, but the decision was made to start with twelve and see how things mapped out. It's worked out pretty well so far,' he adds. 'This place would cost about thirty grand to build from scratch these days.'

As well as professing a deep-seated hatred of poplar trees, ('the big leaves are bastards to clear'), Ian tells me the course was designed by a man called Rob Stanley who also has one of the 12 holes named after him. I explain I'm only here to play one hole, and wonder whether *Stanley's* is the one.

'Nah. If it's the twelfth you're after it could be, depending on which course you're playing, but *Stanley's* is right over there. If I were you I'd play *Nonoti*, which leads back up to the clubhouse.'

'Ah, the clubhouse,' I say. 'I've never had a drink at the 13th hole before.'

'You won't today, either," says Ian. 'It's shut.'

He suggests I take a practice up the par four seventh (or first and thirteenth, depending on which version of the course you're playing) named *Manakau*. I reluctantly agree, and with him watching I soon live to regret it. Although he gives my initial drive the thumbs up as it misses the two psychological barrier trees at the front of the fairway, I then take a further four shots to reach the green, whereupon I also manage to three putt for a quadruple bogey eight. Par fours can seem a bloody long way when you're not connecting well, par fives even more so, thus I'm not exactly relishing the prospect of my return to the clubhouse on *Nonoti*, hole 12, especially in this heat. Nevertheless, with a good deal of perspiration and a lack of confidence oozing from every pore, I swing hard with the driver and this time make a good connection. However, the natural hook on my first and second shots somehow manages to bring a pair of silver birch trees into play, and my third shot, an attempt to scoot through underneath them, winds up smacking one firmly on the trunk before shooting off at an angle, fortunately back on to the fairway. One scuffed pitch later and I am almost into Texas wedge country. Almost. Instead I opt for the chip which gets me surprisingly close, and then I three putt again for a double bogey seven. Not bad, but not great, either.

To rejoin SH1 I return to Cheviot and I'm just on my way out of town when a yellow sign by the side of the road tells me I am on the verge of crossing the 'Jedi River'. How fantastic. I wonder which bank is the dark side. To my great disappointment, however, closer inspection of the sign on the south bank reveals that the 'I' has been brilliantly added by some wag, and I have in fact just walked across the Jed River. I can't help feeling a little cheated. Still, that's exactly how these things start. I know there are historical implications to consider, but I'm convinced that an official name change would help to make Cheviot a place of pilgrimage for Star Wars fans the world over. So, come on, local council, why not harness the full power of the force and change the name permanently? Search your feelings, you know this to be true.

Sweltering it is on the dark side of the river, and thirsty am I after all that crisscrossing of fairways, so I am thankful to drop in for some refreshment at **Domett** and the Mainline Station Café. The Mainline Station Café, if you're wondering, is so called because the building, constructed in 1907, used to be the old station house here. When the railways died out the station also fell into disrepair and was used as a farm storage shed. Then it was shifted across to sit beside SH1 and converted into a café. The original kauri floorboards and rimu linings have been lovingly restored to give a hungry and thirsty traveller like me a wonderfully relaxing break. I'm obviously not alone in my opinion either, as a proud Greg is keen to explain.

'It gets very busy here in winter,' he says, 'we usually have four people on in the kitchen then.'

He directs me to a green folder which maps out the full history of the move and restoration in photographs. It's fascinating viewing, even showing pictures of the wildlife nests that had to be removed during the whole painstaking process.

It is a charming spot to take a break from my journey south, a beautiful building where the food is vastly superior to anything I've ever previously eaten in a railway station, and where the only whistle and steam sounds you hear are when the clock inside chimes the hour.

It's quite a drive to my next destination, about a par 2076 by my golfing handicap, but as I pass Greta Paddock and cross the Greta River I know I can't be far from **Greta Valley**, where I drop in at a Shell station with quaint old-style pumps, the ones which only deal with a single type of fuel each. Murray, the affable chap who pumps my petrol, tells me he used to own this entire town. If that sounds impressive, I should also inform you that at the time this entire town amounted to two houses.

'We're officially one of New Zealand's newest towns,' chirps Murray, gleefully screwing my petrol cap back on.

'Only got recognised in nineteen seventy-nine. Junk & Funk across the road used to be the petrol station, but then we moved over here. You should have a look at their shop. Loads of interesting old stuff, if you like that kind of thing.'

I would, but unfortunately Junk & Funk appears closed for the day, although a quick glance through the window confirms a superb collection of signs, old pottery and other general bric-a-brac large and small, including an ancient car sitting outside in great need of restoration.

With the mountains still brooding in the distance, I then pass through **Spye**, a place Greg at Domett had never heard of, and I'm not surprised as nowadays it seems to consist purely of a single farmhouse. I'm entering the Waipara Valley, the southern part of the Hurunui district, and an area becoming renowned for its glorious wine. As I reach **Omihi**, then, it seems only right to call in at the brand-spanking-new winery of the man who was the first to see the potential in the limestone-rich slopes of this region.

Daniel Schuster trained in Europe as a winemaker and viticulturist. With over 30 years of international winemaking experience, he has worked in many of the world's finest wine regions including Burgundy, Bordeaux and the Napa Valley in California. He is also the author of several industry-renowned text books on the subject of wine and grape growing, and a leading consultant to some of the top estates around the world. So what, I ask myself, is he doing in North Canterbury? There is only one way to find out.

The approach to the Daniel Schuster heartland is fairly unassuming. A modest sign points the way between the vineyards to the winery itself. I am immediately greeted by a rather intense young man who introduces himself as Nicholas and beckons me into the tasting room. Three refined, middle-aged people are performing their very own tasting session just outside the main door.

Inside, Nicholas launches into his spiel about the district and its soil before reaching for the Petrie Vineyard Selection Chardonnay. It's a case of so far, so good on the wine adjective front, and my trusty 'buttery' seems not to offend his sensibilities. But when we launch into a selection of the Schuster speciality, the Pinot Noir, I'm totally out of my depth.

'How do you find that?' asks Nicholas of the Twin Vineyards Pinot Noir.

'Mmmm. Quite dark,' I say unconvincingly.

Nicholas raises his right eyebrow just a shade and pours us each a small amount of the Waipara Pinot Noir.

It's rich and deep. I want to say oaky, too, and indeed I wish I had. Instead I ask Nicholas how he would describe it.

'Velvety,' he replies expertly. 'This one is fermented in open wooden vats and matured in French oak barriques.'

'Yes, I thought maybe oak,' I say forlornly, and I can tell Nicholas doesn't believe a word.

He has saved the best for last.

'The Omihi Hills Vineyard Selection, two thousand and four vintage,' he says with a flourish, and rightly so. Produced from only the finest Pinot Noir grapes in the surrounding vineyards, this is a fantastic wine which thankfully spares me the need to grope unceremoniously for any further adjectives.

'Wow,' I say, Scandinavian-like. The adjective works. Nicholas immediately insists that I meet Daniel Schuster himself who, it happens, was one of the three tasters standing outside as I came in, the other two being members of the Hull family, who established their vineyard here under the masthead of Daniel Schuster Wines in 1998.

After a brief and bizarre chat about soccer of all subjects (Daniel is Czech by birth), the meister whisks lady Hull away to inspect some vines, leaving me to chat with the amiable male Hull.

'So why of all places did Daniel decide to come here?' I ask, hoping not to offend.

He considers a while, then turns to me with great austerity. 'Have you ever heard the term 'Goldilocksian'?'

I reply that I have, pertaining to conditions being 'just right' for life on earth to flourish. Not too hot, not too cold. But never in reference to wine.

'Well,' he explains, 'this region is Goldilocksian for the Pinot Noir grape, second only in soil suitability to the Burgundy area of France. And that man,' he adds, pointing down to where Daniel is busy amusing his female companion, 'that man is a genius. A maestro. Since he set up here in 1985, the whole district has taken off.'

He's absolutely right. There are now a dozen or so wineries in the Waipara area, their reputation growing year after year, and I pass a great many of them en route to my next stop.

In the late nineteenth century the town of **Waipara** was home to the formerly inglorious Glenmark sheep station, owned and run by another namesake, one George Henry Moore, a Manxman by birth. Although extremely rich (his station at one time boasted more than 90,000 animals), Moore was known for allowing his sheep to suffer from scab and was thus christened 'Scabby Moore', a fact which I'm sure will please my son George greatly.

The only station around here these days is one of the two termini for the Weka Pass Railway, a historic rural railway, run by volunteers, which journeys through 12.8 kilometres of incredible natural beauty up to the nearby town of Waikari. Restored gradually since the 1980s, during summer months the fabulous old A428 steam locomotive performs two return trips every Sunday and public holiday, and at this time of year departs usually every other Sunday of the month. It should therefore come as no surprise to you that I have turned up here on a Wednesday afternoon when the station is deserted.

I take a quick peek around the station and the carriages which sit motionless on the tracks. Apparently some similar to these have been fitted out as accommodation a little further up the road at Waipara Sleepers, but unfortunately I must hit Christchurch by tonight.

In the absence of any real story here owing to my usual ineptitude, I shoot a few hundred metres up the road to the Waipara Gardens General Store to ask about the possibility of finding moa bones in the area. It was on George 'Scabby'

Moore's land that a grave of literally thousands of moa bones was found beside the 'muddy waters' (wai para) of the river beside an old wooden bridge. It's news to Sarah, though, who not only runs the store and post shop but also grows and sells GE and spray-free vegetables. I can tell she wants to help me, but she is nonplussed by the whole moa thing, and thankful when Darryl, a local sheep farmer, arrives to shed some light on the subject. He also demolishes a Magnum ice cream in under a minute, and asks cheekily for it to be put on his account.

'Yeah, my brother found some moa bones just up by the river,' he says. 'Took the kids out for a walk and came back half an hour later carrying quite a few.' He's a little more modest about his own subsequent efforts, however.

'I've tried for hours and found bugger all. I guess you have to know where you're looking,' he adds, which kind of puts the kybosh on any potential efforts from this quarter. I have enough trouble finding my shoes in the morning.

Past Wattie's Road and I'm just a short squirt from **Amberley**, where I am looking forward to a sit-down and a nice cup of tea at the much-vaunted Nor'Wester Café, situated in a 1928 bungalow. When I arrive at the heart of this busy township I discover, inevitably, that the café is shut for refurbishment. But when I enter **Leithfield** I get to visit a subject very close to my heart.

The Old Leithfield is a beautiful old English-style pub just off the main highway down Mill Road. It's busy this evening, both in the bar and in the charming little garden area, possibly because tonight is $5 pizza night, a great idea if ever I heard one. Old bar flies and young families alike are mixing happily in the friendly atmosphere, and as I order at the bar it's easy to imagine myself back in the Cotswolds of England. There's even a dodgy old carpet and a pool table. I am in my element. I gratefully accept my drink from the patriarchal landlord and shuffle on through to unwind at one of the garden tables. Outside some kids are playing tag while old fellers in checked shirts argue about fishing techniques. I could gladly stay all night and maybe scoff a pizza or two, were it not for the fact I must sample a rather different kind of drink before nightfall.

No prizes for guessing the origins of the name **Saltwater Creek**. Originally called Northport, also for obvious reasons, the port was officially opened in 1859 and had a chequered career. A disastrous flood in 1868 was followed in 1874 by the government deciding to build the railway a few kilometers to the west of the port through what is now known as Sefton. This pretty much spelt the end for Saltwater Creek as a going concern, and the town has been in decline ever since. In fact today, as far as I can make out, the main feature is the bridge over the creek, and a car park where several free-campers have decided to pull over for the night. God alone knows why. There must be better spots. Maybe they've heard that I'm laying on entertainment, although somehow I doubt it.

My task here, as you may have guessed, is simply to taste the water from the creek for saltiness, which I do at great risk, and to the bemusement of those watching. And yes, I can confirm it is indeed salty. So there you have it. Job done.

I'm soon over the considerably more impressive Ashley River and into **Waikuku**, where a left turn takes me down towards a dramatic stretch of coastline. A few other solitary walkers dot the beach, gazing in awe at the great headlands of Christchurch looming to the south in the half-light of dusk.

At **Woodend** I visit the St Barnabus Anglican Church, an unassuming white building dating back to 1932, now with an obtrusive modern add-on. Closer inspection reveals that a statue of St Barnabus himself sits over the main entrance, but as the door is locked I go round the back to ask a guy on a mower if he can fill in the gaps in my knowledge.

'Nah. Not really,' he states apologetically. 'All I know is that the grass here grows at a hell of a rate.'

Instead I head on out past Stalker Park, which sounds to me like a particularly dangerous place to go jogging, and on to the historic town of **Kaiapoi**.

Only about 50 Maori were living in the Kaiapoi area when

the first Europeans arrived, having been scattered by the marauding raids of Te Rauparaha. With the aid of the river and its famous woollen mills, however, the town soon flourished and believe it or not, the population of Kaiapoi once exceeded that of Christchurch. For a while in the mid-nineteenth century it was even expected to become the main centre of population in the central South Island, but that was before the railway bypassed the town. And that, as they say, was that. Its growth stunted, Kaiapoi nevertheless prospered in a more settled manner and milling continued until 1978. Nowadays, though, up to 60 per cent of the town's residents commute into Christchurch every day, effectively making Kaiapoi a suburb of its more illustrious neighbour, and happy to remain 'just country enough not to be city'. It seems to work well.

Today the river remains the focal point of the town, and it is vital for tourism. Willow trees line its picturesque banks, and a number of historic walks have been set up. But Kaiapoi's crowning glory is surely the MV *Tuhoe*, a twin-masted, steam-powered schooner built in 1919 and now lovingly restored for public cruises. Of course I have arrived far too late in the day even to climb aboard, let alone take a trip down the river. No, tonight I must content myself with a contemplative viewing of this glorious old ship from the shore.

It really is getting dark now, and it's time to ring my mate Stephen in Sumner to check if I can stay the night.

'Of course,' he says at the other end of the line. 'Do you fancy going to the pub, too?' Never mind Daniel Schuster, this man is a true genius. He's just read my mind. Before I can oblige I just have one hellish mission left to perform: crossing the River Styx in **Belfast**. Daunting though it may sound, it turns out to be a fairly simple task: I simply drive along in my car without the need for Charon the ferryman to help transport my soul to the kingdom of Hades, at least not just yet. Now how the hell do I get to Sumner?

Christchurch to Timaru.

So far on my journey I've come to the unerring conclusion that it's much easier to set out keenly in the morning when you've been woken by the sun streaming in through your bedroom window. Back in Kaitaia I thought nothing of rising at 7 am for a leisurely breakfast followed by some cursory planning and being out on the road by 8.30 am. Here in **Christchurch**, and especially after last night at Wakefield's Bar, I've noticed that the temperature has dropped markedly even since Kaikoura. As a result my best-laid plans have slipped by at least an hour. I don't suppose copious amounts of Monteith's Pilsner and chatting with Tim, the landlord, into the wee small hours has helped either, but the fact remains that it's cold here. The spring wind whips in off the sea in icy gusts, and like a diesel engine I seem to need the extra time to warm up.

As well as being hampered by sharp pin-pricks behind the eyes, my quest for today's 'thing' has been further compounded by circumstances beyond my control. My initial plan was to interview the famous Wizard who used to stand and preach daily in Cathedral Square, and is also credited with invent-ing the upside-down world map. I had all manner of probing questions to ask him, such as 'Are you a good wizard or a bad wizard?', 'Have you ever played Quidditch?' and 'If you had a fight with Gandalf, do you reckon you could 'ave 'im?' But then he went and retired, and nowadays the spot where he used to stand, according to my mate Stephen, is occupied by 'an altogether lamer sort of nutter'.

Then I struck on the idea of visiting a nitrous bar. To my knowledge Christchurch was, until recently, the only place in the country where it was legal to go along to a designated café and inhale laughing gas from a balloon for recreational purposes. But of course the powers that be saw fit to stop that particular avenue of pleasure, so I am in something of a quandary. Luckily for me, I have a resident expert to advise me.

'So, go ahead, Stephen, advise,' I say.

'What about punting on the Avon?'

'Nah,' I snap ungratefully. 'I've done that in Cambridge. How about a tram ride?'

'Nah,' he echoes, 'too clichéd.'

'I think the trams here are pretty cool,' I continue, 'especially the way they disappear down inside little shopping malls.'

'Ah, shopping malls,' he says. 'This is a shopping mall town, so why not go to a shopping mall?'

I don't even bother answering.

To avoid further deliberation on hungover brains we eventually decide simply to go into town and see what we can see. We skirt around the fantastic Hagley Park, which last night was alive with touch rugby players, before parking to take a wander around Cathedral Square with its soaring Chalice. The square used to be the domain of the Wizard, but today there seems no-one willing to take on his eccentric mantle. Then as we round the corner into Montreal Street I immediately know I have found my '1 Thing' for Christchurch.

I can't say enough in praise of the new Christchurch Art Gallery, Te Puna o Waiwhetu. From the moment you spy Graham Bennett's rotating sculpture to the steel-and-glass frontage of the gallery itself, you know you're in the presence of some of the finest modern architecture in the southern hemisphere. Bennett's *Reasons for Voyaging* consists of seven steel poles inset with panels of ancient totara, with large curved vanes at their summits to echo the forms of Polynesian canoes and reference ancient navigation systems as they rotate to a new position at each new moon. An elegant feature in their own right, they also complement superbly the curving wall of the gallery, whose shape is inspired by both the Avon that flows through Christchurch and the Maori koru, symbol of new life.

'Remember the past, embrace the future,' as someone clever no doubt once said, and architect David Cole certainly seems to have taken this advice to heart. Not since Paris have I seen such a strikingly beautiful modern building which blends in so effortlessly with its more traditional surroundings, and I can't help thinking that Wellington's Te Papa should hang its metaphorical head in shame. Christchurch Art Gallery even has its own typeface. How cool is that?

The inside is equally impressive, although once you get past the spacious feel of the entrance hall you soon realise it's nowhere near as big as its Wellington counterpart. Thankfully size isn't everything, and Stephen and I manage to while away a very pleasant hour wandering around the different exhibits. My personal favourites are Ronnie van Houtt's bizarre house, school and UFO video installation, and Dick Frizzell's *From Mickey to Tiki, Tu Meke*, in which Mickey Mouse morphs into something expressly more Kiwi. Stephen likes the full-size bull made entirely of corn beef tins, and vows to make one for his living room. Good luck with that, mate.

Later that evening, I tell my host I can't resist a peak at Lyttelton, the port where the *Edwin Fox* Robert Moore first set a rather seasick foot on New Zealand soil. As it turns out, there's a bar over there Stephen wants me to see, and as Lyttelton turns out be a quick trip over the hill from Sumner it all works out very nicely, thank you.

The WunderBar is an odd place, and receives a weird and wonderful mixture of visitors, too, what with Russian, Korean and ships of many other nationalities docking literally on its doorstep on a regular basis. Once you've ducked down the alley towards the harbour from Lyttelton's main street, you're faced with a zigzag climb up the ramps to the top of the building. The outside deck offers fantastic views of the port, but it's inside where things start to get really interesting. There are cosy booths all around the main bar, human torso light sculptures hanging from the ceiling, and running along the back wall is a strip skylight which must make this the only bar in the world with its own fish tank view of supermarket shoppers.

The next day an even later start sees my new travelling companion Stephen and I head out through the suburbs to rejoin SH1 near Hornby, which I am delighted to note has a railway running through it. From here it is a short distance to the flat, almost Roman-like straight road that runs across the Canterbury Plains from the outskirts of Christchurch pretty much right down to Timaru. You'd have to try hard to get lost on such an arrow-like section of highway, but Stephen is already trying his best to achieve this by making a pig's ear of the map. I get the feeling this could be a long day.

First stop is **Templeton**, a town built on the success of chicory production by the Trent family. There's even a Trent Road here to commemorate their contribution to the local economy, but who wants chicory when you can have cookies?

Cookie Time cookies has been a real New Zealand success story ever since Michael Mayell teamed up with brother Guy in 1983 with a dream to spread cookie joy throughout the country. In 1996 they even managed to bake the World's Biggest Cookie, officially recognised by the *Guinness Book of World Records*. It measured 24.9 metres in diameter, contained over 2.5 tonnes of chocolate and weighed more than 13 tonnes. How do I know all this? Because the Cookie Time Factory Shop is right here in Templeton, and Nona has just told me. She's also shown us the scale display model of the record-breaking attempt, allowed us to sample most of the range, and suggested I try on a rather fetching cookie shirt from the rack in the corner. I can tell Stephen quite fancies it for himself. Then again, I think he'd buy the whole shop if he could, especially the boxes of what he has been calling the 'food of the future' ever since we arrived. One Square Meal (OSM for short) is the new 'meal in a bar' phenomenon he's read about recently – a balanced, nutritious meal you can fit in your pocket. Stephen seems quite excited by it, and considering our different body masses (he's built like a rake, I'm not) I suppose I should be, too. If only I didn't have a problem with apricots. Nevertheless, we buy one in case it should come in handy at a later stage of the journey. Oh, and a shed-load of cookies, too, which we propose to consume willy-nilly.

'Cookies for breakfast,' says Stephen contentedly as we make our way back to the car. 'Well, well, well. It doesn't get any sweeter than this, does it?'

On the way to **Weedons** Stephen introduces me to the 'Dead Thing' game, a firm family favourite. The rules are simple. If you see a roadkill – possum, cat, hedgehog, whatever – and shout 'Dead Thing' first, you score points. But if you claim an object as roadkill and it turns out to be, say, a dropped scarf or a discarded jam sandwich, you lose points.

'Dead Thing!' he shouts as we pass a squashed possum. I am focused more on the Air Force transmitter stations to our right, and also on locating a sign for the Weedons Domain. My search, unlike the OSM bar, appears fruitless, however, so we turn off and stop to ask a lady down on her hands and knees with a trowel in her front garden. That's right, she is actually weeding in Weedons. You couldn't make this stuff up.

Over the ear-piercing din of her yappy dog she kindly tells us she has no idea where we can find the local cricket pitch, which surprises me. Our whole reason for being here is because Weedons boasts the oldest cricket club in New Zealand, formed in 1879, something I'd assumed every local would know.

'Your best bet is to go up to the Country Club and ask,' she says. 'There's bound to be some old buggers up there who can help you. The place is teeming with them.'

She's not wrong either. The car park is chocker, especially considering this is a weekday morning. I brief Stephen not to even think of mentioning the phrase 'Dead Thing' before we march up to the clubhouse and soon locate Derrick, a well-groomed gentleman in a bright red blazer and badge which tells us he is a past president of the club. I ask him where the cricket club is. He is immediately more than helpful and we're soon crunching up a driveway towards a humble white pavilion building with an equally humble sign which simply states 'Weedons Cricket Club'. No grand claims, not a great batting pitch either by the look of it. In fact some of the golf fairways appear in better nick, albeit off season. Somehow the modesty and understatement of it all seems typically Kiwi.

On the way out of the domain I narrowly avoid hitting a cat that runs across the road in front of my car.

'That's one rule I didn't tell you,' remarks Stephen. 'You're not allowed to create your own Dead Things. Just so you know.'

Back on the old straight track, we're soon approaching **Rolleston**, 'Town of the Future' as it rather grandly calls itself because the population has grown by over 1000 people in the last 10 years. That's no mean feat for a South Island town. It soon becomes evident just how this has been achieved as we turn off left and pass through a set of gates strangely not too dissimilar to those at the end the street on which the McFly family lives in the 'Back to the Future' movies. Spooky. I wonder if this has been done on purpose.

Building work is going on everywhere as we drive down to the new part of town. It appears that Rolleston has styled itself as a commuter belt town for Christchurch, providing a haven from scandalously high house prices, and good luck to them, I say. Some of the new architecture offends in that nondescript modern way, but over there has to be the hugest New World supermarket either Stephen or I have ever seen. The Library Centre looks welcoming, too, so we decide to give that a shot.

My opening question is innocent enough: I say I'm writing a book and ask whether they have anything on the history of the local area. The lady behind the desk begins very obligingly, returning with a copy of *Selwyn: From the Hills to the Sea*, which looks like a thoroughly informative, locally produced tome on every town in the Selwyn district. It is so informative that I ask whether I could perhaps purchase a copy, whereupon she goes off to check if they have any spares. She returns with a small stack. 'You're in luck,' she says. 'I've just found five that I never knew we had.'

'Great,' I say, and ask her how much.

'Ooh, I'm not sure. Let me just go and ask.'

It is at this point that something, or someone, goes terribly wrong. Another lady, one of the big guns, is mucking up the deal in the background. In the meantime, a queue of innocent library folk is forming behind me, necessitating another librarian to be called from his computer screen and into action.

'Are you dealing with this?' he says to my initial lady. It takes me a moment to realise that he is referring to me. I have become 'this'.

'Yes,' she replies, and turns to me apologetically.

'I'm sorry, sir,' she says. 'I'm not allowed to sell it to you unless you're a Rolleston resident.'

'Never mind,' I say, 'maybe I could just have a quick read of it while I'm here.'

'I'm sorry, sir,' she repeats. 'If you go leafing through it then you might crease the pages and no-one will want to buy it in future.'

'But I want to buy it now.'

'I'm sorry, sir, we don't have enough copies to sell you one.'

'But five minutes ago you didn't even know you had one copy, let alone five.'

'Apparently someone did, sir. I'm sorry.'

So not only will they not let me buy it now, they won't even let me look at it. At this point I'm willing to try anything to get it, including borrowing, photocopying, even a generous donation to a worthy local cause, all to no avail. If this kind of ridiculous bureaucracy is what the town of the future has in store for us, then maybe we should all remain firmly in the present.

'I'm sorry, sir. You could write to the mayor. He might send you a copy.'

So, much later, I do, and thankfully Mayor Michael McEvedy brings a voice of reason to the whole sorry episode by very kindly furnishing me with a free copy of the prized book. Now, finally, I can tell you that as well as a future, Rolleston has a thriving past to relate. Like so many South Island towns it was a mainline station stop on the route south, but also the main interchange for the western route, which means at one stage it probably played a vital role in supplying steel to Sheffield and helped to put the initial spring in Springfield.

Of course this information comes to me after the event. Back in Rolleston I am still stumped as to what my '1 Thing' should be, and the ideas I'm having at the moment could actually land me in trouble with the police. Instead, I leave it up to Stephen to save the day and he obligingly comes up trumps.

'This is the town of the future, right?' he reasons.

'So they say,' I reply, sulkily.

He pulls the OSM bar out of his pocket. 'And this is the food of the future, right?'

He doesn't have to say anything else. In silence we lean against the car and munch on our respective halves of the snack. It must be those damn apricots, but just at this moment I'm not keen on anything to do with the future, meal-wise or town-wise. In contrast Stephen polishes his half off in next to no time, and the remainder of my half – surprising, really, because it is very filling.

With the aid of a few cookies my gloom is all but diminished by the time we reach the Military Camp at **Burnham**. Somehow I doubt they'd appreciate us dropping in unannounced though, so we kick on to **Norwood** where, not for the first time on this journey, I have every intention of cheating. I've noticed that a mere 10 kilometres of straight road inland you can find one of New Zealand's more accidental and eccentric tourist sites. Charing Cross is a point in the middle of the countryside where nine roads converge. (It's also the name of the railway station I travelled to and from every working day for five years during my time in London.) Basically I just want to see how its Kiwi counterpart compares, so I turn right up Telegraph Road and drag Stephen off for what I think will be a quick photo opportunity. To my disappointment Charing Cross is a bit of a non-event. The aerial photos I have already seen do the place much more justice, but I fire off a couple of shots before we zip off back the way we came. About a kilometre down the road we both hear an unusual clunk from the back of the car. It is then that I realise that in my rush to get back to the main highway I have had a senile moment and left my digital camera on the roof. Bugger.

Poor Stephen. Instead of enjoying a cosy lunch and a leisurely afternoon, he spends the ensuing three hours helping to comb every inch of the grass verges up and down that darned road, all to no avail. By the time I have resigned myself to losing $1000 worth of kit through my own stupidity it's actually closer to teatime. There's nothing left to do except report it to a very understanding policeman back in Rolleston, and then limp onwards for tea and self-sympathy at the White House Café in **Selwyn**, the district town named after the one and only bishop of all New Zealand. As well as the obligatory cup of tea, Stephen wants to eat here, too, but I persuade him to hold fire until we reach the café at our next destination, **Dunsandel**, which ironically turns out be yet another bad idea as they've just had a fire in their kitchen and can offer only a limited menu. When it rains, it pours, and seldom when you need it.

I'm sorry to say I can't wait to get out of the Selwyn District as a whole. So a quick sausage roll or three later we move on at speed through the once thriving rail town of **Bankside**, now seemingly reduced to its former train station sign at the side of the highway, and prepare to try to lift our spirits with one of Stephen's car games.

Spanning 1.8 kilometres of once lethal river, the **Rakaia** bridge is officially the longest in New Zealand. A.H. Reed tells us that between 1840 and 1870 a horrifying 1115 people died attempting to cross here, a figure so high that drowning became known as 'the New Zealand Death'. It was even suggested in Parliament at the time that drowning be classified as a natural death. The original bridge was built in 1873 to a low-cost design by an English weaver called William White, then subsequently widened to accommodate both rail and road traffic. In 1939 this was replaced by separate road and rail bridges, and again despite or maybe owing to its length, budget seems to have played a major factor in the design. In other words, it's nothing much to look at, but blimey, it is long. Just how long we are about to find out as Stephen's game involves trying to hold your breath for the full length of the bridge. I think we actually start a little late for official qualification, but even at a steady 95 kilometres per hour I'm struggling. I'll flatter myself and say we are roughly halfway before I fold on the premise that it wouldn't be a good idea for the driver to pass out. Stephen manages just over a kilometre before he sadly follows suit, puffing and blowing in a manner which would suggest he'd be more at home on the rail bridge over to our right.

'I've never done it yet,' he wheezes. 'One day ... '

'I wouldn't hold your breath, mate.'

Nestled on the south bank of the river, the settlement of Rakaia is renowned as the salmon capital of New Zealand, which explains the large fish sculpture in the centre of the town. In addition to serious salmon and trout fishing you can also go rafting, jet boating or even rock hounding (whatever that is) near the Rakaia Gorge. Such energetic pursuits seem far away today, with the town bathed in sleepy afternoon sunlight.

There's not a lot going on at **Overdale** today. Hang on, though, what's this? A little to the south of town sits a notice for a FAR Field Day, and not far beyond this we see a group of grown men standing in a circle in a field to our left. One might suspect suspicious activity were it not for FAR being the Foundation for Arable Research. I wonder what they're discussing today. Stephen reckons maize, but I'll plump for pea production. Somehow I don't think we'll ever find out.

The town of **Chertsey** played host to the fabulously named and original NZ Woollymunchers Fine Wine & Lambfest in 2005, attracting such stars as Peta Mathias, Jordan Luck and Shrek the sheep. But sadly, in 2006 the honour passed to larger neighbour Ashburton which has managed to secure Goldenhorse and Hello Sailor. I note that Shrek the sheep is conspicuous by his absence, so maybe in its inaugural year the munching became a little overenthusiastic. The only other points of interest in the town appear to be the tavern, and the school which opened in 1879. We decide to take a quick look at the latter where today a young lad is busy out front mowing the lawn, as kids should be made to do everywhere in my opinion. I wonder if he's on detention.

Back on SH1 the police are out in force trying to capture speeders, when some of them at least should surely be out there looking for my camera instead of hiding behind hedges and playing with their own. We spot at least four cop cars in the short distance to **Dromore**, home of the range-reared turkey. I remember seeing a TV commercial for Crozier's Turkeys recently, which should be a dead giveaway for the time of year. Maybe the turkeys saw it, too, as there are none on view in the fields today. I guess they must all be safely locked up in the barn for the evening. Either that or already in the deep freeze at the Food Processing Unit at **Fairton**, almost too conveniently just down the road.

Ashburton, which an ex-resident who wishes to remain anonymous recently described to me as 'a big, black hole', appears on first impressions perfectly pleasant. Then again, I didn't grow up here. Nonetheless I'm sure the original founders of Ashburton, and no doubt most of the present inhabitants, too, would be mortified to hear their town talked about in such a way, especially as it was founded on such grand designs.

The land on which Ashburton now stands was originally obtained from the Canterbury Association in the 1850s with the aim of building a Church of England settlement like back home in the Mother Country. I'm not sure which English town they had in mind, possibly Basingstoke, but anyway it was pioneer settler William Turton who really got the ball rolling in 1858 when he established a ferry station here, and built an accommodation house, too, right next to where the modern bridge stands. There is supposed to be a plaque here on the exact site of his house, and this is what I am here to see.

WILLIAM TURTON'S ACCOMMODATION
HOUSE, THE FIRST BUILDING IN ASHBURTON,
WAS ERECTED HERE IN 1858.

I expect some locals aren't even aware of this modest little plinth on the north side of the river, but this is the spot where it all started. I would take a photo if I had my camera.

We drop in at a local café bar for a cheeky half, and do you know I'm quite enjoying this so-called black hole of a town. Too soon however, we must away, although I have a sneaky feeling I'm not entirely done with Ashburton just yet.

Across the river at **Tinwald** we head for the domain, a real hidden treasure of a park with tall, stately trees enclosing a picturesque lake which, bizarrely, is perched higher than the green expanses around it. We're looking for two particularly stately trees near the entrance, oaks planted by the then Duke and Duchess of York (later to become King George V and Queen Mary) on their royal visit in 1901 (which also included that loose remark about Bulls, as we know). It doesn't take us long to locate them, along with their accompanying plaques, and I'm delighted to relate that after 100 years both are still going strong, which is more than I can say for the royal family.

Happy with the ease of our discovery, and as it will be our last stop together, I decide to treat Stephen to the ice cream he has been pestering me about for the last two hours. Apparently he remembers a dairy around here that bestows you with overly large scoops on your cone. We find the shop and Stephen pushes his luck by asking for a double of Goody Gumdrops and Strawberry.

'Go on then,' I say, 'seeing as you've been such a good boy today.'

'As long as he eats his tea,' quips the lady behind the counter, opening the freezer.

Alone on the road again, I push on to **Winslow**. There's a big old derelict building here that may or may not have something to do with the railway's auspicious past, otherwise the Winslow Feeds Factory dominates in these parts.

With the mountains clearly visible off to my right and dark, scudding clouds threatening ahead of me to the south, I then pass through **Windermere**, notable only for vast quantities of sheep in its fields, and then **Hinds**, where the 'Shake Hands' Gallery also shows few signs of human life. So I drop in at the On the Spot shop to ask where I might find the Hinds Craft Gallery. The ladies behind the counter stare at me as if I am completely mad, and maybe I am, having driven mostly in straight lines for the past three days. I mutter an apology and leave them to continue pinning some felt onto a board.

Just the other side of town a kink in the road for no apparent reason gets me rather excited. Unfortunately it turns out to be nothing more than that, a kink, and I continue on my monotonous, arrow-like way, past the brilliantly named Frisby Road and on to my next stop where I hope to find some airborne phenomena of a rather more exotic nature.

At 4.02 pm New Zealand time on 31 March 1972, the Soviet Union launched *Cosmos 482*, an A-2-e type rocket carrying a spacecraft destined for Venus. For whatever reason the launch failed and the spacecraft eventually re-entered earth's atmosphere at around 11 pm on 2 April of the same year. Uncannily, with the entire Pacific Ocean at its disposal, it chose to descend on a diagonal trajectory across the South Island where many keen-eyed Kiwis reported spotting everything from meteorites to UFOs streaking across the sky. The following morning John Lindores, a farmer from Huntingdon just south of Ashburton, returned home to find a strange metallic sphere lying in a field just 200 metres from his house. He called the police who took it away and, fearing it to be radioactive, locked the mystery object in a cell overnight until the experts could be called in.

The find proved to be the first of around eight 'spaceballs' discovered in the area over the next few weeks, including one right here in **Ealing**. At the time the Iron Curtain ensured a total denial of any ownership of the spaceballs; thus they were eventually returned to their finders. All of which means that with any luck there may well still be one sitting proudly on a mantelpiece or propping up someone's gatepost here today. A long shot maybe, but it's got to be worth a try.

My quest begins badly. Ealing isn't exactly a metropolis and the first three houses I try seem empty. At the fourth house, however, I meet a young chap home for his lunch.

'Ooh, I couldn't tell you,' he says. 'I've only been here for about two years.'

I'm tempted to ask whether he is a migrant from Northland, but I'm on a fact-finding mission and this is no time for flippancy. He suggests I try the Reith family back up the road, so I call in on Nigel Reith, a third-generation farmer here. He vaguely remembers something about the spaceballs from his youth. He says his father, Alan, would probably know more, and kindly gives me his number.

'Either that or you could try the Ashburton Museum,' he says. Now why didn't I think of that?

On returning to Ashburton I meet Rita, the curator of the museum and a lovely lady who goes out of her way to furnish me with newspaper clippings on the subject, past and present. One of them from 1988 carries a photograph of Rita herself leaning against two of the spheres, on loan to the museum at the time. She tuts modestly at the image, although I think she looks quite hot.

'We had them on display here for quite a while,' she says. 'Actually, I think they've still got one up at the Aviation Museum. I'll just ring Jim for you.'

This is going fantastically well. Perhaps a little too well, come to think of it. Yep.

Jim, it turns out, is on holiday. Also, the Aviation Museum only opens on Wednesdays and Saturdays. Today is Monday.

'I'm stuffed, aren't I, Rita?' I say.

'Not necessarily,' she replies. 'You could always just go up there on the off-chance.'

So I do. Sure enough, the Aviation Museum is shut, but there are a few people at the airfield next door, so as a last resort I give that a whirl. Some elderly gentlemen there are very helpful. One of them makes a call and then passes the phone over to me. On the other end of the line is Neil Stukely, President of the Aviation Museum. It just so happens someone's having a do there tonight, and he'll be down in about an hour to open up. I'll be more than welcome to drop in and have a look at their spaceball.

'You can pick it up if you like,' says Ron.

In front of me on a modest display at the corner of the hangar is a small metal sphere, about 15 centimetres in diameter, a fuel tank for one of the manoeuvring engines, apparently, made from titanium alloy. Amongst the other information on the noticeboard behind is a map of where other parts of the rocket were discovered across the South Island, and there I can see the one in Ealing. This, however, is the first one found in Huntingdon.

Nervously, I lift it. It's surprisingly heavy – 13.6 kilograms, the noticeboard informs me.

'If you look underneath you can see the scorch marks where it heated up on re-entry,' says Ron, proudly.

This is incredible. I've touched a piece of moonrock in Florida before, so smooth from human contact it could have been anything really, but I've never held anything like this, a piece of space age history, something that's actually been up there and back, albeit unintentionally.

Outside I chat on, elated, with Ron and Neil. The spaceball is very popular with kids, apparently.

'More so than the planes we have here,' says Neil, a little ruefully. 'I can understand why, though. It's not every day you get a piece of rocket land in your back yard.'

Before long I have returned to the source of my quest, and

I realise that in all the excitement I've forgotten to ask anyone whether you can actually go eeling in Ealing. Ah, well.

Similar in design to its longer Rakaia neighbour, I could probably have held my breath over the **Rangitata** bridge, had I known it was coming. Unofficially marking the border into South Canterbury, the river below has always been renowned as treacherous, although less so these days as part of its mighty force has been diverted for irrigation purposes. A few kilometres upstream, however, I really fancied taking on the gorge, one of New Zealand's most impressive Grade 5 white-water rafting experiences, only yet again I am thwarted by the off-season. I will return one day, though. No, honest.

There's a MOO-seum for sale at **Orari** just down the road, along with a notice which mourns the recent demise of Orari School, gone the same way as the large sheep dipping station here which in 1899 used to be able to cope with 7000 sheep in a day. And there was me thinking an Orari was a mechanical model of our solar system.

At **Winchester** I drop in at the local store and ask Allan what he knows about the history of the town.

'Ah,' he says, 'you want Alan.'

Alan Patrick, the other Alan, is a lovely old boy and quite a name in Winchester. With another chap, Dave Butler, he recently spent five years filming, collating and narrating a video history of the town. It started out as a casual hobby and then snowballed, and although it has been time-consuming, Alan has few regrets about undertaking such a mammoth task. The video, he says, was just something he felt he should do, having spent all his life in the area.

'There's not many old buggers left here now,' he comments philosophically. 'Hopefully in fifty years someone will think "those old buggers did all right there" and appreciate it.' I hope so too.

Among many, many other facts, Alan tells me that the town has produced one All Black (Dickie Stewart), was originally named Waihi Crossing, and was founded in 1865 by a Major

John Albert Young. As well as having a saucy wife (tomato, that is – Mrs Young made it commercially for a while), it was he who was instrumental in setting up the sale yards, two hotels and the Masonic Lodge here, although not the flour mill, one of Winchester's more enduring commercial ventures. Harrison's Mill lasted here for over a century, and although defunct relatively recently, a part of it will always live on as the original millstones were used as the base of the war memorial a little further up the road.

We also talk about the time when A.H. Reed walked through the town. Alan is pretty sure his wife went out with a glass of water for the hardy octogenarian as he passed through. It's my first direct link to the man in whose footsteps I am driving.

Alan then takes me out back to his garage to show me his next venture, an old Crossley motor car that was shipped over here in the 1920s for a royal visit.

'They sent six in all,' he says, 'but this is the only six-cylinder model. She's all here, it's just a matter of finding the time, you know.'

I guess visitors like me don't help, so I thank Alan, wish him luck and tell him I'm off to Temuka, but not before stopping for a quick look at the war memorial and its historic circular base.

Temuka I find to be a cute, active and typically Kiwi little town, with its wonderfully diverse, awning-covered shops spreading haphazardly up King Street, the main central thoroughfare. Although many Kiwis may not know where it is, they will surely have heard the name of the town before and this is due in no small part to its world-famous pottery. You can still visit the factory today, a little to the west of town, or, like me, simply choose the easier option of the dedicated Factory Shop just off SH1.

The original items produced here in the 1800s were brown or grey, and if you come across any in a second hand shop you can expect to pay through the nose for them. These days, however, Temuka pottery comes in an array of vivid colours as I discover when I enter the shop and nearly have to put my shades back on. The bright oranges, yellows, blues and greens are quite beautifully arranged, and my only real quandary is which household item to choose. I eventually plump for an orange-and-blue sugar bowl and take it up to the aptly named Jade at the counter, whose greeting nearly causes me to drop it on the floor.

'Are you Bob?' she asks.

I'm flabbergasted. I've never met this girl before in my life.

'Yes,' I reply suspiciously.

'It's just that a man was in here about five minutes ago looking for you. He left a note.'

She passes it to me. It's from Alan. It reads: *Bob. Colin Hawke (rugby ref). Born & bred in Winchester. Alan P.*

Bless him.

No trip to Temuka would be complete without a quick mention of its most famous son, Richard Pearse, local farmer, inventor and aviator. He was nicknamed 'Mad Pearse' or 'Bamboo Dick' by his contemporaries (the latter thankfully due to his use of bamboo in construction), and many still believe that Richard Pearse actually achieved powered flight at the turn of the twentieth century, just before the Wright Brothers. He built his flying machines in his own humble workshop and then flew them from a nearby hill. It was a phenomenal achievement for a man who received no financial backing and sadly remained unrecognised as a genius during his lifetime. Nowadays of course, everyone has cottoned on and there is a memorial to him, a reconstruction of his original plane, to the west of town as you drive out. The original is housed in the South Canterbury Museum in Timaru, suspended from the ceiling at the exact height he is thought to have flown, but I'm happy I took the small detour to see this one, for reasons which shall soon become clear.

The town of **Arowhenua** straddles the famous Opihi River. It is rumoured that generations ago local Maori were the first to introduce the predominantly West Coast treasure of greenstone to the area. Today, like so many rivers down here, it is more renowned for its trout and salmon fishing. I'm looking to wet my whistle rather than my boots today though, for a couple of reasons. The Arowhenua Hotel was, for three years, run by Major Young of Winchester fame. It is also mentioned very favourably by A.H. Reed in his book, in which he describes stopping here for a glass of lemonade. As such I feel it is my duty to do the same, possibly with something a little stronger as a chaser.

A huge, beautifully sculpted 'fmthmthm' tree (I'm sorry, I don't know which type it is) is the first thing I notice as I pull up in the hotel car park, closely followed by a huge lumbering labrador dog who barks unthreateningly as I walk up the steps to the main entrance.

'Shut up, you deaf old bugger,' comes a voice which I soon find out belongs to Richard, who is looking after the place this afternoon while landlady Karen is 'in town'.

I look around the walls in vain for a picture of A.H. Reed while Richard pours me both a glass of Sprite and a lager (I don't think A.H. would begrudge me that), and ask whether the old fellow's trip is ever still discussed in these parts.

'You'd be better off asking Karen, mate,' says Richard, before racing around my side of the bar to deal with two young birds that have inexplicably flown inside and become entangled in the net curtains.

'Sorry about that. I do know they used to call this place Disneyland,' he continues, once the birds have been liberated. 'The old landlord used to be a real joker. He had an old trumpet behind the bar that he used to play to amuse the locals, and all sorts of other silly bugger tricks.'

I retreat to the garden, leaving Richard to carry on with his vacuuming, and sit and sup my lemonade in a Reedesque fashion. I then down my lager in a very Mooresque fashion and continue on my way.

Washdyke is so called because early settlers and sheep farmers George and Robert Rhodes used this location as a dam or dyke for washing the sheep from their station. Today it is more noteworthy for the Phar Lap Raceway, named after the wonder horse born near here which went on to win 37 out of 51 races, including the Melbourne Cup in 1930. Like many Kiwi-born heroes, Phar Lap was adopted by the Australians and subsequently made it big in the States before getting into trouble. That said, Russell Crowe's phone incident was nothing compared to the suspected poisoning of Phar Lap before he could race in the Kentucky Derby. For a fuller insight into his life, and death, I suggest renting the very watchable 1983 movie *Phar Lap*, a forerunner of *Seabiscuit*. Except it's Australian, of course.

Timaru to Oamaru.

So where were we? Ah, yes. Leaving Washdyke and on to **Timaru**, town of champions, and no, I'm not joking. As well as Phar Lap, Timaru has produced some notable athletes of the human variety as I discover when I scan a leaflet from the Info Site in the centre of town which today, Saturday, seems abnormally quiet. Even the museum is shut, so I can't go and see Richard Pearse's plane. Maybe everyone's away playing sport, and it wouldn't surprise me with this pedigree.

Of Cornish descent, Timaru blacksmith Bob Fitzsimmons took the middleweight boxing world title from the legendary Jack Dempsey in 1891. He also went on to win the heavyweight and light-heavy-weight world crowns, and has the unparalleled pugilistic honour of being mentioned in James Joyce's *Ulysses*.

Born in 1910. Jack Lovelock, better known as New Zealand's first ever Olympic gold medallist, attended Timaru Boys' High School. In the 1936 Berlin Games, in front of Adolf Hitler, he ran the race of his life in the 1500 m and a world record time of 3 minutes 47.8 seconds.

See what I mean? What with a couple of All Blacks as well, they obviously breed them hardy round here, and I think it only right that I should do these two champion names justice by entering into some sort of pilgrimage. Which is lucky, because as you'd expect, both now have monuments erected to them.

Fitzsimmons' is a short walk away on the corner of Stafford and Strathallan Streets, showing 'Ruby Robert' in suitably regal pose with his dukes up. It was funded by Sir Robert (Bob)

Jones, and my friend Nick has told me a funny story about the run-up to its unveiling, so you can blame him if it's not true. Apparently a reporter chasing a story hired a helicopter in order to zip out to the wilds and instigate an interview with Bob Jones during the latter's fishing holiday. When the reporter arrived, Jones promptly punched him on the nose. You couldn't make this stuff up, and I trust Nick hasn't.

Jack Lovelock's statue stands in the grounds of his former school, not far away from where they planted the oak tree which was presented to him as a sapling after his victory in 1936, supposedly (but not actually) by Adolf Hitler, and which still stands today. Not far past the imposing Basilica, I also spy a boxing club. It's good to see that the old sporting traditions continue in Timaru.

As I pass over another Saltwater Creek to the south of the town, I note that the irrigation machines in the fields look strangely reminiscent of Richard Pearse's plane, albeit on a much larger scale. There's no time to dwell upon the fact, however, before I turn off at **Normanby** in search of another monument, this time to the memory of perhaps the greatest Maori chief of the South Island.

Tuhawaiki of the Ngati Mamoe and Ngai Tahu, affection-ately known as 'Bloody Jack' for his fondness for that exple-tive, was based on Ruapuke Island in Foveaux Strait. Noted for both his honesty and his shrewdness, he was one of the few chiefs to defeat Te Rauparaha on his southern marauding ven-tures, and in 1840 signed the Treaty of Waitangi aboard the HMS *Herald*. After helping to negotiate the sale of Otago land to Pakeha in 1844, he drowned the same year on the coast at what is now known as Jack's Point.

Despite directions, I find the monument on Scarborough Road with some difficulty, mainly because I am expecting something grander. The stone is small, with a short inscription in Maori. It is, I think, my failing and lack of understanding of Maori traditions to think that such a great and humble man would need anything pompous or ostentatious to honour him.

At **Pareora** I am again faced with the inevitability of my own ignorance. Stephen, my erstwhile travelling companion, has previously suggested that this town was the first place to render L&P world famous in New Zealand. Either he was taking the mick out of the dumb Pommie guy, which I greatly suspect, or he is sadly misinformed. Or both. As I drive up the main street there is nothing to suggest that a fizzy drink ever materialised here rather than in Paeroa, and the only evidence of industry is the Food Processing Plant. I would suggest therefore that the only relevance of L&P in the vicinity would either be at the local dairy, or as an abbreviation of Lamb and Pork.

Feeling suitably foolish, I continue on to **St Andrews** which, inevitably, is in possession of a golf course. I note that none of the holes is named similarly to those of its more famous ancestor in Scotland, although I may well be wrong, especially given my L&P episode just now. In the town proper I am rewarded with a signpost to an historic building – one of the country's first-ever concrete buildings. Now just an empty, roofless hulk, the New Zealand Australian Land Company Granary was built in 1878 to store grain before sending it by rail to Timaru and beyond.

Judging by the size of its cemetery, the town of **Otaio** was once a much larger concern than today. However, one name you won't find among these gravestones is Jeanie Collier who in 1855 – in her early sixties – emigrated from Scotland to New Zealand and took up a sheep run here just to give her orphaned nephews a good start in life. This incredible lady slept in a tent until a permanent home could be built, occasionally waking in the morning to discover her nightcap frozen to the pillow. Nevertheless, she managed to steer her wards towards prosperity before succumbing to blindness and dying in 1861. She is buried further inland, on her run as she wished, and the site has since been declared a historic reserve.

Past Woolshed Valley Road and some particularly old painted farm buildings, and over Horseshoe Bend Creek brings me into **Makikihi**, where I can see the legend 'Makikihi Fries

Ltd' emblazoned on the roof of the chip factory. There is a hotel here, so for my '1 Thing' I could simply pull over and eat a bowl of chips in the bar, but despite the fact it's lunch time already I'm not all that peckish. My waistline could certainly do without the helping hand, too, so instead I call in at Country Crafts and wake up Sue who is having a nap behind the counter.

Now, I'm no doctor, but Sue has obviously come down with 'flu or something. It's by no means a cold day – I myself am in a T-shirt – and yet here she is shivering away with her portable gas fire on full. She should be tucked up at home in bed, and I tell her so. She agrees, especially as she's only had two customers all morning. Yet such is her affability that she still manages to talk to me for five minutes about, among other things, the local church and the soil erosion that is clogging up the region's river mouths. The latter is obviously an issue which concerns her greatly.

'I just don't know what will happen,' she shudders, and turns back towards her gas fire.

I take this as an invitation to leave and allow Sue to catch up on her sleep.

On the short drive to **Hook** I manage to build up an appetite, convenient as I'm due to stop at the famous Cup & Saucer café, a local institution on the other side of town. I am one of a number of enthusiastic customers at the counter, and at my turn to order the lady behind it asks me how far I am travelling. When I tell her from Picton to Bluff she very kindly adds a free cup of tea to my order under the laudable nationwide Driver Reviver scheme. I munch through my bacon and eggs, entertained by an amusing conversation among a group of 'old buggers' reminiscing about their glory days at rugby. When I leave I nod an acknowledgement in their general direction and realise that although I may have just picked up two free cups of tea I have singularly failed to use a saucer on both occasions. There may be bacon and eggs in my stomach just now, but there is no poetry in my soul.

Passing Studholme Junction on my left, I am soon into **Willowbridge**, site of another piece of Kiwi sporting history, and one that horse-racing enthusiasts will appreciate, for it was here that the first-ever New Zealand Grand National was staged. On the corner of Bradshaw and Willowbridge Roads a modest plaque reads 'This stone marks the site of the first NZ national Steeplechase 18th May 1875'. I can't help thinking it would be interesting to be supplied with more information on the actual layout of the course, but there we are.

Back on SH1, I arrive at **Glenavy**. The Carriage Restaurant here, which as it sounds is a restaurant inside an old railway carriage, would provide a welcome stop were I not already filled up on free tea from Hook. Instead I fill up the car at the Caltex station and ask the lady there if Glenavy is famous for anything else.

'Nah,' she says, 'not really. Fishing, I suppose.'

Her slightly contradictory statement gets me thinking. Thus far in the South Island I have driven past many a great angling waterway without once dipping a rod. During my home research I did look into the possibility of a guided fishing tour, but was put off by the website of one chap (who shall remain nameless) charging up to $600 a day. Consequently I have assumed that fishing here is out of my league, both financially and piscatorily, but I resolve from here onwards to at least make further enquiries whenever I stop.

Between **Hilderthorpe** and **Richmond**, two small towns south of the Waitaki River, lies a fairly monumental point in terms of world geography. For here, as you'll see if you look in an atlas, is the 45th parallel, the exact midway point between the South Pole and the Equator, and again it is marked with such modesty that I drive straight past without noticing and have to double back. Oddly, the small stone plinth states that the Pole is 5011kilometres to the south, and the Equator 4999 kilometres to the north. How does that work, then? Maybe it's something to do with the slight flattening of our planet at the poles. I can't work it out. All I can say is that it certainly doesn't feel any colder in Richmond than it does in Hilderthorpe.

Pukeuri is famous for just one thing, the freezing works, although I note as I drive through that the town also boasts the Landon Creek Bird Sanctuary and Gardens. Today, however, I am in search of a different species of bird: one that can't fly, is an excellent swimmer, and smells of fish.

'I'd like to see the penguins, please.'

'Have you booked?' says Helen, with the slight hint of a West Midlands accent and, I'm hoping, a greater slice of irony.

'No,' I reply, 'you said I didn't need to. I phoned this morning.'

'Did you?' By now there is a definite wry glint in her eye.

'Yes.'

'Did I say that?'

'If it was you on the phone, yes.'

'Oh,' she says, and her face breaks into a beaming grin. 'Just hang around here for a while, then. I'll give you a shout when it's time to go through.'

The **Oamaru** Blue Penguin Colony lies at the southern end of the town. It's an eco-friendly site, of course, positioned on an old disused quarry which supplied much of the rock for the nearby harbour, and a place that afterwards the penguins naturally gravitated towards, so much so that in 1992 it was decided to formally recognise it as a protected area. Nesting boxes have been provided for the penguins should they prefer a prefabricated home and the scheme has proved a fantastic success with the population increasing from 33 breeding pairs to over 100 in just 13 years. Not to say there haven't been some setbacks on the way.

The blue penguin is the world's smallest penguin, standing around 30 centimetres tall which, when on land, makes it easy prey for cats, ferrets, weasels and the like. In fact a few years ago tragedy struck when 74 penguins were killed here in one night by a local dog. Thankfully, further measures have since been taken to safeguard the welfare of the penguins, so hopefully the birds will continue to flourish in the future, aided by passionate conservationists like Helen and a steady stream of inquisitive punters like me.

'I'll have to ask you to stay very quiet when they arrive, and please no photographs,' says Helen into her radio microphone as we funnel through to the subdued lighting of the purpose-built wooden grandstand at the rear of the complex. 'Please remember this is their natural habitat and we don't want to go scaring them away with clicks or flashes.'

Several of my fellow voyeurs zip up their camera bags, others make vague efforts to gag their young children.

'Also, there's no smoking, either, as the penguins don't like the smell. And no cheap aftershave,' she adds, mischievously.

In the morning, your average blue penguin will get up, shake down its feathers and head off up to 25 kilometres out to sea where it will remain alone all day, hunting for food and endeavouring to elude its own natural predators, namely seals and sea lions. After a hard day's fishing, it will then join up with its mates about a kilometre out to sea before returning to the ranch en masse around dusk, which is exactly what we're all hoping to see in the next few minutes.

Until then, and Helen assures us it won't be too long now, she will just continue to 'waffle on' about penguins in general. She then notices I am taking notes, comes over to see exactly what I am writing, and hits me reproachfully on the arm for observing that she is indeed 'waffling on'.

We wait. Thankfully only a short waffle later the first raft of about 30 penguins scuds chaotically on to the beach, literally on the crest of a wave. They stand there, quacking and surveying the scene for potential predators. After what seems an age one begins to scuttle clumsily up the sand and the rest follow, all stooping at an angle of 45 degrees, drunk on fish to feed the family. Halfway up the ramp to the nesting area they stop again, not for as long this time, before waddling up the final slope and dispersing to their respective hidey-holes.

Did I say all? Not quite. Whispers of concern are echoing around the spectators. Three penguins are still on the beach, languishing in the surf. What's going on? Are they hurt?

'No,' says Helen. 'They must be adolescent males. They've got no family to feed so they're just messing around, playing. Because they can.'

With the main event seemingly finished, some of the crowd begins to move towards the exits. They think it's all over. But what's this? More penguins are on the beach. The high-jinx of the three stragglers are interrupted by a larger and noisier raft crashing the party. The new group of 40 penguins performs the same ritual, sweeping the stragglers along with them, until they, too, disappear into their nests, no doubt to vomit their catch into eager young mouths.

'If you hang around you might get to see some mating behaviour and watch the adults preening themselves,' says Helen hopefully, but I think the majority of us have had enough of the cold. Besides, it's the second NPC rugby semi-final tonight, Otago *vs* Canterbury, and if I hurry I might just catch the second half.

The lights are bright in the centre of town, casting shadows on the famous whitestone architecture and lending the buildings an even more regal air. I nip into the Brydone Hotel to drop off my stuff, and then, as recommended by my friendly receptionist, straight back out and across the road to Fat Sally's where I settle in at the bar and order the hugest light meal I have ever seen in my life.

To everyone's amazement and delight, Otago are beating Canterbury for the second time in a matter of weeks, and the atmosphere here is fantastic. I strike up a conversation with my neighbours at the bar, who I discover to be a fellow Bob and his wife Julie. We hit it off straight away (Bobdom is a great icebreaker, I've always found) and after buying each other rounds, swapping jokes and a good deal of life history, Bob leans in conspiratorially.

'What are you doing now?' he asks.

'Nothing much,' I say. 'Going back to my hotel.'

'No, you're not,' he says. 'You're coming with us. To see a bit of the real Oamaru. Do you like penguins?'

The Penguin Club is a cool little venue near the waterfront, a place where all the bands that play Oamaru play Oamaru. Muso heaven. It gets its name not just from the colony down the road, but because some penguins, those with a penchant for music presumably, actually nest underneath it.

'If you listen out you can sometimes here them squawking,' says Bob.

I'd be hard pushed tonight, though, what with all the rival squawking from a local band on stage. Nevertheless, the crowd seems to be into it, or out of it, and what a diverse crowd it is. Respectable looking middle-aged women mix with hardened bikies in full leathers. There's even a guy in the corner wearing an eye patch.

Shouting to be heard above the noise, the conversation somehow comes around to fishing. I tell Bob I'm disappointed I haven't got around to doing any in the South Island yet. His eyes light up, and he almost chokes in mid-swig of his drink.

'I'm going this Sunday,' he says. 'Taking my boys. You'd be very welcome.'

I turn to Julie. 'I know he's pissed,' she says, 'but he wouldn't say it if he didn't mean it.'

I'm struggling to focus, too, so I decide to call it a day and stagger back through the old main street to the hotel. I'm just admiring the beautiful old buildings with their fabulous, imposing columns when a small figure flashes in front of me and darts behind a parked van. Cautiously I lean around the bonnet to see a penguin, cowering under the wheel. I salute the little bugger that gave me such a fright and meander onwards to bed.

My alarm goes off at 5 am. Fishing. Thankfully both Bob and I have had a day to get over our hangovers, although Bob is still complaining about feeling rough all yesterday.

'I must be getting old,' he says, to smirks of assent from Grant and Mark, his two teenaged sons. 'Don't mind those piss-takers,' he adds. 'They'll start on you once they've got to know you.'

We follow the **Waitaki** upstream as far as Kurow, then cross the bridge and cut along the other bank until we arrive at a grassy field beside the river. It's a sharp, fresh morning and as we get out of the car, our breath is clearly visible as the sun's first rays begin to poke over the mountains.

'What a beautiful day,' says Bob. 'Let's get fishing.'

And we do. Bob's boys prove to be just as kind and generous as their father, helping a fishing novice like me set up the rod they've lent me, giving me the best spot and coaching me in what to do. Bob seems very eager for me to catch something. I get the distinct impression he feels responsible for me enjoying my little fishing trip – silly, really, as I'm happy as Larry. Quite apart from the angling, the views here are breathtaking and I couldn't imagine a more idyllic way of spending a crisp spring morning. I'm resigned to the fact that with my technique I should consider myself lucky to catch a cold, when wham! I get the first bite of the day.

Bob is ecstatic. Grant appears at my side.

'Reel her in slowly, don't rush it,' he says. 'We should see her jump in a minute.'

A silver flash arcs up out of the water.

'Wahey!' shouts Bob. 'Thar she blows!'

Following advice, I coax the fish slowly into the shallows. Bob wades in further and prepares to pounce. And then suddenly, inexplicably, my prized fish manages to squirm its way off the hook and it's free, flapping on the pebbles in the extreme shallows. Bob does his best but with another quick flick its of powerful tail it's gone.

'Bugger,' says Bob, and I can tell he's disappointed for me. 'I thought we had that one. Still, a great start.'

'Beginner's luck,' I say. And so it proves.

While the others expertly bag a handful of fish between them over the ensuing few hours, I manage to cover myself in mud, water, grass, and in fact anything but glory. My dismal casting means I break two bubble floats on the rocks, and then after Grant and Mark have patiently fixed every problem, I hook my *pièce de resistance*, an overhead telephone wire, causing a degree of justified hilarity. As far as I know, the bubble remains there to this day, which I hope gives Bob and the boys a good laugh every time they go there.

Before long it's time to call it a day. The fish are gutted, brown and rainbow trout alike, and photos taken. Mark asks me if I want a shot of the phone line as it's the only thing I really caught all day.

'I told you they were cheeky bastards,' says Bob.

We drive back in high spirits and I can't thank these guys enough. What a fabulous morning I've had. I'm invited home for a quick cup of tea, after which I'm off to see a woman about a sheep.

Oamaru to Dunedin.

For the first time in many a kilometre on the way out of Oamaru I encounter a gradient, a welcome change from the flat, open monotony since Christchurch. A couple of hundred metres south of town is Awamoa Creek, so named by Walter Mantell after he found a rake of moa bones in the vicinity, and then **Alma**, where the fresh veg store appears closed, and the road begins to challenge me with gentle corners and undulations. Up ahead of me now I can even see a hill, a monument sitting atop it in full view of the entire surrounding area. It draws ever closer as I skirt around its right flank into **Totara** and the historic Totara Estate. At the old men's quarters, now converted into a reception area of the museum, Hazel comes out to greet me wearing a Victorian maid's bonnet and a large grin.

'I'll just put the video on,' she says, after wrestling gainfully with the EFTPOS machine.

The Totara Estate should hold a special place in every Kiwi's heart. For it was here, during the Great Depression of the 1870s, that two men hit on an idea that saved the country, and has continued to prove pivotal to New Zealand's economic success ever since: the export of frozen meat.

As visions go, they don't come much bolder than that of William Davidson and Thomas Brydone. New Zealand had a surplus of meat and very few people to eat it, whereas in London and the rest of Europe the opposite was true. Food was in great demand, the logic undeniable. All it needed was for someone to work out a way of keeping meat frozen for the entire journey halfway around the world. Which is exactly what they did, processing the sheep here at the Totara Estate and then ferrying them straight to the port. And so, on 15 February 1882 the *Dunedin*, converted into a refrigerated ship for the purpose, set sail on the 98-day journey to London. By the time it arrived the 5000 sheep carcasses inside were still frozen hard and, for the second time you might say, Davidson and Brydone made a killing. And a $4.5 billion industry was born.

Despite the historical significance I'm not expecting too much from what is, after all, ostensibly an old farm and meat factory. but, dodgy fake beards aside, the video gives a fascinating insight into problems overcome, and into just how much the meat industry has advanced since those pastoral days. More than 30 million sheep are slaughtered and processed in New Zealand every year, a staggering number in anyone's book. One clip shows shanks of lamb being sliced with frightening accuracy by a robot knife arm, a contraption that wouldn't look out of place in a 'Terminator' movie.

Suitably sobered, I opt for some fresh air and head towards the old stables and granary, walking past some different early breeds of sheep which today, thankfully, are here for informational purposes only. Look, I do feel slightly hypocritical for feeling squeamish about the raw facts of eating meat. After all, I'm one of the biggest carnivores I know. But even I have to draw the line at the redeveloped museum-style slaughterhouse, complete with sound effects.

I return to reception where Hazel is looking forward to the meal her husband is cooking her at home.

'Lamb, is it?' I ask.

'Pork, I think,' she laughs.

You could definitely describe the countryside as rolling now; it's much more pleasing to the eye and not a little reminiscent of England, especially with the rain, as I enter **Maheno**, the most sweltering leg of A.H. Reed's walk but far from it today. Unfortunately the Maheno tavern is shut, so I drive on out the other side and past a house rather grandly named Monte Cristo. No doubt some rich Count lives there, I think, and head onwards towards the distinctive Otago hills.

My chances of successfully completing the task I've set myself in **Herbert** would seem to be negligible, but I thought it worth a pop: to spot a rare breed of New Zealand sheep known as the Herbert Sheep. The trouble is that although these sheep are known to live somewhere around here, they are a feral breed, no longer farmed, and so it's unlikely I will see any as I travel lazily down the highway. No, it's no good. I do spot a replica moa outside a shop, though. That will have to do. (It is still raining, you know.)

At **Waianakarua** things promise to be much simpler, as for this task I won't need even to exit the car. Built in 1874 from local stone, the bridge here is the oldest still in use on SH1, and by the look of it it's getting a facelift today, along with having its road realigned. Great news for the bridge, not so good at present for the beautiful Mill House Hotel, with dust from the roadworks coating its magnificent green shutters.

Yellow and blue flags and balloons outside one house on the way to **Hampden** are a gentle reminder both of the other night's rugby, and that I am entering the Otago heartland country. Down at the Hampden Reserve is a beautiful little picnic area with a long sandy beach nearby. If you're down this way camping or in a motor home I can heartily recommend stopping for a while. Me, I follow the loop all the way back round to the highway and on to **Hilgrove**, which promises little and doesn't disappoint on the delivery. There's another historic bridge signposted here, just after Baghdad Creek, but no further information, or bridge, or town for that matter, seems to be forthcoming. Or maybe it's just me missing something because I'm getting so excited at the prospect of seeing for the first time one of New Zealand's more bizarre natural phenomena.

Concentrated on two main areas of the beach here, the **Moeraki** Boulders are remarkably spherical concretions of calcite formed over millions of years within the surrounding sedimentary rocks. No, it didn't mean a lot to me either. Big rock balls that used to be under the seabed, then, but whatever you call them you can't fail to be impressed by the two-metre giants that sit proudly at the edge of the surf on this windswept beach. Unless, that is, you're a Goth and his particularly sullen girlfriend who frown dismissively at them, and are possibly the first people I've met in a remote location in New Zealand who haven't said hello.

The Maori belief is that these huge spheres are washed-up cargo – food baskets (kaihinaki) and gourds – from the wreck of the great canoe *Arai Te Uru* after it foundered in these waters during a storm. The hull of the canoe supposedly forms the reef further up the coastline.

The scientific explanation is that they were not washed up on the shore at all, quite the reverse in fact: they are coming out of the eroding cliffs behind the beach. I take a look and yes, there are two more just waiting to pop out and trundle on to the sand within, ooh, the next 200 years or so. A kind of slow rock and roll, you might say, even slower than a Bon Jovi ballad, although possibly not as tedious.

Some of the boulders are perfectly preserved, others have either been worn away by the sea to a turtle-shell pattern, or broken open to reveal a strange, orangey crystalline mantle with a completely hollow core. The surf that beats against the ones closer to the shoreline has also formed an odd, white foam around them, almost like soap suds. Maybe that's what scared the Goth away, I wonder, before returning the long way to the car park.

The town of **Katiki** is a simple drive down the highway from the boulders, but to reach the Katiki Point lighthouse, a feature of which no doubt the crew members of the *Arai Te Uru* would have been grateful, you have to branch off onto the headland through the Moeraki settlement and avoid missing the clearly visible signpost off to the right. Then, to do the whole Virginia Woolf thing, simply follow the lengthy gravel track and ensure you and your vehicle get 'to the lighthouse' with the minimum of fuss and expletives. The view from up here at dusk on a pleasant evening such as this is enough to calm the most enraged mind, with the beautiful Katiki Beach, a sliver of sandy coastline, stretching off to the south. Jacket collar raised to fend off the chilly wind, I wait, perfectly alone, until the lighthouse illuminates, and then I drive off, satisfied.

Back on SH1 the next morning, and past the Trotters Gorge turn off, I notice both road and rail skirt alongside Katiki Beach. I cross Back Creek, which I always thought was something my mum complained about after a night out at skittles, and make for the next peninsula, the intriguingly named **Shag Point**, which offers another beautiful detour whose history includes housing an old Maori settlement and later a coal-mining area, the remains of which are still visible today.

At the further of the two car parks a sign suggests not to err from the marked pathways or I could find myself plummeting down an old mineshaft. So I pick my way carefully down the boot-worn route to see if I can spot my prey on the hull of the Maori canoe, the reef. I'm not convinced I know exactly what a shag looks like, but there are helpful information boards down here at the viewing site. Apparently, too, I have a choice of shags here for my entertainment. The Stewart Island shag, that must be that one there; the spotted shag, again there he is, and, oh, the sooty shearwater. I could see some yellow-eyed penguins further along the headland, but I'm not convinced that I'll bother, not today. There must be seals around here someplace though – that smell is unmistakable.

From Shag Point it's a short trip to **Bushey** and my first glimpse of the Sir John McKenzie memorial cairn atop the towering Puketapu hill. It's not until I get to **Palmerston**, however, that I also spy a fair selection of mad buggers who this morning are running up and down its steep slopes in some kind of a race.

'If you'd been here a bit earlier you could have joined them,' smirks the woman in the Info Centre. Watch it, lady, I haven't had any breakfast yet. And you've just told me the gold mine

I've been looking forward to visiting here is a) miles away and b) shut today. What am I to do now? Watch the race stragglers come in along with the rest of the dwindling crowd? Or discover what all the squawking is about at the Butterfly and Bird Haven? Hmmm, tricky.

The culprit turns out to be a cockatoo belonging to a supremely affable, silver-haired man called Charley Block who apologises for the lack of fauna on display here today.

'We've only just opened, really, but we have big plans,' he says.

Funny, I've never talked to a man with a cockatoo on his shoulder before. I think maybe they should rent one out to that chap with the eyepatch in Oamaru. Maybe the cockatoo doesn't agree, mind, as it lets off another eardrum-perforating screech. What's that, Charley?

'I said, we'll be adding better signage, heating all-year round for the butterflies, and lots more birds and insects, too.'

I wish him the best of luck and get out while I still have ears, across to the pub for a snack and a pint. There, I am accosted by a man who notices I am carrying a Macraes Gold Mine tours leaflet.

'It's not open today,' he says helpfully.

'No, I know,' I reply.

'Open tomorrow, though.'

'Yes.'

'You should stay here the night and go in the morning. There's karaoke at the pub tonight.'

I'm sure he means well, but for so many reasons I am gone from Palmerston in under two minutes.

Wairunga appears not to be here. To make sure I'm not missing anything I double back through the Goodwood loop road and re-emerge right back by the Butterfly and Bird Haven in Palmerston. I can still hear the cockatoo screeching inside, but thankfully I'm not stopping, not even for karaoke, and I drive on to have another go at locating the town. It's all to no avail, but when I get to **Tumai** I see a signpost off left for some historic buildings. I'm on Edinburgh Street, driving past Glasgow Street, Forfar Street, Aberdeen Street, Perth Street and oh, there's a golf club. No prizes for guessing which European nationality settled here first.

The historic buildings turn out to be Matanaka, Otago's first farm set up in the 1840s by trader, whaler, ship owner, village setter-upper and general entrepreneur Johnny Jones. Several of the original buildings are still standing, as I soon find out after another winding gravel drive and then a short tramp through a wooded copse and out on to the headland. The final stage of the walk takes me across a rich pasture with a collection of glorified corrugated shacks at the far end – the old stables, granary, privy, store room and school house. They're all painted that familiar, deep rust-red. Rudimentary dwellings you might say, up here in their splendid isolation, but ones that helped forge a community and give so many new settlers their first real home in New Zealand. The farm is long gone, of course, and only the privy is open today, although sheep still graze here and a few eye me suspiciously as I circle the buildings.

'They're part of Waikouaiti, really, those buildings,' Mary at the **Waikouaiti** library tells me.

I ask her if she also knows anything about the huge stash of moa bones found in the vicinity in 1846, and again in 1849.

'You'll probably find out more at the museum,' she says. 'The old Bank of New Zealand building up the road.'

At the museum I meet Helen, the curator. After a brief scout around among glass display cases jam-packed with memorabilia, from the historical to the trivial, I ask about moa bones.

'We used to have them out here but there wasn't a lot of interest,' she says. 'Hold on, I think they're locked away in the back.'

I'm left to muse on how items such as watches, pipes and thimbles can be deemed worthy of exhibition and yet not the bones of one of the largest birds ever to have existed, and one which, were it not extinct, would have tourists from all around the world flocking in their droves to see its immense stature.

'The kids liked them, but we don't get many kids in here,' says Helen, struggling through with a large cardboard box, which she unceremoniously dumps on the counter. Scrawled on the side in felt tip are the words 'MOA BONES'. I look at Helen, expectantly. She looks at me. We neither of us move. Then I realise that she wants me to sift through the box myself. I'm really not sure I should be doing this, and I tell her so.

'Ah, I'm sure you're more qualified than me,' she says with a dismissive gesture.

I'm pretty bloody sure I'm not. Still, I delve in and pull out what looks like a leg bone, only it's longer than any leg bone I've ever seen before. I pass it to Helen, whose arms drop with surprise.

'It's heavy,' she says. 'I thought birds' bones were hollow.'

There's a cow's skull in the box, too. Maybe these bones are just plain old cow bones, and the felt tip is lying. Felt tip never lies, though, does it?

'Huh,' harrumphs Helen, handing the bone back to me. 'Well, I wouldn't know. I'm not a bird, I'm an animal.'

Soon afterwards we're joined by Marie, President of the museum, who continues the great moa debate by filling me in on Maori hunting tactics.

'These bones were found up at the mouth of the Pleasant River, I think. They reckon the hunters used to drive them downstream until they had nowhere left to go, then slaughter them there.'

We chat on, we three, for another 15 minutes about everything from the local racetrack to the now defunct Seacliff Lunatic Asylum ('You couldn't call it that these days'), at which point I realise that I have been casually holding the moa leg bone in my hand and even gesticulating with it to help illustrate the odd point. I put it gently back in the box, slightly ashamed, although neither Helen nor Marie seems bothered in the slightest.

The first thing I notice at **Merton** is a large cross on a hill, closely followed by the turning for Evansdale Cheese. Hang on, according to my list **Evansdale** is the next stop *after* Merton. Let's investigate. Turning off right I find The Grazery, the Evansdale Cheese factory café. It looks shut, and it is shut. The factory looks none too active either, although one of the hatches is open. I call inside several times, to no avail. Then I hear the sound of a radio from a small house-cum-Portakabin across the way. The door is open so I go over and knock.

After a short wait, an old geezer shuffles to the threshold.

'That is the cheese factory, right?' I ask, pointing vaguely behind me.

'Yep,' says the old geezer.

'There doesn't seem to be anyone there. Do you know what's going on?'

He visibly tightens. 'Nothing to do with me,' he says.

'Do they still make cheese here?' I ask.

'Yep,' he says, 'I think so.'

'So, what—'

'Nothing to do with me,' he interrupts, and shuts the door.

I go back for one last check of the factory. There are boxes of cheese waiting to be loaded at the hatch all right, but still no response to my cries. I guess it's just hard cheese, then.

Once through Evansdale the fabulous stretch of water on my left is Blueskin Bay, a tidal lagoon flanked by the creeping fingers of bush-clad hills, named after a particularly well-tattooed old Maori who lived here in the early days of Pakeha settlement. At the far end of the bay is **Waitati**, a variation on Waitete, the Maori name for this area meaning 'Lake of the Grey Teal'. It seems apt, then, that my lightweight task here should be spotting the duck mural on the bus shelter as I drive through, skirting the beautiful, rocky river as the road starts to climb. And climb. And climb.

These must be the famous Otago Hills I've heard about, a mass of welcoming yellow gorse in today's sunshine. But I am warned of more inclement times when I see the sign that informs travellers whether the road – and this is SH1, let's not forget – is open or not.

Dunedin must be close now, I think as I pass by **Pigeon Flat** (possibly worth a few points in Stephen's Dead Thing game), and then I'm at the crest of the final peak and, wow, there is **Dunedin**, huge and basin-like, spread out before me, its chocolate-box houses dotted over every available hillside, drawing me down, down, down the hill again towards the heart of this vibrant Victorian harbour city. Not quite yet, though. Before I approach the centre proper I have just one small task over in the North East Valley suburb of town.

At a gradient of 1 in 1.266 (that's about 38 degrees if you're into geometry) Baldwyn Street is officially the steepest suburban street in the world, an honour accredited in the *Guinness Book of World Records*. I am also informed that on its most precipitous section the seal had trouble adhering to the road, and was thus concreted over. Some reports say that cars and people have to be careful to avoid rolling over. Armed with such intriguing facts I can't resist a quick peek, so I turn up North Road and start counting the streets on my right to Baldwyn Street, the tenth. But it's not a street, it's a cliff with houses.

I drive up it first, about 150 metres in first gear all the way. No point in taking any chances. By the time I reach the bottom again I'm sweating almost as much as the two mad joggers I've passed, and I haven't even begun walking it yet. This takes me a further 15 minutes and reminds me of the dreaded cross-country runs at school, the shin pains on the way up, and the deadlier downward canter working tragically under-used leg muscles to stop myself going arse over tip. Pleased just to be alive, I stumble around the corner to the local store.

'I know what you've been doing,' says Kevin, cheerily.

Once I've got my breath back five minutes later, I quiz him on the various events that take place here each year.

'Well, of course there's the Gutbuster Race. The record for that is one minute fifty-six seconds,' he says, matter of factly.

'What, to get to the top?' I pant.

'No, that's up and down.'

Holy crap.

'Some guy's also ridden up and down seven times continuously without getting off his bike,' says Kevin, 'and then there's the Jaffa rolling for charity. It's never dull around here.'

'What do the residents think,' I ask, 'of people traipsing up and down outside their front doors all the time?'

'Oh, they're mostly okay with it. Some are inclined to get uppity, mind,' he says, without even noticing his pun, 'especially if some joker decides to screech up and down in his car at two o'clock in the morning.'

The perils of living next door to a tourist attraction, I guess. Speaking of which, it's time I picked up my official certificate for walking the world's steepest street and staggered onwards.

There was a time when Dunedin could quite proudly say it was the commercial and industrial capital of New Zealand. Even before Pakeha came here the area was popular with Maori for its bountiful fishing, hunting (especially moa) and greenstone, and then when gold was discovered, well, for a while there was no stopping this thriving settlement. Originally earmarked to be called New Edinburgh, Dunedin sprang from the old Gaelic name for that fairest of cities, and even today there is something uniquely stately, slightly dour and downright Scottish about the atmosphere in the centre as I drive in. Apart from the fact it's sunny, of course.

Monuments to former and present glories surround me as I cruise down Cumberland Street North and past the university, New Zealand's first, now the training ground for the nation's doctors. The Hippocratic Oath must have been taken here more times than you could shake a stethoscope. Study would seem to be furthest from the minds of the hundreds of students on show today though, all out drinking, laughing or playing touch rugby on the college grounds, and who can blame them on such a fabulous afternoon. Feeling comparatively old and envious, I push on to one of Dunedin's historic landmarks, only this one has definitely seen busier times.

Dunedin Railway Station sings its past in grandiose style, a vision in grey and white from the outside, and inside, now fully restored, a reminder of just what used to be achieved in public buildings when money was no object. Royal Doulton mosaic floors, stained-glass windows, kauri carvings, clay tiles shipped over from Marseilles, and I defy anyone not to be transported back in time as they enter the incredible ticket hall. What a shame, then, that with such a beautiful Flemish Renaissance-style building, they are unlikely to be transported anywhere else from Dunedin Railway Station these days, with the notable exception of the scenic Taieri Gorge. Indeed, I did consider such a trip as my '1 Thing' to do in Dunedin, this or maybe the museum, but both were ultimately rejected in favour of beer.

The Speight's Brewery is situated in Rattray Street, a short walk from the historic central Octagon. At the ticket desk I note a few other loiterers for the tour, mostly males it must be said, busy studying the paraphernalia on the walls.

'We'll be starting in about five minutes,' says Keith, our ebullient guide for today. 'You're welcome to take photos on the way round if you like.'

I explain that I've lost my camera.

'Oh, and I did my hair specially today, too,' he says, stroking his bald head in mock disappointment.

The tour kicks off with a briefing downstairs. 'Welcome to one of the few gravity breweries in existence,' he says,'which means we can start with the ingredients on the top floor and work our way down chronologically through the brewing process. If you all behave you'll get some beer at the bottom, too,' he adds. Faint smiles ripple through our group of seven, apart from one Australian man for whom beer is obviously not a joking matter.

It was for the local newspaper, though. Water for the brewery comes from a bore right here on the premises. There's a tap on the wall outside and apparently people come from far and wide to fill up their water bottles for free.

'A few years ago the *Otago Daily Times*, the local newspaper, played an April Fool's trick,' Keith relates. 'They printed a story that for one morning only the Speight's tap would be flowing with free beer instead of water. We had queues around the block that day.'

As we pass traditional milling machines and stills, all of which remain an active part of the brewing process, Keith adds that the local students treat this building as a place of worship. They hold a bizarre kind of initiation ceremony for freshers, blindfolding them and bringing them here to kiss the hallowed stone walls. Those crazy kids.

Down, now, to a room full of old kauri gyles, huge open brewing vats recently refurbished to produce the range of Speight's Distinction Ales in celebration of the company's centenary and beyond.

'They were always here but no-one knew how to work them,' says Keith. 'We had to drag in Norrie, a previous employee, to help us work out what to do.' A previously outdated brewing method, gyles are now very much back in fashion. 'Since one of our blokes was a keynote speaker at a brewing conference, things have just gone mad. We've had camera crews in here from all over the world.'

A circular staircase winds down through the middle of one of the old kauri vats, taking us to the final, and some may say most important, section of the tour, the bar. Here we get to pour our own beers, and sample as much of the different types as we please. My easy favourite is the Chocolate Ale, specially produced for an expo at the local Cadbury's factory.

'Yes, a limited edition, I'm afraid. Only available at Speight's Ale Houses,' says Keith. Shame. I'd buy a bottle or 12 at the drop of a hat.

Outside I finally get to spot the famous Speight's water tap for myself. In fact I don't know how I missed it, really, it's right next to the front door. I would sample the water for myself, but there's quite a queue just at the moment and I'm bound for Invercargill.

Dunedin to Invercargill.

The road out of Dunedin takes me past the hallowed turf of Carisbrook (House of Pain, home of Otago rugby), before climbing the only hill I've ever seen with a speed camera on the upward slope. **Green Island** comes next, named after an island away off the coast to the south of here. At **Fairfield** I snake over the crest of Saddle Hill before plunging down past the Hollywood-style Mosgiel sign to **East Taieri** and its inviting fish and chip shop. We're back into open countryside now, the Tokomairiro Plains, and as Gary at the Baldwyn Street shop informed me, 'It's all pretty flat from here on down.'

I know there's a network of descendants from Polish settlers in **Allanton**. Oh, and a Honey Shoppe. And the turn-off for the airport. **Otokia** doesn't appear to be here but I'm so intent on finding the place that I dogleg over the Taieri River and miss the turn to my next destination. Luckily another presents itself further up the highway, and I'm soon cruising slowly over a lovely old wooden bridge and into **Henley**.

My task here is to find the White Horse Hotel and Inn that A.H. Reed mentions in print, an establishment at which he had previously hired a boat for a river trip with his wife. But before I start my search I think I'll just appreciate the setting. The river beside me is beautiful, a perfect strip of blue across the bright green plain. You can see why some homesick Brit saw fit to name this place after Henley-on-Thames, although thankfully it appears posh blokes wearing ridiculous stripey blazers were not considered part of the deal. Unless they happen to own the pub, of course. Let's have a look. No, not a whiff of a pub, especially not a two-storey one, as I trawl the main street,

SH1 in Reedy's day, nor any person to be seen either, unfortunately. Hold on though, who are those two?

Alan and Marty, 'The Henley Terrors' as Marty refers to himself and his accomplice, profess not to know much about the town. They've only lived here for 10 years, they say. I expect in another 30 or so they will have sorted that out. In the meantime, they think the pub may have been somewhere down near the bridge, and that it may have flooded, and may have shut down in the 1970s. They also tell me Henley used to be a thriving little settlement, as did Otokia just up the road. 'Now you drive through and you'd hardly know it was there,' says Alan. I couldn't agree more.

Dragging myself away from Marty's mad spaniel, I check out their theory by driving very slowly down the road trying to spot pub-like buildings. I'm eyed warily by a large group of people about to embark on a hearty BBQ. A few of them, presumably having lived here for at least 20 years, are more than qualified to confirm Alan and Marty's suspicions.

'It flooded originally,' says one of the men, launching thirstily into a beer, 'and they had to rebuild the whole thing on a mound just here. Just here.' He indicates a spot not 10 metres from where we're standing.

'Yeah but the rebuilding cost all the money they had so the landlady sold the licence, and then I think the pub burnt down,' says another. 'She opened a second hand shop in Mosgiel, I think.'

'Ah, but she's retired now,' pipes up a third man.

'Anyway,' says the first man, picking up the story again, 'see that little outbuilding there, that's all that's left these days.' He points to a small, open shed-like structure. I can't help feeling a little cheated, as do the locals I expect. A good, traditional pub by the river here would be idyllic. Still, I mark it down as another partial success, say my goodbyes and leave these good people to it.

'OHAU – it's closer than CORONET' reads a sign just past Henley, and I still have no idea why so I guess I'll just have to take their word for it and keep moving south, past the **Titri** Motor Cross Track and on to **Waihola**, where another sign in a more humorous vein declares the town to have 'NO HOSPITAL. NO DOCTOR. ONE CEMETERY'. I do know from my research, though, that they definitely have a pub here, and having missed out at Henley I resolve to rectify that omission forthwith.

The Waihola Tavern is honest and functional, much like its nachos actually, and that's not a criticism. Together with a cool, crisp Speight's (I'm getting quite a taste for the stuff since Dunedin) they're just what I need to fuel another fearless adventure into uncharted territory, or in this case to fend off my hunger while I sit and look at a beautiful lake.

As one of New Zealand's finest shallow water lakes, Lake Waihola makes for a rowing course of international standard, boaties' heaven, you name it. People and black swans flock here to enjoy its beautiful surroundings and rich wetlands respectively. The name Waihola is a corruption of the Maori Waihora, or 'Spreading Water', which seems a perfectly apt description of the calm expanse of blue ahead of me. I sit here on a wooden picnic bench, belching soft, satisfied nacho belches in the first chill of early evening and contemplate what it would be like to holiday in this part of the country sometime, just for the tranquillity of it all. My God, I must be getting old.

The town of **Clarendon** ain't exactly Dallas these days, although at some stage in the past, with the lucrative fertiliser industry in full swing, I bet it wasn't far off, as the remains of the old Ewing Phosphate Co. Ltd building would no doubt testify if they could. I pass Phosphate Road, and soon afterwards have to force myself to blink twice at a sign to my left which points off to a place called Kapiti. We're a long way from Paraparaumu here, Dorothy.

From the remnants of a phosphate company to one still in existence (into which, incidentally, Ewings was merged), Milburn Lime of Milburn have been producing 'Superior Lime since 1875', or so they tell me. Certainly the quarry looks to be fully active when I drive through the middle of it, via the imaginatively named Limeworks Road. My quarry (ahem) today has also been excavated from the lime deposits, although no prizes for guessing what it is I'm after at the Whale Fossil Lookout. A single-track, winding gravel road takes me up to a gate at the crest of the hill, and never mind the fossils – the lookout really lives up to its name. The views back down to Lake Waihola, its surrounding hills and the lush plains beyond are quite breathtaking. I take my time drinking it all in before turning my attention to the whale jawbone, and the display boards that give a brief history of the quarry down the road.

The view of the hills to the south is not to be sniffed at either, especially not with the clouds of dust my car is kicking up as I drive back down to SH1. Less appealing is the brutally honest Southkill Abattoir on the outskirts of **Milton**, where I pull over to admire the Toko RFC rugby stand, one to strike jealousy in the very heart of even the proudest Sansonian.

'Yes, it's a beauty, isn't it,' says Nancie at the Information Centre. 'There's a cricket pitch and showgrounds up there, too. All beautifully kept.'

Milton, originally Milltown, came into being after the opening of McGill's Flour Mill here in 1857. That was soon joined by the Alliance Textile mill, which continued in business long enough to celebrate its centenary.

'A hundred years in business and it closed down two months later,' says Nancie sadly. I'm about to lament the demise of once-strong industries in rural parts of the South Island when she adds 'they've re-opened now, and they employ fifty people.' Things are obviously looking up, although it's doubtful they'll ever again reach the boom times of the 1860s when Milton, like so many towns in Otago, caught gold-mining fever.

'There used to be a gold mine just west of here,' Nancie continues. 'The tunnels are still all over there in the hills.' Gold in them thar hills, then. What happened?

'Some of the shafts caved in during an earthquake and trapped some miners. They got everyone out but no-one wanted to work it again. Goldminers are a superstitious lot.'

A case of paradise lost for Milton. Still, it's a pleasant town with its fair share of historic buildings as I discover on a short walk before topping up my tank at the Caltex station, where I meet Clare.

'Make sure you mention the prison at the north end of town,' she says. 'We call it the Milton Hilton. Now, do you want your windscreen cleaned or will that just make the rest of your car look even dirtier?'

To my delight there used to be a railway station over the Tokomairiro river at my next stop, **Clarksville**, although you'd never know it now. What's more, I'm told that the last train to Clarksville occurred around the time The Monkees released their hit in February 1967. Today the town consists of three houses, one of which tragically burnt down last week. Mind you, from what I can see Clarksville still has at least double the number of residences of **Crichton**. I call in at the only house I can see, a farm, with the vague hope of meeting a Michael so I can make some lame gag about Jurassic Park. But there's no-one at home.

A beautiful retreat set in 10 acres of gardens and woodland park, Garvan Homestead looks extremely tempting on the right-hand side of the road at **Lovell's Flat**. That said, any-where that boasts a name like Old Sod Cottage, right opposite, is always going to win hands down in my book. I stop to inspect its recently restored lemon-yellow walls and corrugated iron roof, a sight once shared by miners heading to the Tuapeka Goldfields. Inside, a period display has a bed to one side, a dining table and chairs to the other with the obligatory dummy sitting in one of them.

Not content with a flat, Lovell also has a stream named after him, or so I note as I drive on to another body of water, **Stony Creek**, where down to my left I can see what looks like pottery chimneys.

'You're absolutely right,' says Gary at the **Balclutha** Museum. 'That's Benhar Pottery, or at least it was until they went bust. Some property developer wanted to knock it down recently, but a gang of local protestors joined hands to stop the diggers.'

A mine of local knowledge, Gary tells me the works was originally started by two partners. After a short time one of them left to set up Temuka Pottery, leaving Mr McSkimming (who sounds suspiciously like a character in a Two Ronnies sketch to me) on his own to continue with mostly ceramic toilet and sink production. Nevertheless both, it seems, were flushed with success. So, what am I going to do here? Gary is in no doubt as to the town's most important feature.

'The bridge,' he says without hesitation. 'It's the whole reason this place exists.'

Balclutha, literally 'spanning the river Clyde' in Gaelic (there's that Scottish connection again) was originally known as Iwikatea or 'bleached bones' by Maori in honour of a great local battle, and then for more obvious reasons as Clutha Ferry by early European settlers. James McNeil it was who set up the first ferry crossing here in 1853, no doubt plying an honest and passable trade, but again it was the gold rush that saw the settlement really take off. All of a sudden Balclutha took on huge strategic significance in the ferrying of men to and from the goldfields, so much so that the first bridge soon followed in 1868. A simple wooden structure, it lasted only 10 years before being washed away in one of the mighty river's more extreme floods. Eighteen months without a bridge followed, 'during which time poor old Mr Thompson had to row across every day with the bread,' laughs Gary. Normal service was resumed and Mr Thompson's arms spared in 1881 when a second wooden bridge was erected, not to be superceded until 1935 by today's noble structure which I crossed on the way into town.

'It's a six-span concrete arch bridge,' says Gary, proudly, 'the only one of its kind in New Zealand,' and a fitting, elegant tribute to what is after all New Zealand's biggest river. Such an accolade also explains why the powers that be have decided to call Balclutha 'the Big River town', although Gary's not overly impressed with the moniker.

'They had to simplify it, I suppose,' he says, resignedly. 'At least they didn't plump for the 'Lord of the Rings' connection. There's a Balclutha mentioned in *The Two Towers*, you know.'

Gary shows me around the multitude of items on display in the museum before I head off to take another look at Balclutha's *raison d'être*. I've been told you can still see the remnants of the previous two bridges and sure enough, there they are, lonely wooden pilings poking up through the blue, an echo of the town's golden years.

Just beyond Balclutha the road eases me gently around to head due west, running parallel with the beautiful Kaihiku Ranges to the south, a mass of crumpled, undulating green, and the Blue Mountains straight ahead of me in the distance. Yes, the countryside is spectacular again here, as is the strength of the wind, which I find surprising given today's wonderfully clement weather. Great gusts buffet me along past the tiny settlement of **Kaihiku** and on to the turn-off for the marginally less tiny **Waiwera South**, where I've decided that it should be a fairly simple task to locate the hot pools, right? Right? I really do walk into these things sometimes.

In the centre of the settlement sits a stream, or is it a pond? Promising, I think, but I see no evidence of bubbling heat or steam rising from the surface, so I decide I'll have to ask someone. I plump for a house from which I can hear the familiar drone of a lawn mower, and open the gate to be greeted by Mr Farquhar, a large, jovial man in shorts and a vest, his nipples poking out either side of the straps.

'Hot pools?' he says, wiping his brow. 'Not that I know of. We'd better ask my mother.' He beckons me up to the house, where an elderly lady comes frowning into the kitchen.

'No,' she affirms. 'No hot pools that I know of. We've only been here twenty years, mind. You want to ask Tom Whiteside in that house over there.'

Tom is not at home, but his wife Anne suggests I phone later, so I do. Does he know of any hot pools in the area, and if not, why then is the town named after the Maori for hot water?

'I'm not sure,' says Tom apologetically, 'but I think it may have something to do with the name of a Maori chief who lived around here. He drowned in the river, by all accounts.'

Back on SH1 I cross the allegedly lethal Waiwera Stream and continue on to **Clinton**, self-proclaimed three-horse town in honour of its agricultural heritage. Bill Clinton has dropped in at least once, and maybe twice, according to Ethan, a very helpful teenager I bump into at the local dairy. 'I know he's been to the school and the fire station. In between hanging out in Queenstown of course,' he adds with a knowing raise of the eyebrows far in advance of his years. In honour of Big Bad Bill's visit the stretch of the road between here and Gore has been christened the Presidential Highway, a name that would have proved even more apt had Al actually beaten Dubya in the 2000 election.

Ethan also suggests that I talk to a local historian lady if I want to find out more, but time is marching on and I feel the need to be in a populous area before nightfall. And so, ladies and gentlemen, let me tell you now I did not have social relations with that woman, instead preferring to carry on to **Wairuna**, its stream, and Whiteside Road. I wonder if that's at all connected with Tom back in Waiwera South.

According to the sign the bridge over the **Waipahi** River marks the official start of Southland. 'Spirit of a Nation,' it says, cryptically. Still, that's three cryptic words more than the next notice at **Arthurton** which is so faded that I can't read it at all. Judging by the track running parallel with the road around 100 metres to my right I assume there used to be a railway station here, in a time long before 'leaves on the line' was ever considered an excuse for the tardiness of trains. Or at least I hope so, as my next stop **Pukerau** translates as 'cluster of leaves'. I expect it would rarely be a problem down here though, not if today's blustery conditions are in any way typical of the weather in these parts. Even the tussocks in the Red Tussock Scientific Reserve are feeling the battering, and they're only, well, tussocks.

Otikerama, noted for its soil type (heavy silt loam in all horizons, if you must know), leads me on to **McNab**, also discussed in soil circles apparently, but more significant for being named after one of New Zealand's most famous historians, one Robert McNab, a robust Scotsman who in the early 1900s felt it his duty to catalogue the complete European history of his newly adopted home. By all accounts he was a keen temperance supporter, too, which may have made him unpopular with his fellow ex-pat contemporaries, many of whom brought their whisky stills over with them on the boat from Scotland, no doubt looking forward to escaping the dreaded Excise Act imposed upon them by the English. Indeed, had it not been for prohibition proving so in vogue down here in Southland during the past 150 years, it is quite feasible that New Zealand today would boast one of the most prestigious whisky-producing areas in the world outside Scotland. Alas, this was not to be the case, although one illegal distillery at least seems to have slipped through the net, and it is this I'm hoping to find at the next red dot on my map.

New Zealand has already established sister cities all over the world. Dunedin is partnered with Shanghai, Portsmouth USA and Edinburgh (of course), whereas Wellington rubs familial shoulders with Sydney, Hania (Greece) and, strangely, Harrogate in Yorkshire, England. I've been thinking. What if this practice were extended closer to home, between the North and South Islands? The potential would be amazing. You could twin Nelson with Hamilton, after Lord Horatio and his lover Lady Emma. Or smaller towns on my route such as Saltwater Creek and Vinegar Hill.

After an aeon spent in the queue at the **Gore** Information Centre waiting for an over-zealous mother to book her son onto a bus to Dunedin, I finally get to talk to the woman behind the counter. To jolly things along while I'm buying my ticket to the Hokonui Moonshine Museum I test the water with my sister town theory. '… and of course,' I finish, confident of my punchline, 'Gore could be twinned with Bulls.'

She stares at me as if I've had too many shots of the hard stuff already, and says, 'Go through whenever you're ready.'

'I beg your pardon?'

'The Moonshine Museum. It's through there.'

Just as the tax laws had driven whisky production underground in Scotland since the mid-seventeenth century, so in New Zealand by the 1870s the law stated you needed a licence to brew or distil alcohol. For many Scottish settlers this was merely an extension of the draconian taxes imposed by the English, and many chose to ignore it, setting up their own 'stills in the hills' around Southland, and Gore in particular. One family, the McRaes, became well known for their moonshine production, smuggling it around the region in bottles, cans and milk billies from their base in the Hokonui Hills to a discerning and professional clientele. The McRae brew was known simply as Hokonui, a term which then became the accepted slang for illegal whisky in general for the whole area.

When prohibition ended demand for illegal booze waned, and thus, too, did the legacy of the McRae family. In fact it may well have disappeared altogether had not two men, Malcolm Wilmott and Peter Wheeler, boutique distiller and chemist respectively, teamed up in 1989 to resume the manufacture of Hokonui Moonshine to the original McRae recipe. And we know it's the original recipe because it's taken from a handwritten document by a relative of the McRaes which is now on display in the museum here, along with other memorabilia from Gore's illegal distilling days. Historic copper stills, letters, posters, even a video history presentation – all provide a more than comprehensive guide to the infamous moonshine lore. But I think you know why I'm really here. As luck would have it, at the end of the tour there is a bar complete with friendly barman who pours me a not-so-wee dram of the brew that has been described as both 'rough and obnoxious to the taste' and 'smooth as milk – better than Scotland's best', the latter possibly a verdict given after several wee drams.

I give it a good nose first.

'What do you think?' he asks.

Don't say buttery. Don't say buttery.

'Smells like a Speyside malt,' I say. I can't tell whether that's a scowl or a sign of pleasure on his face. No time now, I'll just have to go for it. Gore blimey. That is smooth. Hold on, though. An intensely warm feeling starts to climb my torso and up through my throat, sending me into a stooped coughing fit.

'Very nice,' I gag, much to the barman's amusement.

'Another one, then?' he grins.

Outside in the foyer I buy myself a half bottle of the firewater to inflict on friends. It seems to me that Hokonui Moonshine, much like tequila, will be the perfect dare for a drinking game at some point in the future. I'll bet a good deal of that kind of behaviour also goes on during the Western Awards, an event that attracts over 10,000 people every June.

'Do the cowboys and cowgirls drink it?' I ask the lady behind the front desk.

'They try to,' she says. 'They try to.'

Moseying on, I soon find myself on the lonesome highway down the valley to **Charlton** where I pass the Waitane Food Processing Plant. The next I know I am in **Mataura**, like Gore renowned for its trout fishing, and it's time to turn off left towards another key piece of Maori history at **Tuturau**.

A short way up the Wyndham Road a signpost directs me to the site of the last North *vs* South Island Maori battle in 1836. I drive as far as a farm and discover I've gone too far when a tourist-weary farmer points me back down the way I've come.

'You'll have to park on the grass,' he says, ignoring the fact that the verges are roughly half the height of my car. I do as I'm told (you should never argue with a farmer, especially not on his land), and frog it through knee-high grass across a windswept hillside to where a simple stone monument marks the spot. Ngai Tahu *vs* Ngati Toa it was and, as the plaque is keen to point out, the home side won.

I carry on to **Brydone**, named in honour of our friend from Totara Estate who may even have had a hand in establishing the big freezing works that remains to this day. From here it's over to Low Burn, previously familiar to me only as the oven setting my wife uses to cook parsnips, and on via the Pioneer Highway to **Ota Creek**, spiritual home to another root vegetable in Southland's first-ever carrot crop. Nothing to trouble Ohakune just yet, though.

Edendale rather grandly calls itself 'the home of New Zealand's cheese industry'. Bearing out this claim, a huge, shining metal cheese factory dominates the town, but disappointingly I can see no sign of a cheese shop. Where's an Albert (see **Mercer**) when you need one? Instead, I find an Angela and her daughter Ruby at the Edendale Discount Groceries where, having already unsuccessfully checked the fridge units for local cheese, I decide it best to ask for advice.

'No,' says Angela, Ruby hiding shyly behind her, 'you can't buy direct from the factory any more, otherwise I'd gladly stock it. I think they signed their life away to Mainland Cheese a few years back. You're lucky to get us actually,' she adds. 'I reckon they'll shift the highway to the other side of the factory soon. The trains cause jams, see.'

Darn it. I was rather looking forward to another cheese escapade. Is there anything else here to see?

'There's the tulip fields just up the road,' says Angela helpfully. 'All in bloom just now, beautiful. I walk past them every morning. Go and have a look.'

I do, and she's right. Not far down Seaward Road a whole field is awash with vividly coloured tulips, from yellow to orange and every possible hue in between. So bright are they it nearly calls for sunglasses even on an overcast day such as today. Nearly. Yes, there may be no cheese on offer to the general public in Edendale, but as a Dutchman surely Albert's heart would be gladdened at the sight.

Well I never. There's a Moore Road on the outskirts of Edendale, a topiary moa in a garden too, and then I'm heading west again, on past the old Dunedin Road to **Dacre** where I spot Dacre Hall looking disused to my left. Unsurprisingly since Gore I've also felt somewhat thirsty, so the **Woodlands** Tavern comes as a godsend a couple of clicks further down the road. I drop in for a quick handle of Speights. All the locals are drinking DB Draught from bottles, but no-one bats an eyelid at either my drinking habits or my accent, and I'm left alone to sup quietly in the corner while everyone else watches the racing on a small TV near the bar.

Flat and windy like Holland, conditions appear to be perfect for another brightly coloured tulip field at **Longbush**. Disappointingly there's no sign of an Oval cricket ground at **Kennington** either, just the Niagara Sawmill Company, so I throw caution to the wind and breeze on through the dusk to **Invercargill**, the last major city of my journey. In a compact but comfortable room at the Kelvin Hotel, I notice the bathroom sink is made by McSkimmings of Benhar, before ringing home. My wife tells me a man from Pukerua Bay has tracked me down after seeing my dubious performance on *Close Up*, discussing my failure to find a kauri in Kauri. He's not left a number, just a message on the answerphone: 'I just wanted to let you know,' he says, 'there is definitely a kauri tree in the graveyard at Kauri because both my mother and grandmother are buried beneath it.'

Invercargill to Bluff.

Now I remember. There was a house in the middle of the road as I drove into town yesterday. Fortunately for all concerned it was on the back of a lorry, and continuous traffic flow was never threatened as the streets here are so incredibly wide – up to 40 metres in places.

There's a distinct sense of considered design about Invercargill, the most southerly bastion of urban New Zealand. From the plan view of my map its deliberate street grid system and rectangular central park (Queen's Park) suggest something of a Manhattan feel, on paper at least. The reality, of course, is quite different. With space in no way at a premium on this previously swampy ground, skyscrapers are conspicuous only by their absence. Instead, the town enjoys a selection of fine old one- and two-storeyed stone buildings inherited from its early settler days of the 1860s and 70s. For these we again have a bunch of hardy Scots to thank, likewise for the street names nominated by original surveyor General J.T. Thomson after Scottish Rivers: Dee, Forth, Esk and Tay, for example. Oh, and Queens Park too, I guess.

Oddly an independent state until 1871, Invercargill has always been New Zealand's main centre for meat and wool exports, initially from the city wharf on the Waihopai River to the west of town, and later from Bluff. It's also always been a town in a hurry (speed is presumably of the essence when you're building on a bog), sprouting from nothing to financially independent in a matter of eight years. It's 'a city where dreams are possible', or at least that's what the sign on the way in said, in homage to the movie *The World's Fastest Indian* starring Anthony Hopkins and based on the life of Invercargill inventor and world-record holder Burt Munro. After years of dedication, he travelled half-way around the world to Utah's Bonneville Salt Flats to set the land speed record on a 1920 Indian motorcycle in 1967. I, however, am here in a Nissan Silvia to experience something infinitely slower.

The Southland Museum and Art Gallery, a bizarre pyramid-shaped building, lies at the southern entrance to Queen's Park. 'The largest pyramid in the southern hemisphere,' my guide-book tells me, although to be fair I can't imagine there's much competition. Anyway, I tiptoe past the tulips and towards the foyer. Half-way up, the path opens out to reveal both a statue and a statue-like tourist sitting on a bench beside it, head in hands. Surely things aren't that bad. Maybe he's feeling the effects of last night's Hokonui Moonshine. I don't really care. It's the statue we're interested in. A statue of Henry.

'Henry was born around the end of the 19th century,' says one placard inside. 'He was brought here in 1971. Henry has never wanted to breed and attacks the others so he's kept in a separate enclosure. He is 540mm long and weighs 1.2 kilos, making him possibly the heaviest tuatara in the world.'

Henry is also underground in his bloody burrow this morning and showing no sign of coming out, much like all his fellow tuatara (I hesitate to call them friends). Here at the back of the building the museum houses a special climate-controlled habitat or tuatarium for these ancient creatures and has been instrumental in replenishing their now-threatened numbers through its highly effective breeding programme. In fact the programme has proved so much of a success that breeding has been suspended for the time being, which may explain the apparent lack of lust for life today. No, my mistake. According to information posted here they are nocturnal animals and as such not early risers. It doesn't seem to have done them any harm as a race, either. The tuatara has been referred to as a living fossil, and with good cause. This ancient reptile is thought to have roamed the earth at the same time as the dinosaurs, remaining relatively unchanged in evolutionary terms for the last 225 million years. A bit like Keith Richards, then, only slightly less wrinkly. Unlike Keith, though, it's also the last remaining member of its group, the order Sphenodontia, its relatives having died out around 60 million years ago. As we know, today tuatara is a protected species and can only be found in the wild on certain remote islands off New Zealand. To spot one in captivity, however, you can't do better than come here. Apparently. Hang on, though. What I thought was a piece of wood for a while is definitely a tuatara. Not Henry, but you can't have everything.

I watch the creature through the glass for a good five minutes. By 'good' I actually mean 'at least'. 'Good' would imply that something happens during this time, when in fact nothing happens. The tuatara doesn't move. I can't see it breathing. It doesn't blink. The statue outside was more active.

Still, I've seen one now, and I can leave happy. Before I go I take a quick look around the rest of the museum which houses some very impressive taonga, including traditional Maori fishing equipment carved from bone, as well as adzes, mere and a beautiful old waka. There's also one old paddle (hoe) found recently in a hollow totara tree on the Waiau river, which would suggest the original owner left it there for safe-keeping and then, for whatever reason, failed to return.

Maybe now is a good time to let you in on a secret. As a tribute to the late A.H. Reed, it had always been my intention to walk this last stretch of road from Invercargill to Bluff. It seemed the least I could do considering that when he was in these parts he had already tramped his way practically the full length of both islands. On a map it looks a tiny distance, but now I'm here and it's late afternoon on a blustery day I've reached the conclusion that it is much, much too far to go on foot. Besides, it was a gentler age when Reedy did his walk. Yes, he was in his eighties, but he had people constantly coming out offering him refreshments and respite for his weary head. I have only a bottle of Pump and a steak and cheese pie. I also have the lazy gene. It's a Moore trait, I'm afraid. So, no, it's driving for me.

Passing through the Clifton area of town, I'm soon on to **Woodend** where I presume the wood used to end before it was all cut down to help to build Invercargill. The landscape transforms again at **Awarua**, the largest protected wetland area in southern New Zealand and a haven for water fowl, fernbirds and bittern. Then it's windswept, open country all the way to **Greenhills** where I find a cute little wooden church built in 1886, now beautifully restored. A sign tells me there used to be an elaborate raised pulpit and lectern inside adorned by a red velvet cushion with tassels; the former was removed in 1969 due to borer infestation.

I decide to stretch my legs at **Greenpoint**, so in the fading light at the edge of the windswept peninsula I begin the process of muffling myself up against the sea breeze which is really beginning to bite. Overall it's a clean, crisp evening though, perfect walking weather, at least that's what I'm telling myself as I set off smartly along the gravel path, crossing the train tracks to find a well-appointed wooden walkway down to the shoreline. The rocks here are apparently among the oldest in New Zealand, but I'm more concerned at present with the stench of thick, gooey mud that pervades the air. White-fronted terns flit low across the water as I look out across the bay to the aluminium smelter at Tiwai Point, Southland's unsung money-spinner generating an astonishing $1 billion in export sales every year.

Its lights are beginning to show in the gathering dusk, but such modern industry seems incongruous compared to the sight before me. I've reached Rotten Row, the ship's graveyard, final resting place of once proud vessels of the Bluff oyster and fishing fleet. The *Kekeno, Orewa, Dispatch, Sir William Wallace, Hirere, Comet, Toiler, Colleen, Tartan* and *Marina*, rusting iron hulks and sodden wooden skeletons alike, lie here quietly decomposing in the shallow water. It's a ghostly spectacle in the twilight, but there's a serenity here too, a sense of the sea reclaiming its own.

Through the channel beyond Tikore Island ('the place where you eat dog') I think I glimpse **Ocean Beach** further along the coast. It will have to do, anyway. The light is fading fast now, and in spite of the mud I can smell victory. Finally I am within touching distance of the end of my personal odyssey. In fact I'm so excited that as I start back along the path to the car I actually begin to jog, a rare occurrence in the Bob Moore calendar, I can tell you. I'm soon firmly ensconced in the driver's seat busily steaming up the windscreen with my heavy breathing. This is it, I think, fumbling for the fan control. The final stretch.

Even at dusk the angular facades of **Bluff** seem to take on a radiance. My heightened senses lend them almost a halo effect as I pass the Maritime Museum and Fred and Myrtle's famous Paua House, searching, hoping for Stirling Point. I've never been here before so every slight twist and turn in the road has me holding my breath, ready to clench my fist in delight. And then, without any great fanfare, there it is. I'd recognise that signpost anywhere. The end of the road.

'But this is where the highway begins,' laughs Jane in the Land's End guest house as she fills in my certificate. 'The writing's a bit wonky 'cos I haven't got my glasses on, but is that okay?' She could have written it upside down for all I care. I'm so high I could eat a Bluff oyster, and I hate oysters. Like French-kissing a dead tongue. Dammit though, why not, just this once? I poke my head around the kitchen door.

'Do you have any Bluff oysters?'

'They're off season, I'm afraid,' she replies.

Of course. Thank God for that.

'Actually, we're meant to be closed, too. I only let you in 'cos I was feeling kind,' she adds, and once again I'm left humbled at the generosity and good-natured spirit of a Kiwi soul.

I go back outside in the twilight and sit contentedly on the bonnet of my car. The moon tonight is amazing, a huge scoop of pock-marked vanilla, as big as I've ever seen it, and despite my current penchant for overstatement that's no exaggeration. To my right people scuttle among the rocks on the beach below, possibly in search of paua. And in the distance is Stewart Island, sedate, motionless and State Highway 1-less, and I know I have finished my journey.

I've learnt many things over the past two years. That tattoos hurt, for one. That watching tuatara is not really a spectator sport, for another. Also that I'm not getting any younger. That A.H. Reed must have been a hardy old coot. That kebabs here are respectable food, not merely beer-goggled post-pub closing-time fodder. That you can apply the word 'awesome' to pretty much any situation you want. That second-hand Japanese import cars are probably a good thing. That even slow cars tend to speed up when they get to passing lanes. That New Zealand has some of the most beautiful natural scenery I have ever seen. That although the countryside can change here within a few kilometres, the accent rarely does. That everywhere has an interesting story to tell if you take the time to scratch the surface. That wherever you go in this country you will find people are amazingly friendly, quick-witted and willing to help at the drop of a hat. And that although I'll never really be a Kiwi, wherever I've been I've always felt accepted. And believe me, when you up sticks and move to another country, that's more than enough to make you feel at home.

Right then, that's enough of the sentimentality. There's only one thing left to do. Drive home.

Bibliography.

Anon., *Waipara Valley*. Waipara Valley Promotion Association, 2000

Belich, James, *The New Zealand Wars*. Penguin, 1988

Bentley, Trevor, *Pakeha Maori*. Penguin, 1999

Brewer, Ian H., *Te Rauparaha*. Department of Education, 1966

Brodie, Ian, *The 'Lord of the Rings' Location Guide Book*.
    HarperCollins, 2002

Campbell, John Logan, *Poenamo*. Wilson & Horton, 1970

Carkeek, W. W., *The Kapiti Coast*. Reed, 1967

Chapple, D. L., *Tokoroa: Creating a Community*. Longman Paul, 1976

Chowdhury, Dave, *Driving Scenic New Zealand*. Craig Potton
    Publishing, 2001

Clune, Frank, *Roaming Round New Zealand*. Angus & Robertson, 1956

Cuff, Martine E., *Totara Estate*. New Zealand Historic Places Trust
    Wellington, 1982

de Botton, Alain, *The Art of Travel*. Penguin, 2003

Ell, Gordon, *An A–Z of Kiwi Fact & Folklore*. New Holland, 2003

Ell, Gordon, *Kauri Gum and the Gumdiggers*. Bush Press, 1989

Ellesmere Camera Club, *Selwyn From the Hills to the Sea*. 1999

Evans, Alice, *Mount Camel Calling*. Hodder and Stoughton, 1981

Flaxbourne Settlers Assn, The, *The Flaxbourne Settlement Centennial
    1905-2005: A Pictorial Record*. Blenheim Printing Company, 2005

Grover, Robin, *Alias The Wade: The Story of Silverdale 1839 –1853*.
    1996

Harper, Laura, Tony Mudd, Paul Whitfield, *The Rough Guide to New
    Zealand* (third edition). Rough Guides, 2002

King, Michael, *Whina: A Biography of Whina Cooper*. Hodder and
    Stoughton, 1983

King, Michael, *The History of New Zealand*. Penguin, 2003

Maclean, Chris, *Kapiti*. The Whitcombe Press, 1999

Mander, Jane, *The Story of a New Zealand River*. Whitcombe & Tombs, reprinted 1973

McLauchlan, Gordon (ed.), *The New Zealand Guide*. Insight Guides, 1987

McLauchlan, Gordon, *A Short History of New Zealand*. Penguin, 2004

Menefy, Diana, *Hukerenui ... in the beginning*. Capricorn, 1988

Menefy, Diana, *Kamo: The story of a village*. Kamo Book Committee, 1994

Moon, Paul, *Hone Heke: Nga Puhi Warrior*. David Ling Publishers, 2001

Mooney, K., *From the Heart of Europe to the Land of the Southern Cross: a story of Puhoi*. Puhoi Centennial Publications, 1963

More, David, *The Golden Road to Cape Reinga*. Reed, 1966

New Zealand. DK Eyewitness Travel Guides, 2002

New Zealand Travellers Road Atlas. Kiwimaps, 2003

NZ Historic Places Trust, *Discovering Northland's Past*: 'Route Five – Kaitaia to Cape Reinga'. Pamphlet compiled by Vic Hensley for Northland Branch Committee, 2000

Patrick, Alan A., *Winchester's History*. 1990

Reed, A.H., *From North Cape to Bluff*. Reed, 1961

Reed, A.H., *The Four Corners of New Zealand*. New Holland, 2004

Reed, A.W., *Illustrated Maori Place Names*. Reed, 2001

Riley, Murdoch, *New Zealand Trees and Ferns*. Viking Sevenseas Ltd, 1983

South Canterbury District Committee, *South Canterbury Historical Guide*. New Zealand Historic Places Trust, 1991

Startup, Capt. Bill, with Neil Illingworth, *The Kaikoura UFOs*. Hodder amd Stoughton, 1980

Tobin, Christopher, *Fitzsimmons: Boxing's First Triple World Champion*. 2000

Waite, Hon. Fred, *Pioneering in South Otago*. Whitcombe & Tombes, 1948

Wolfe, Richard, *Moa*. Penguin, 2003

Wood, June A., *Gold Trails of Otago*. Reed, 1970